ISRAEL
IN THE OBLIQUE

SCOTT SHAW

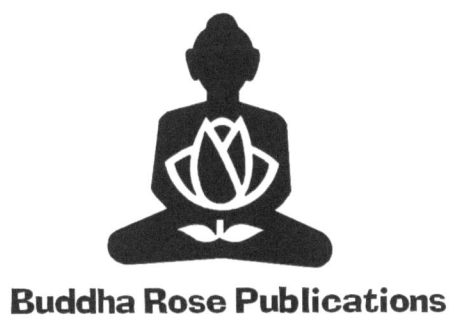

Buddha Rose Publications

Israel in the Oblique
Copyright © 1984 by Scott Shaw
All Rights Reserved

No Part of this book may be reproduced
in any manner without the expressed written
permission of the author or the publishing company.

ISBN-10: 1-877792-61-6
ISBN-13: 978-1-877792-61-8

ISRAEL
IN THE OBLIQUE

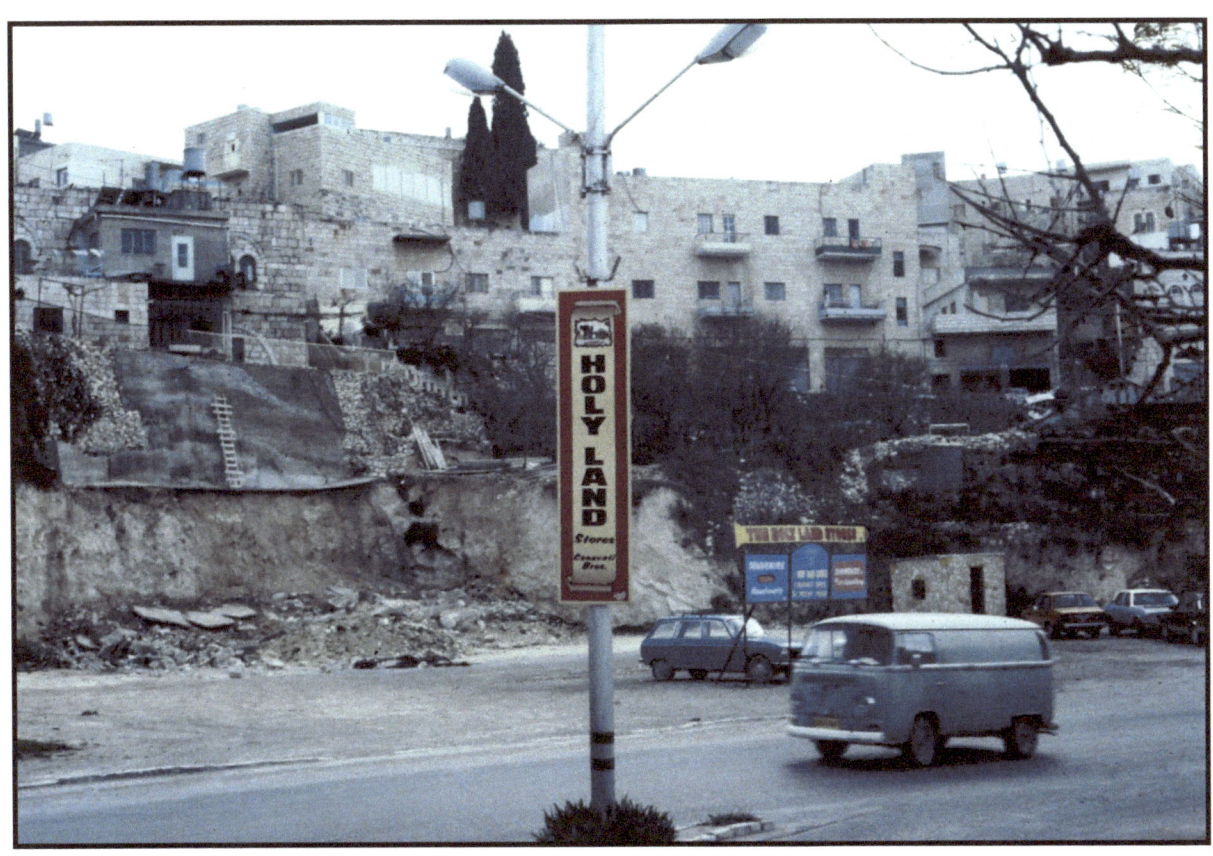

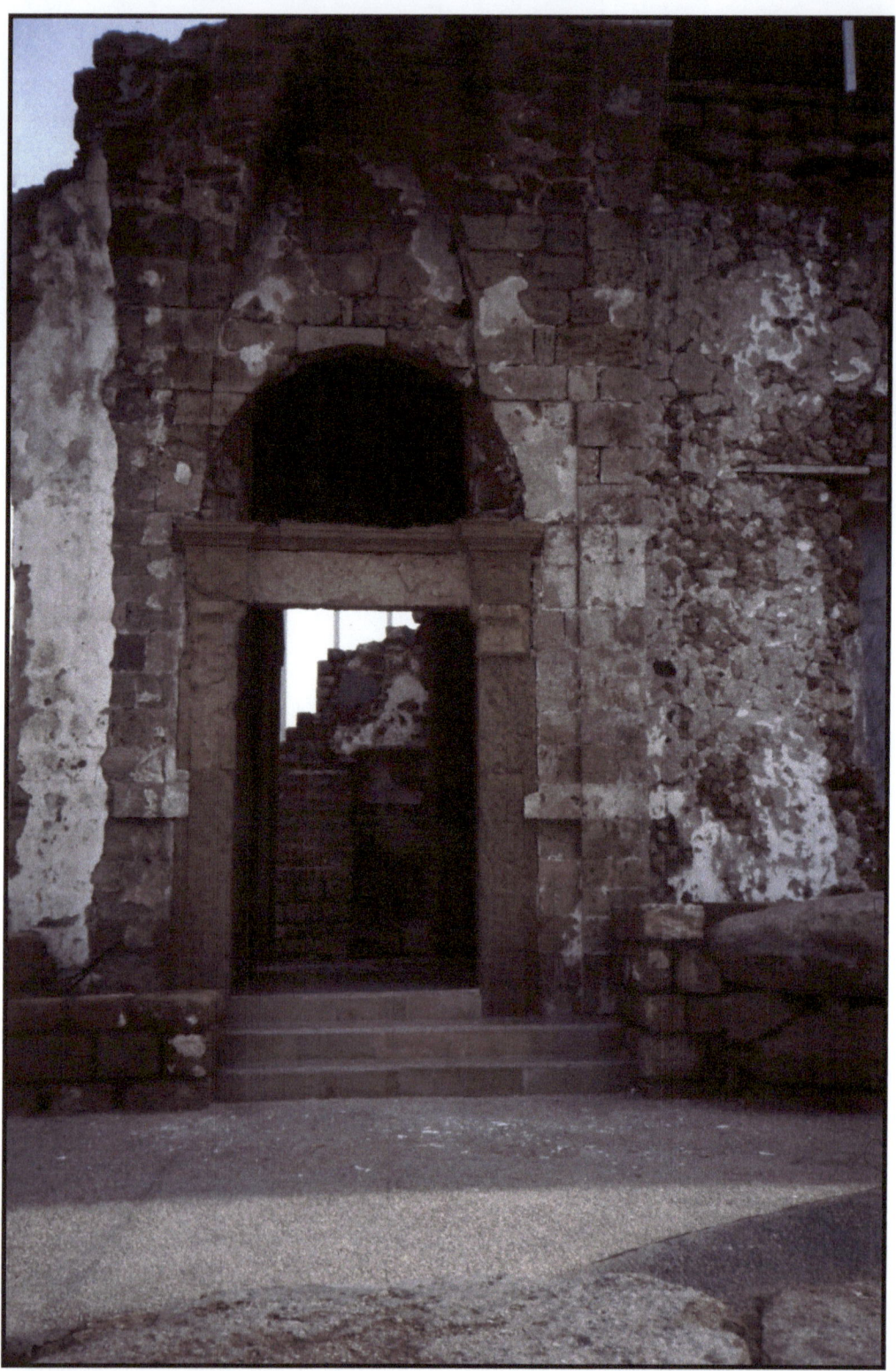

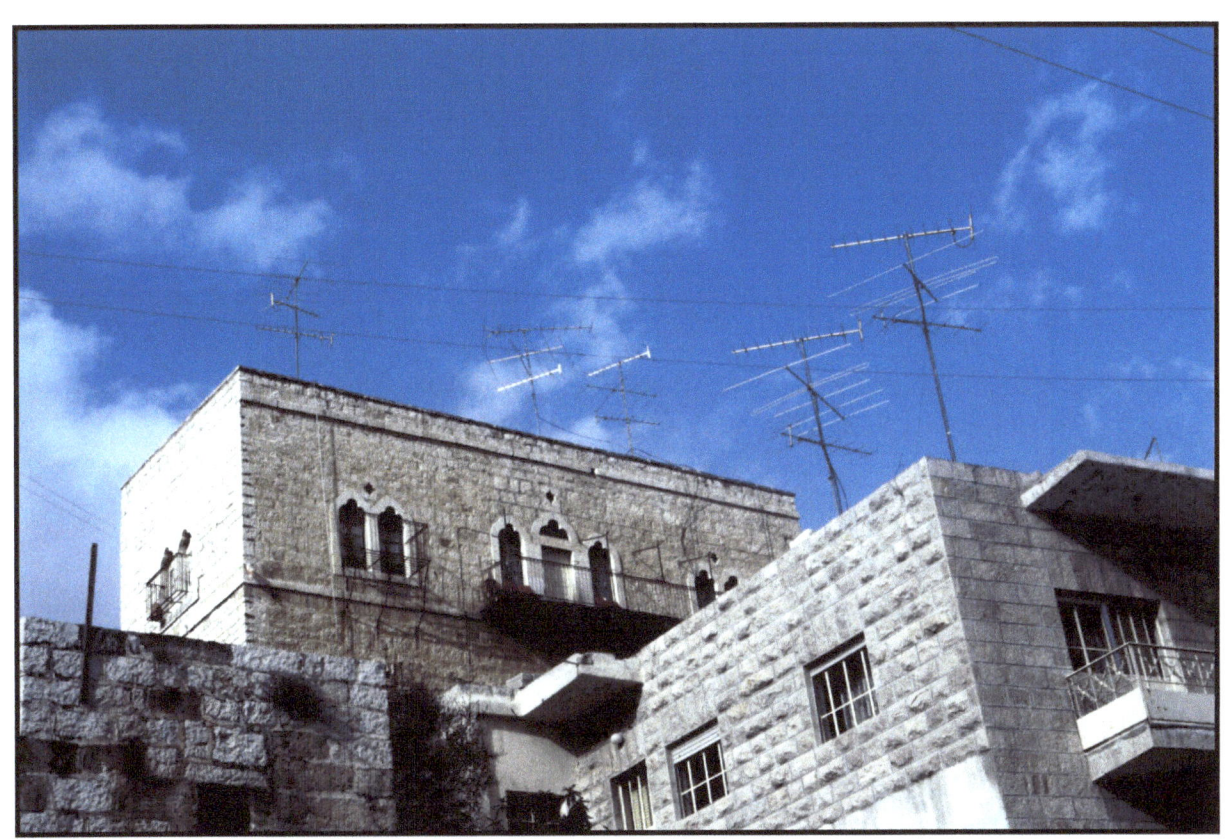

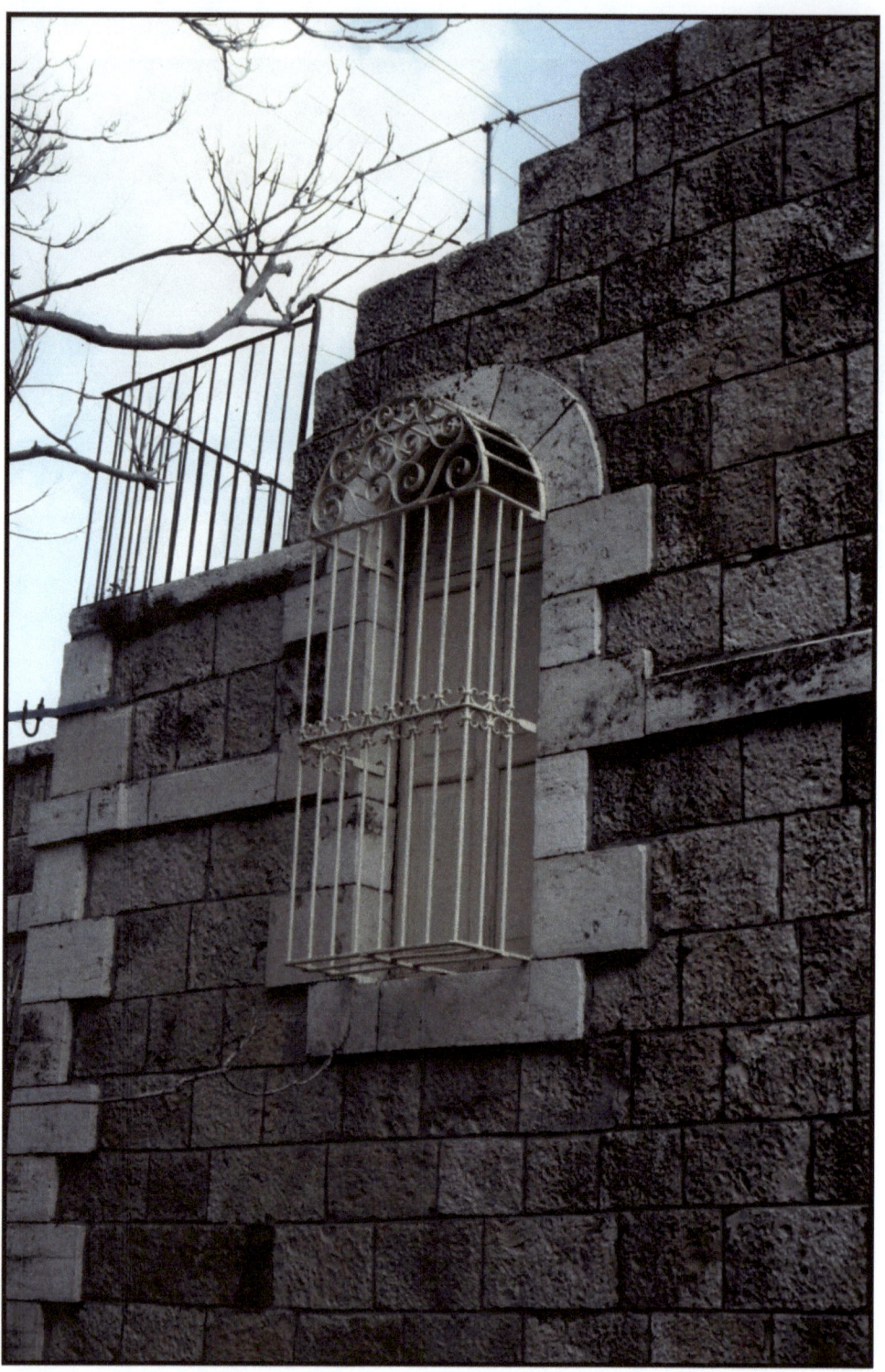

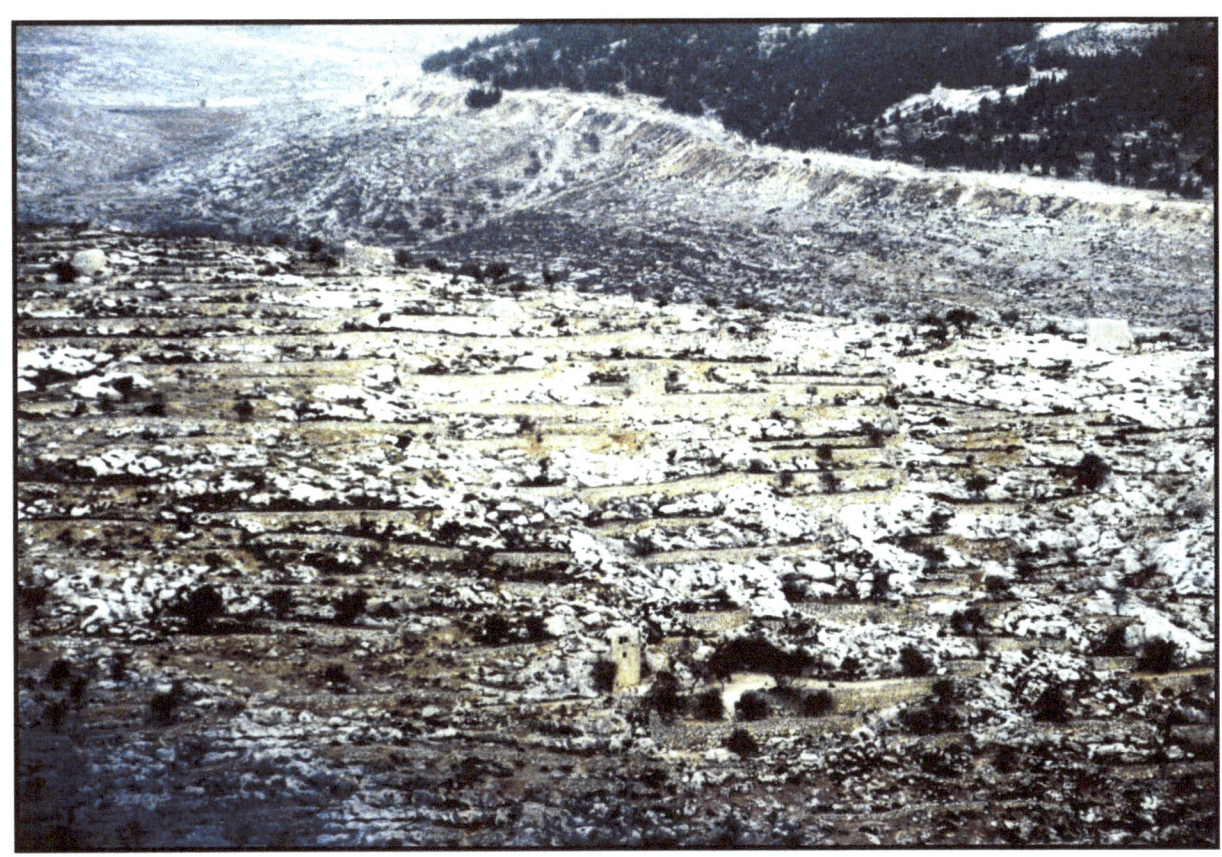

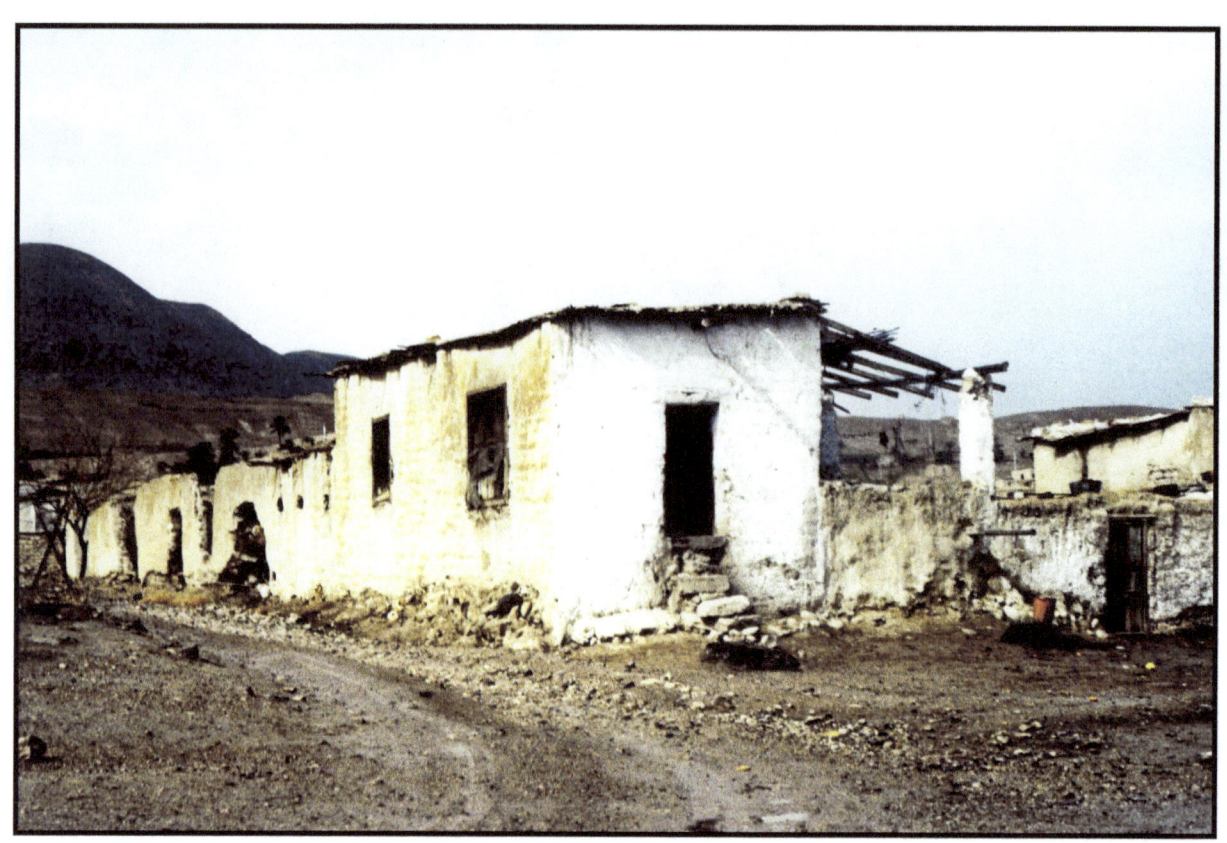

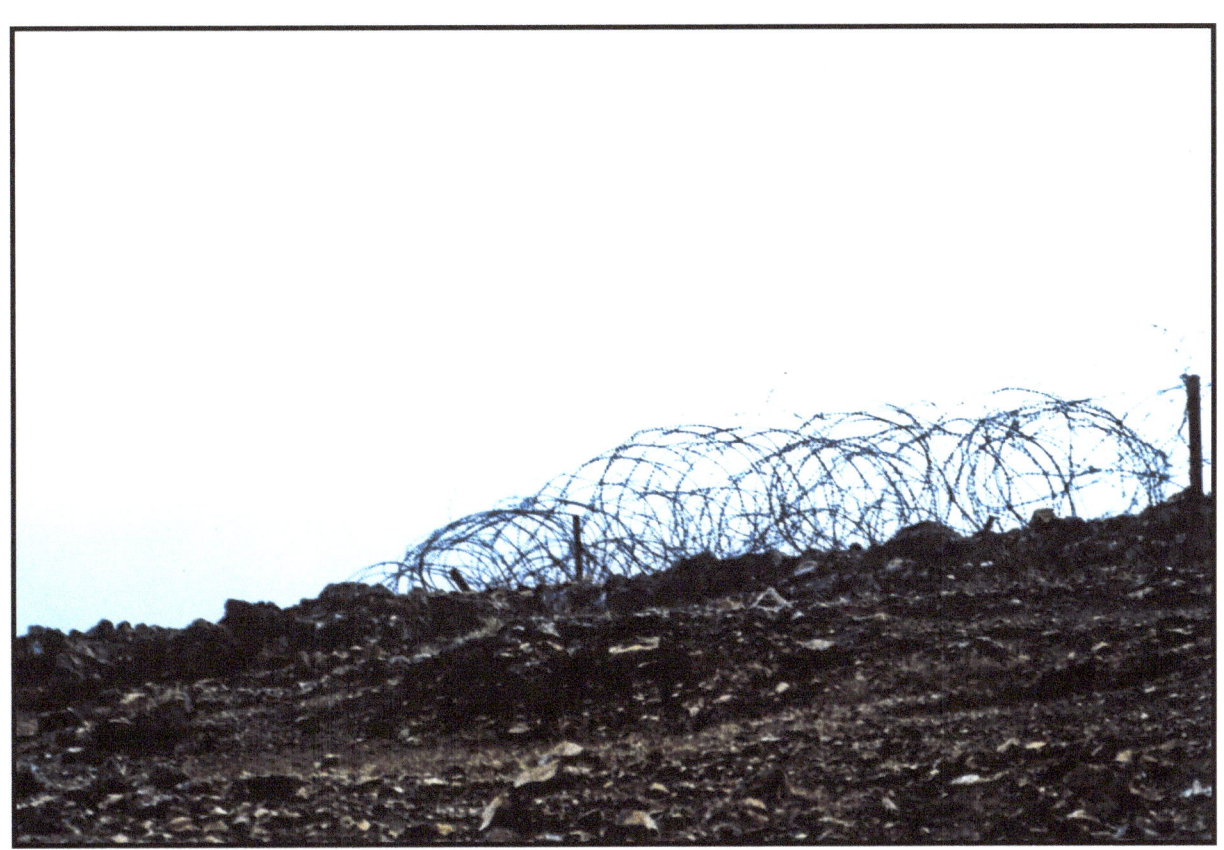

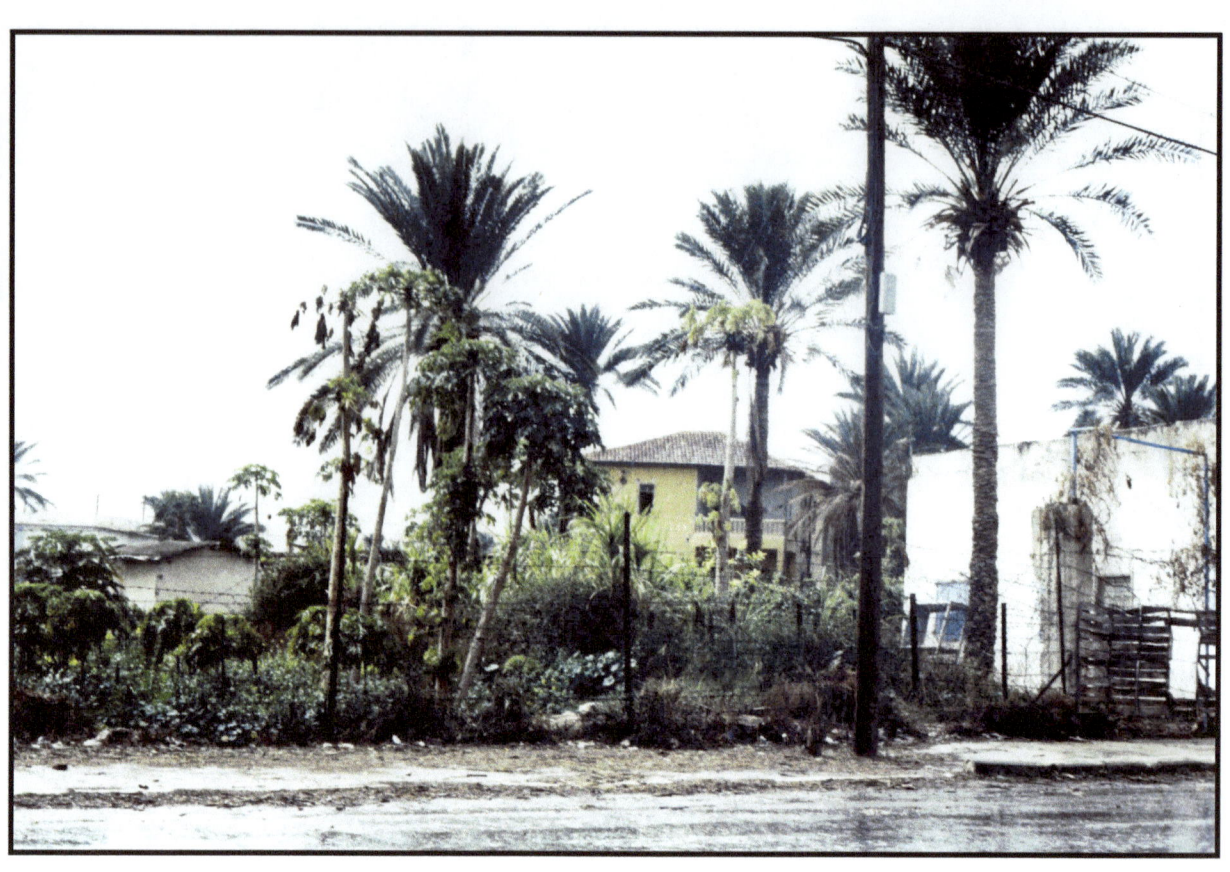

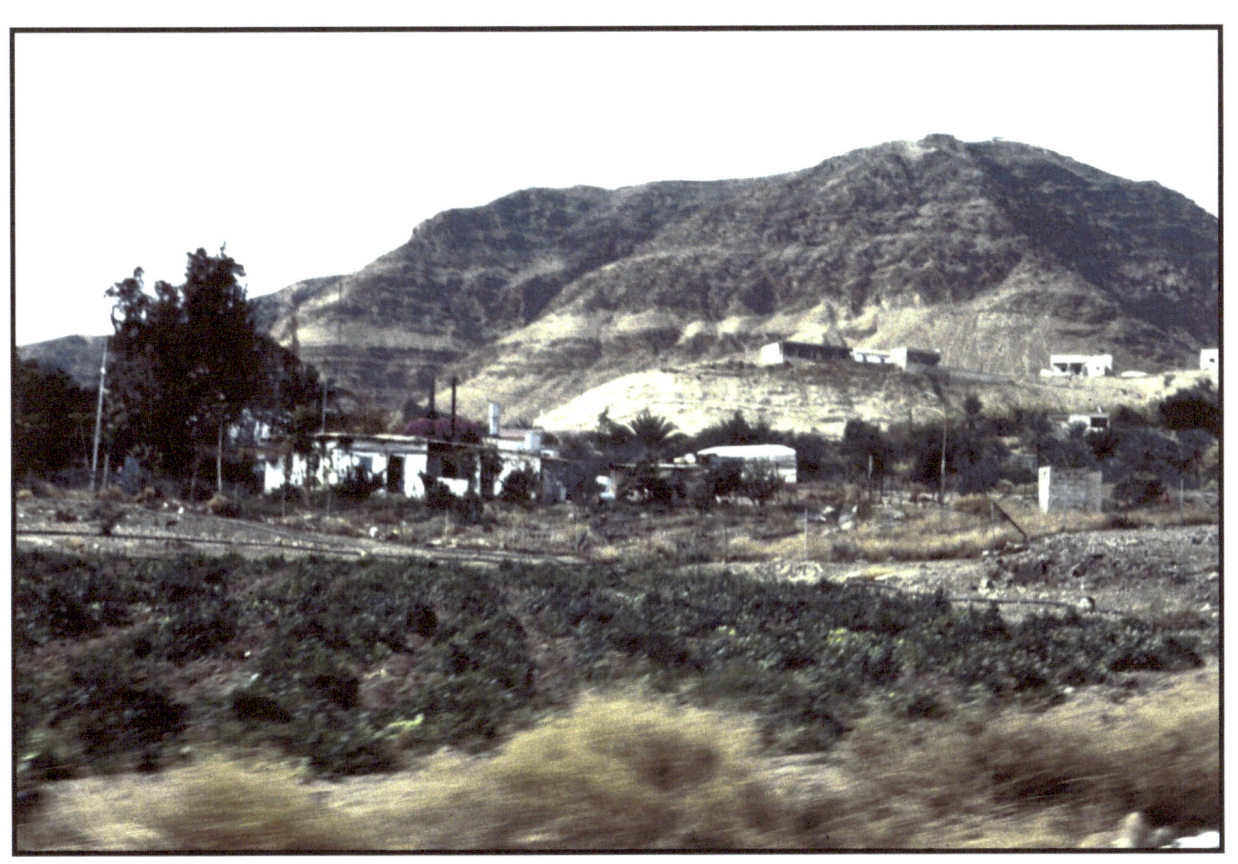

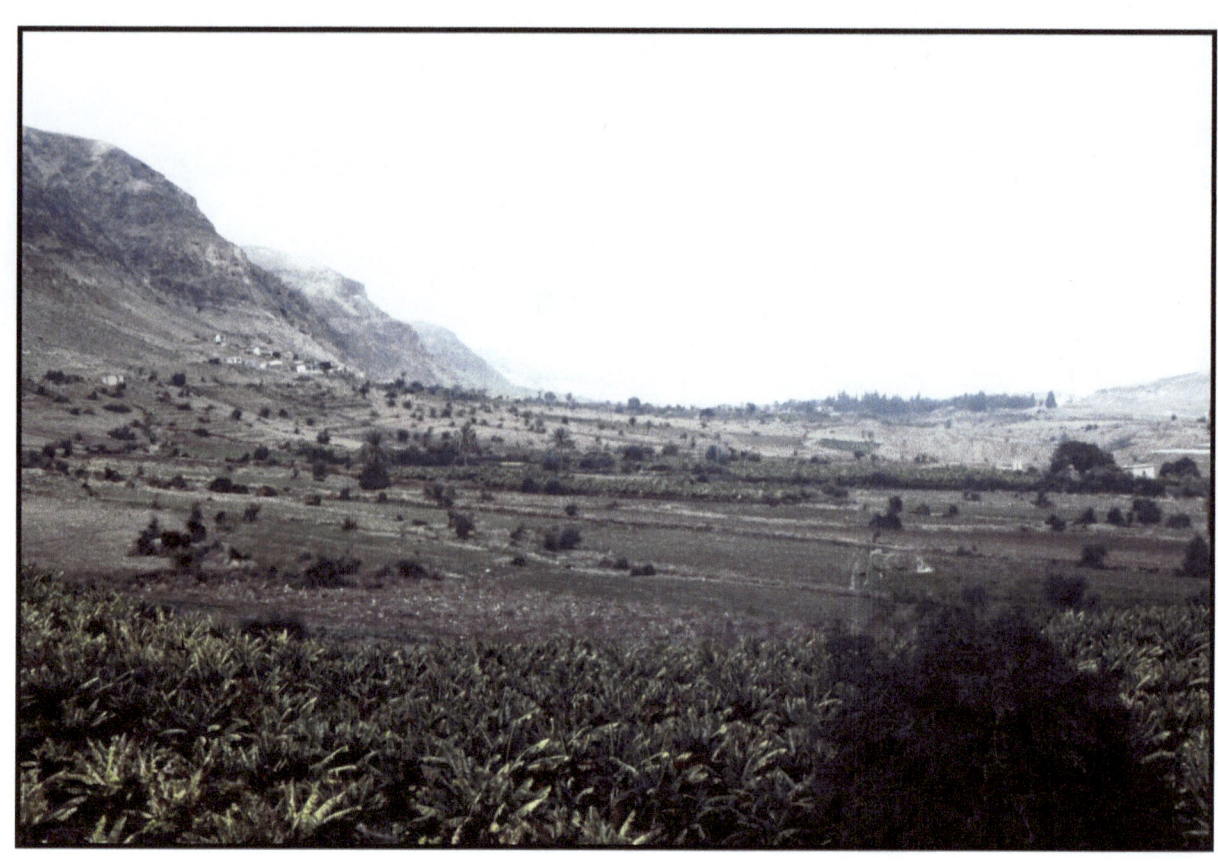

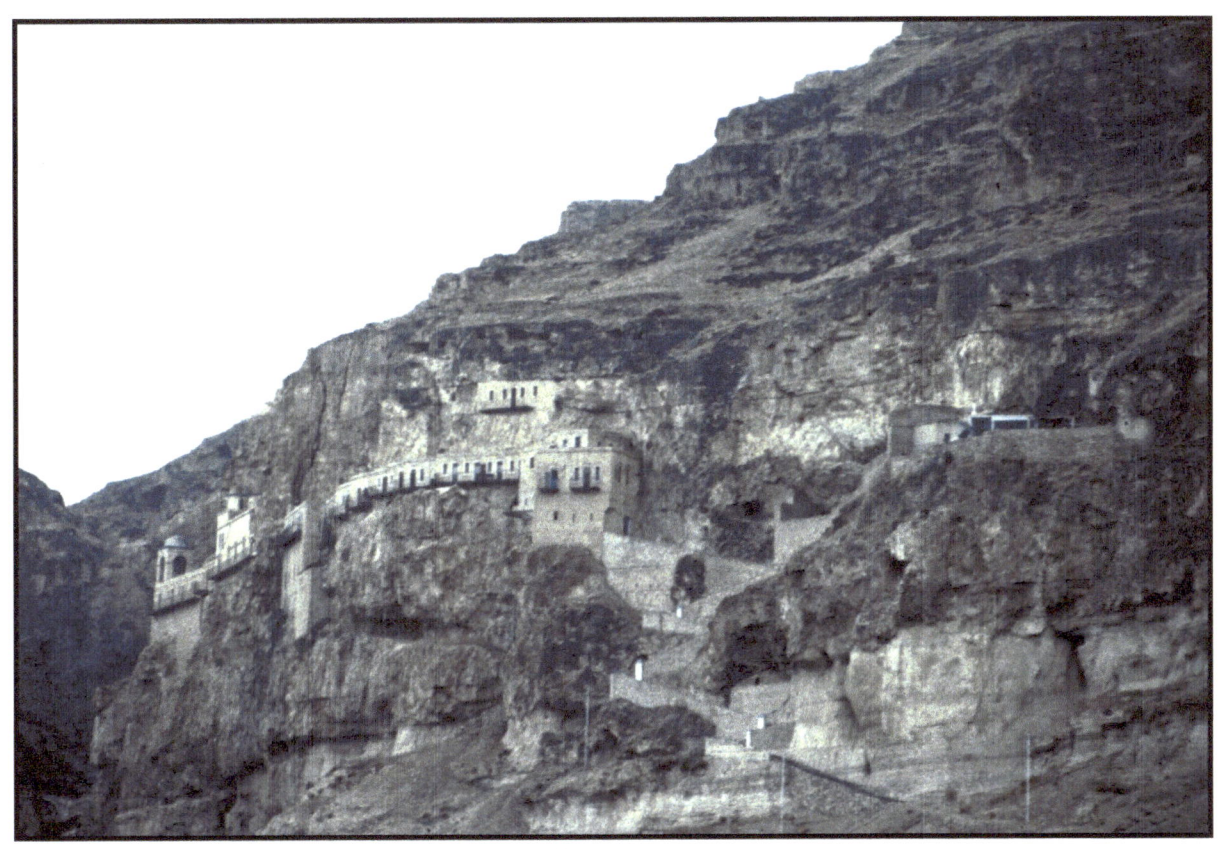

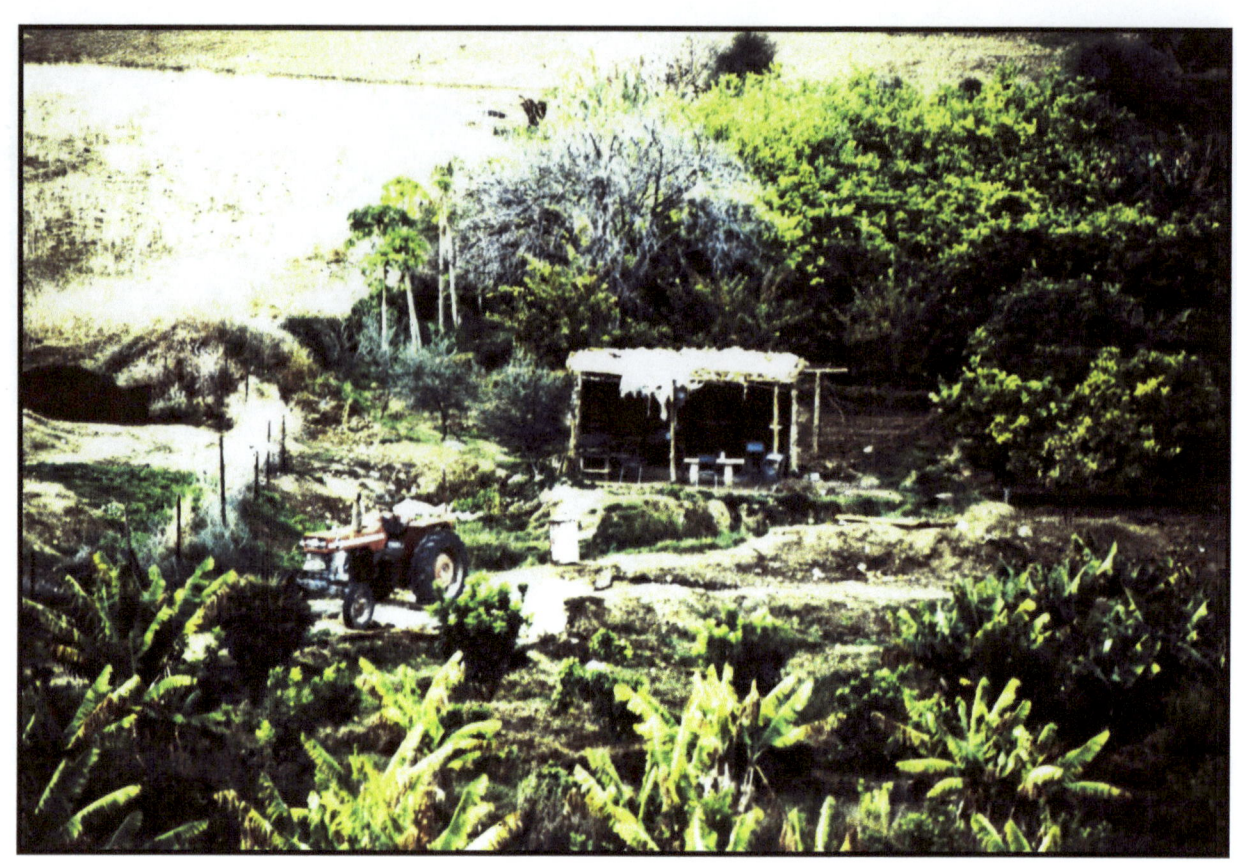

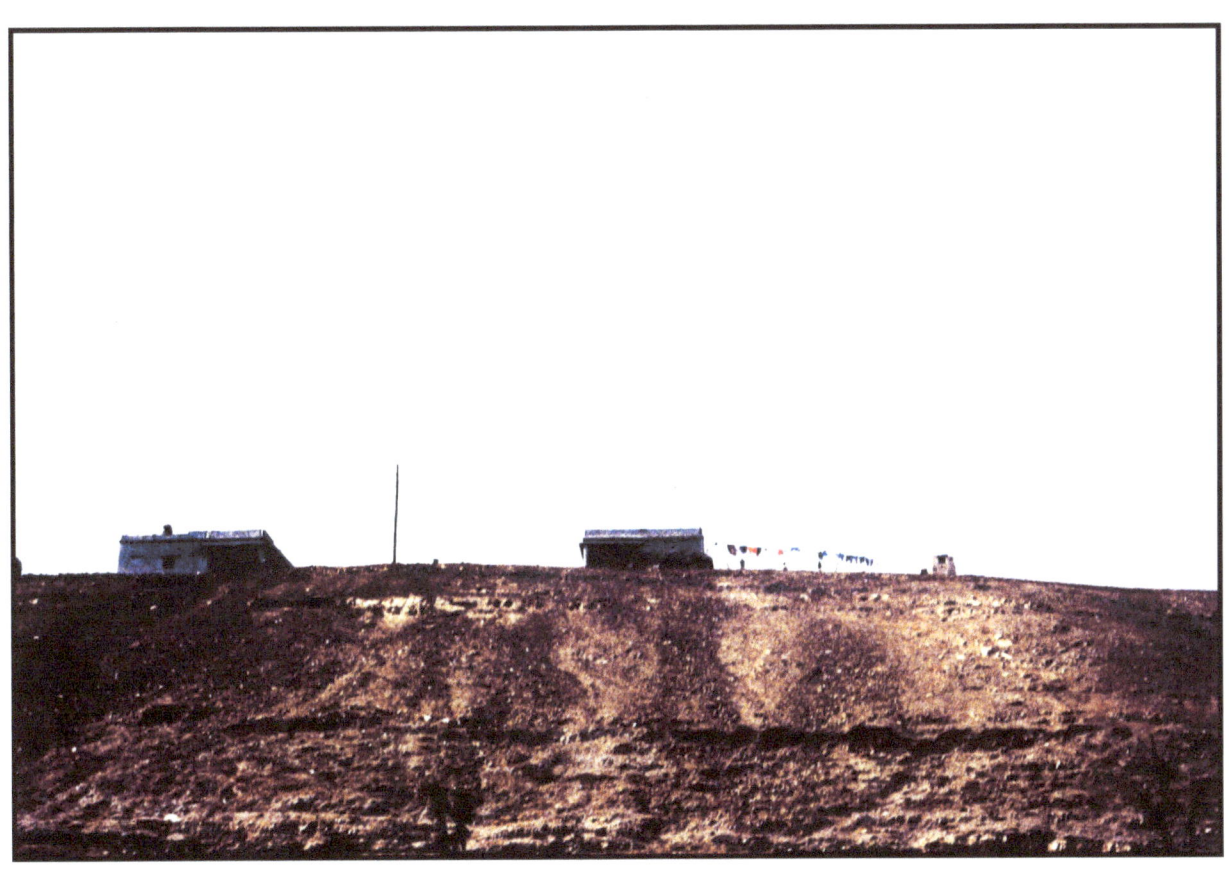

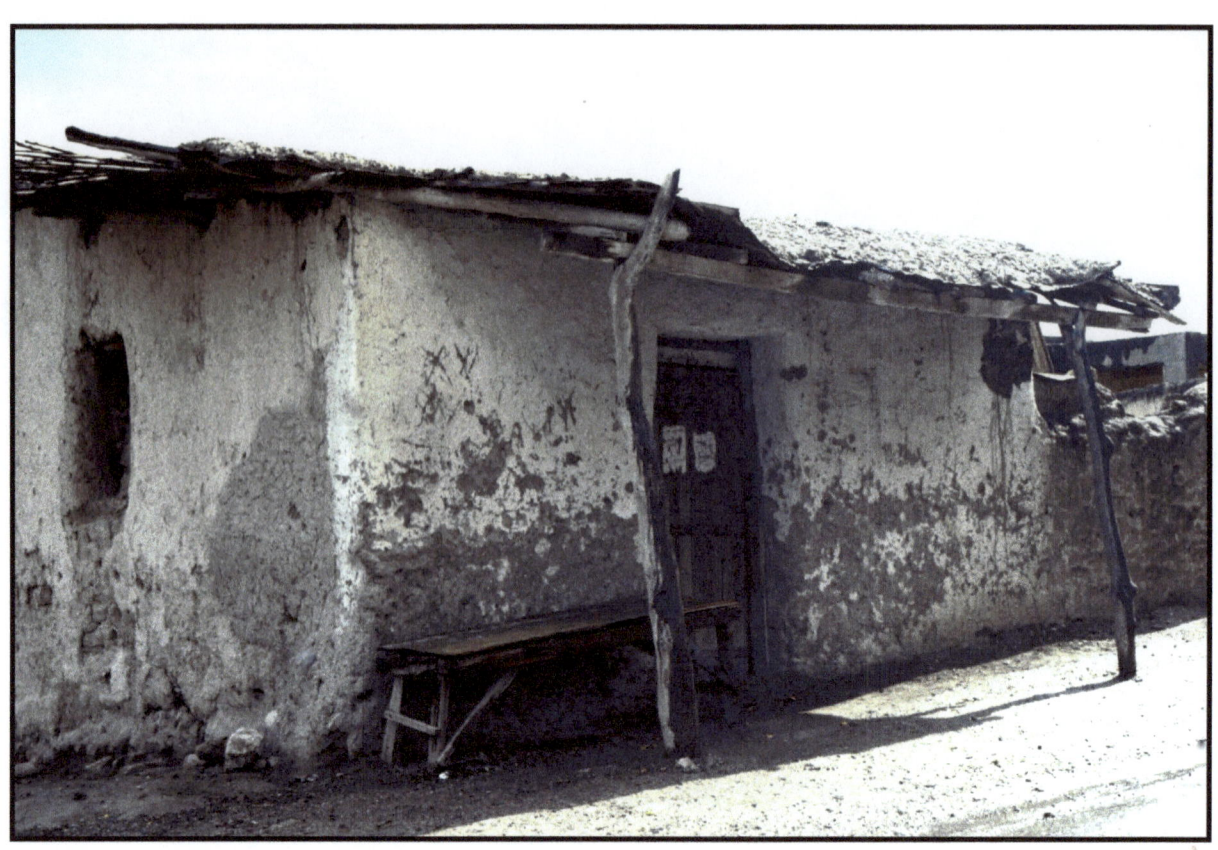

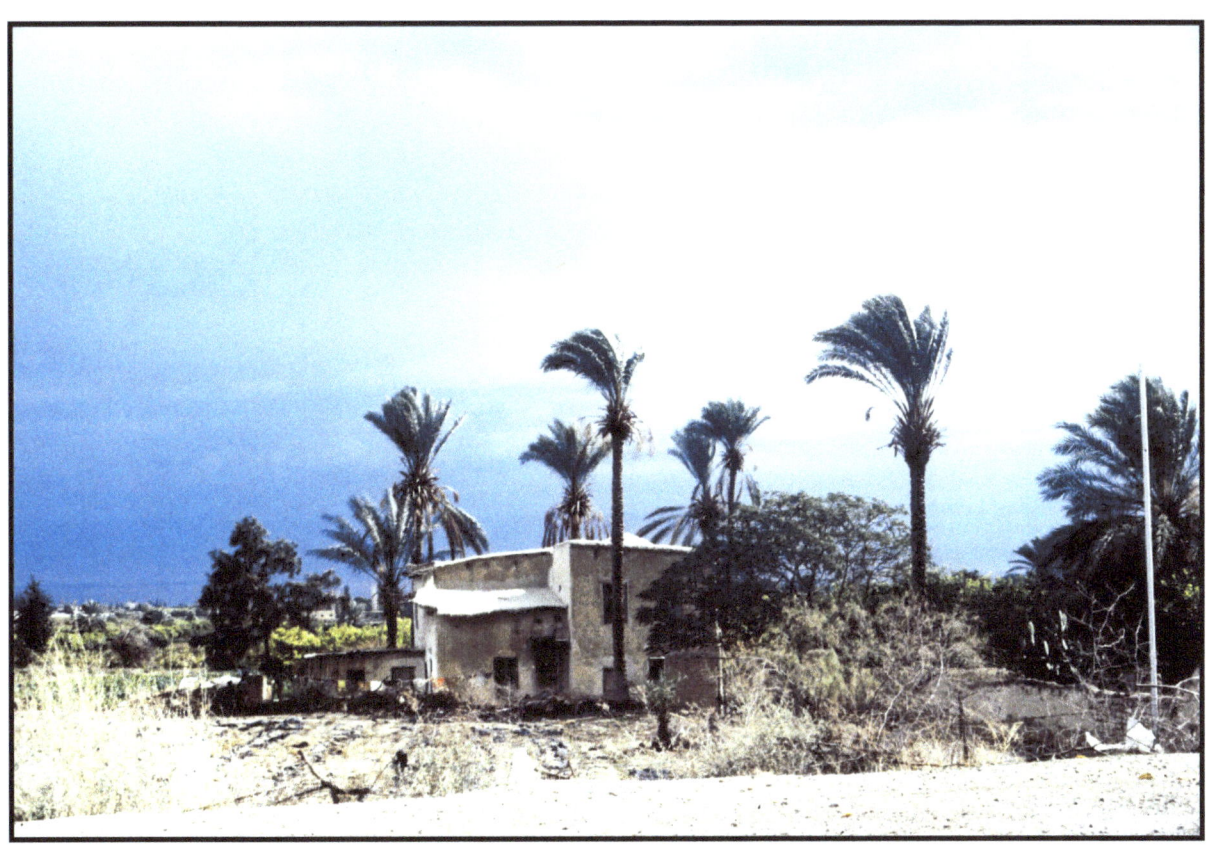

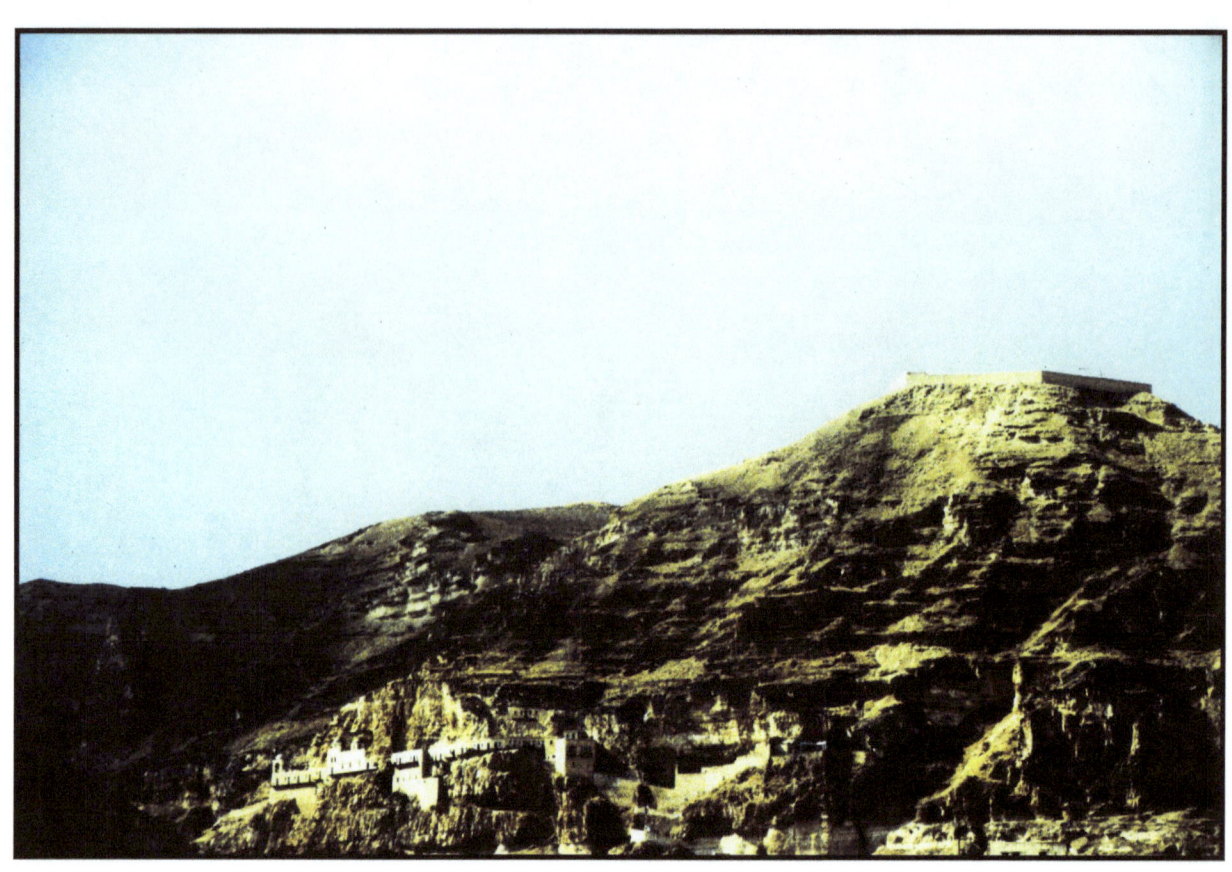

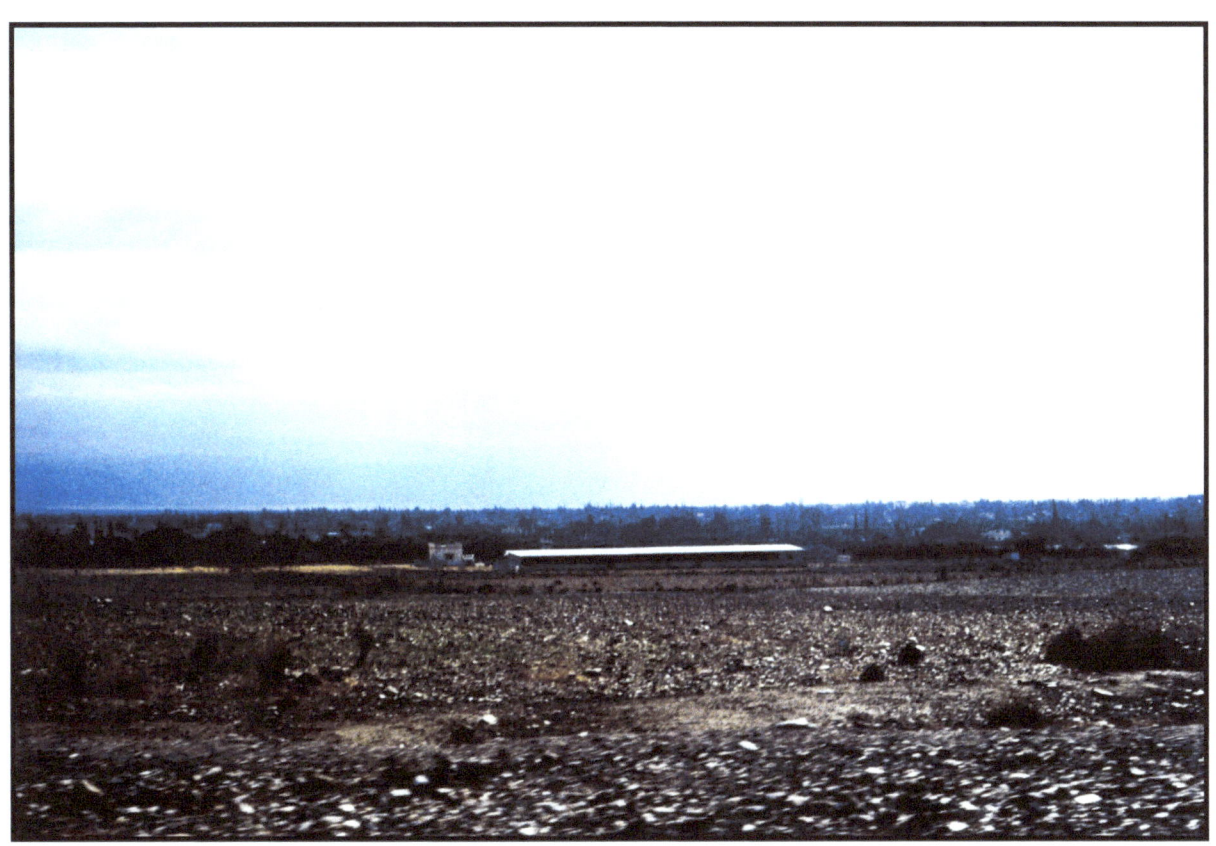

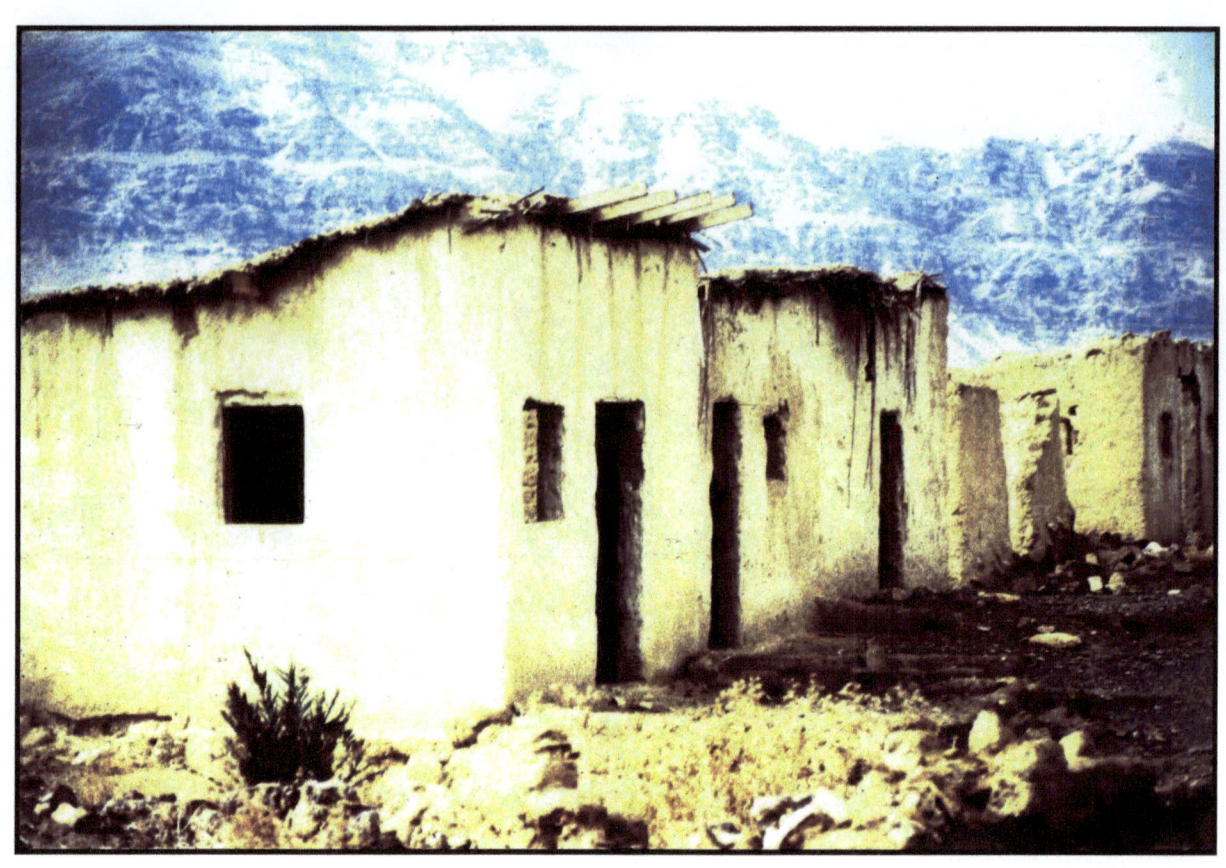

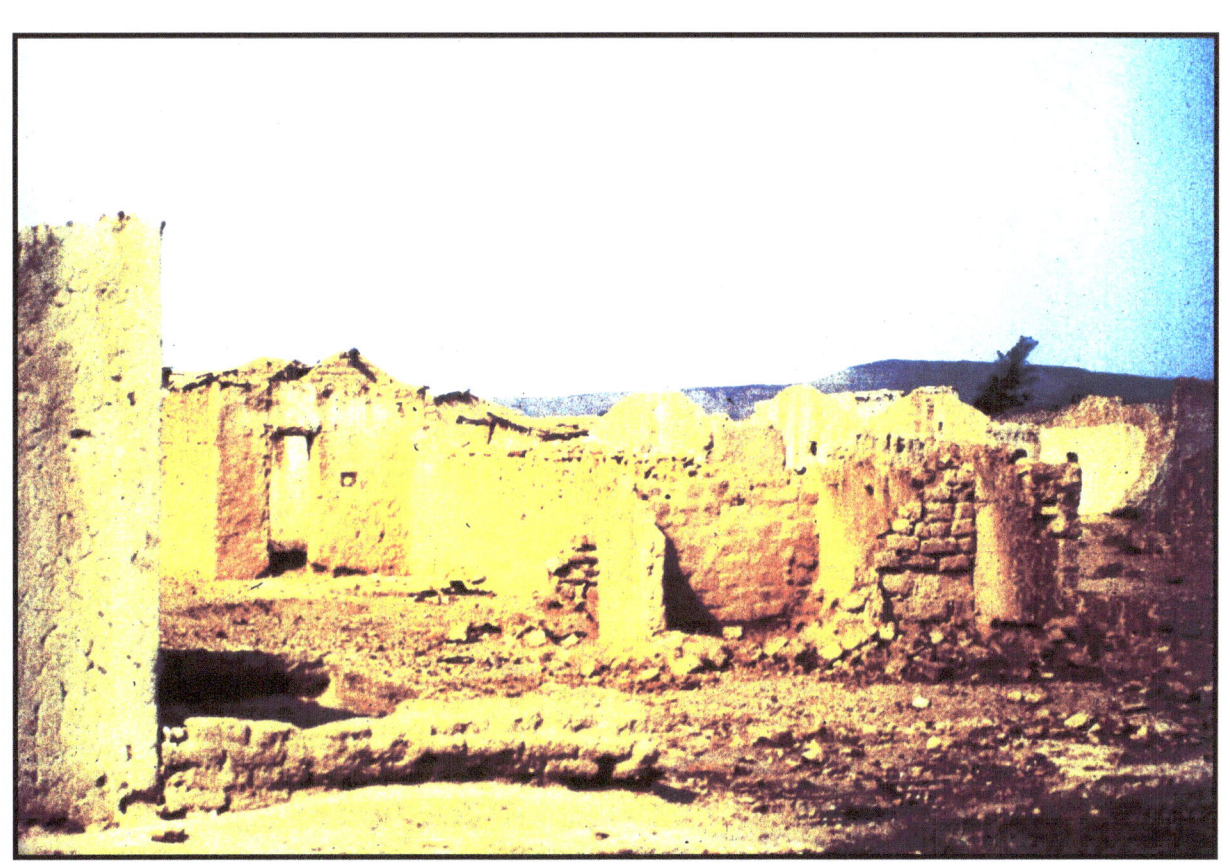

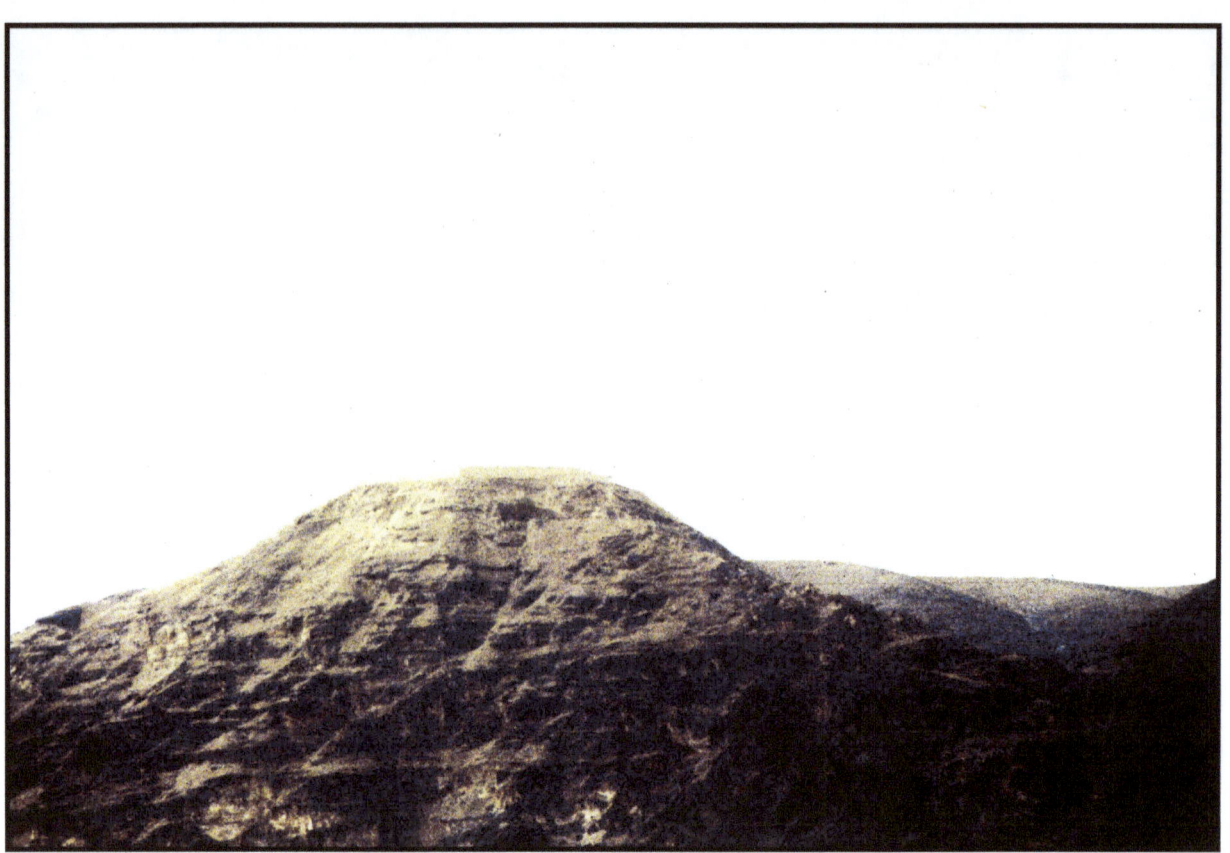

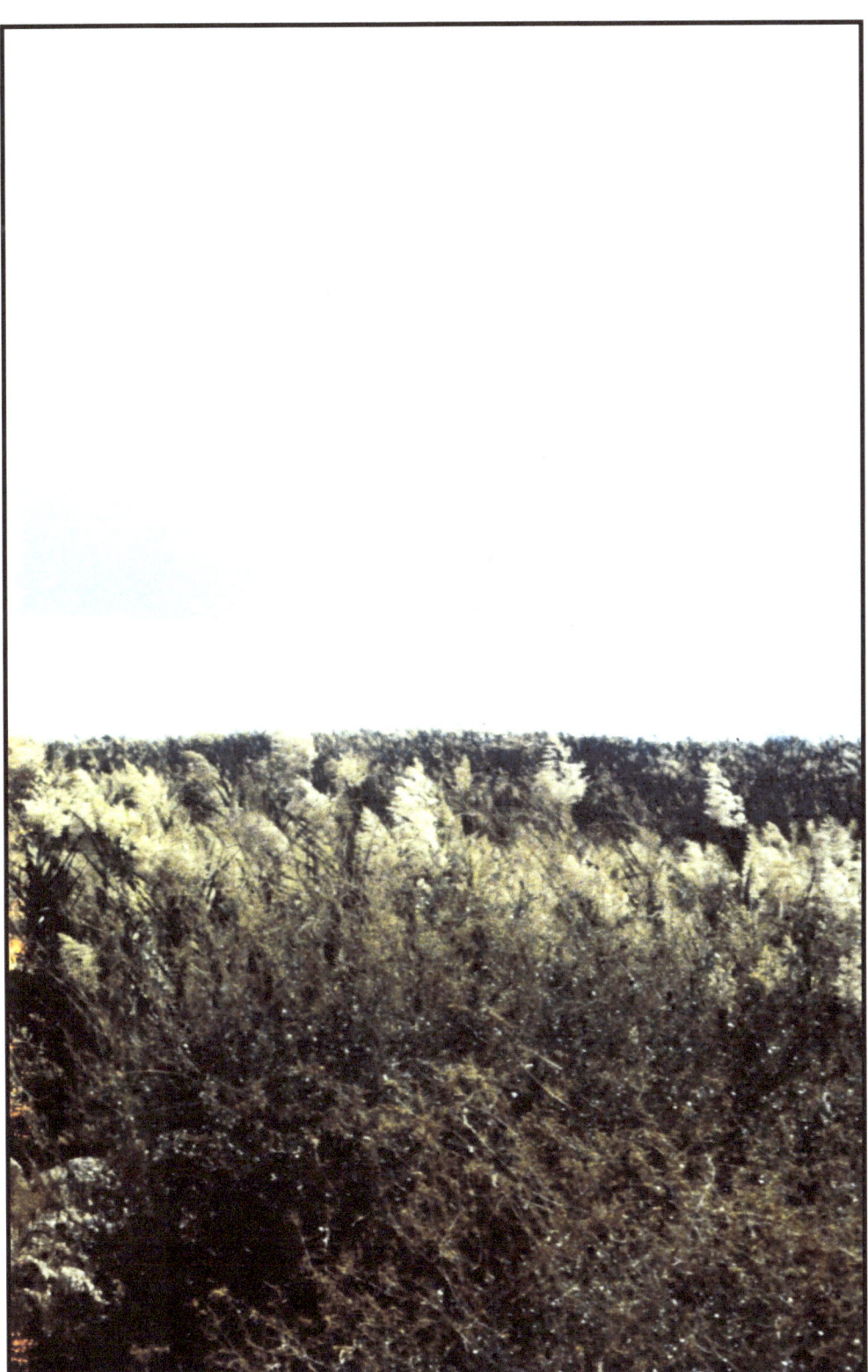

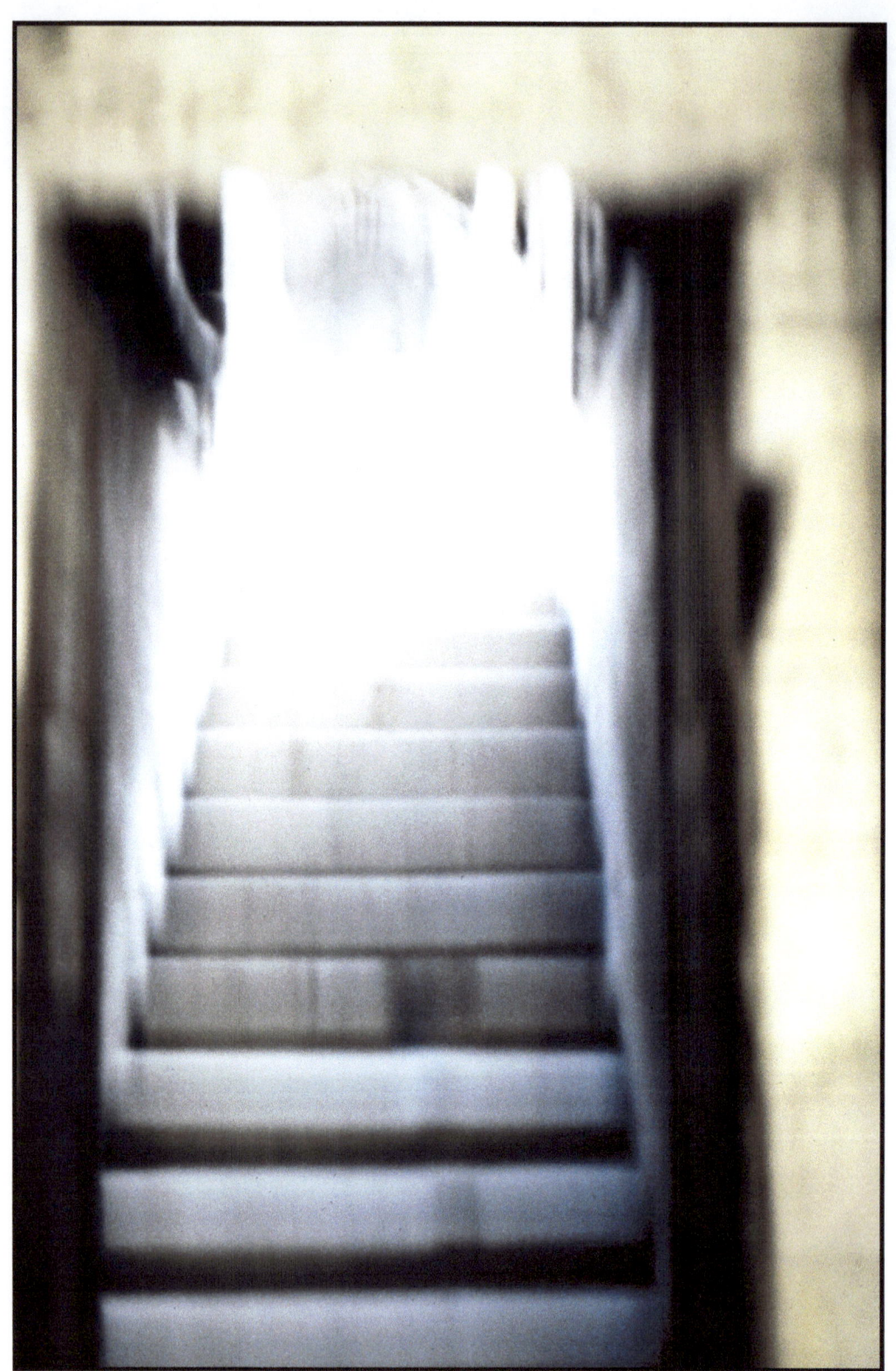

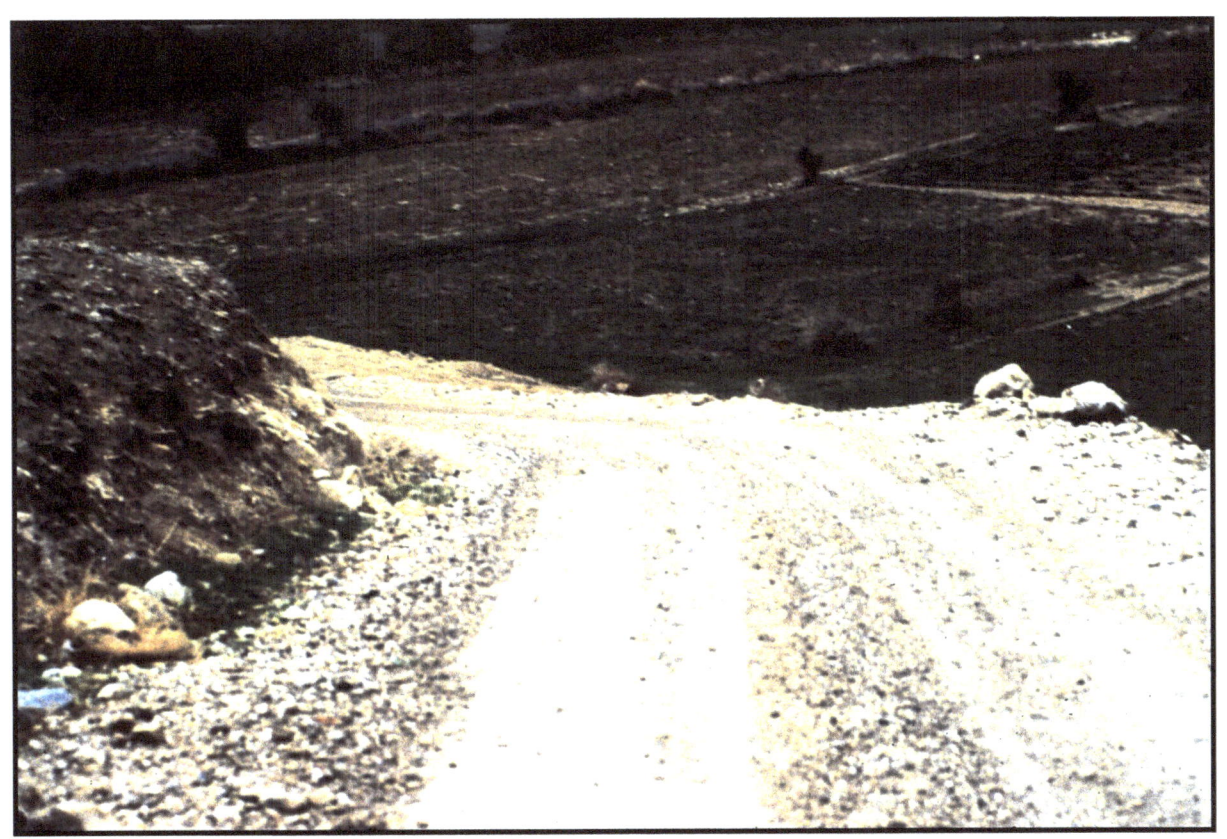

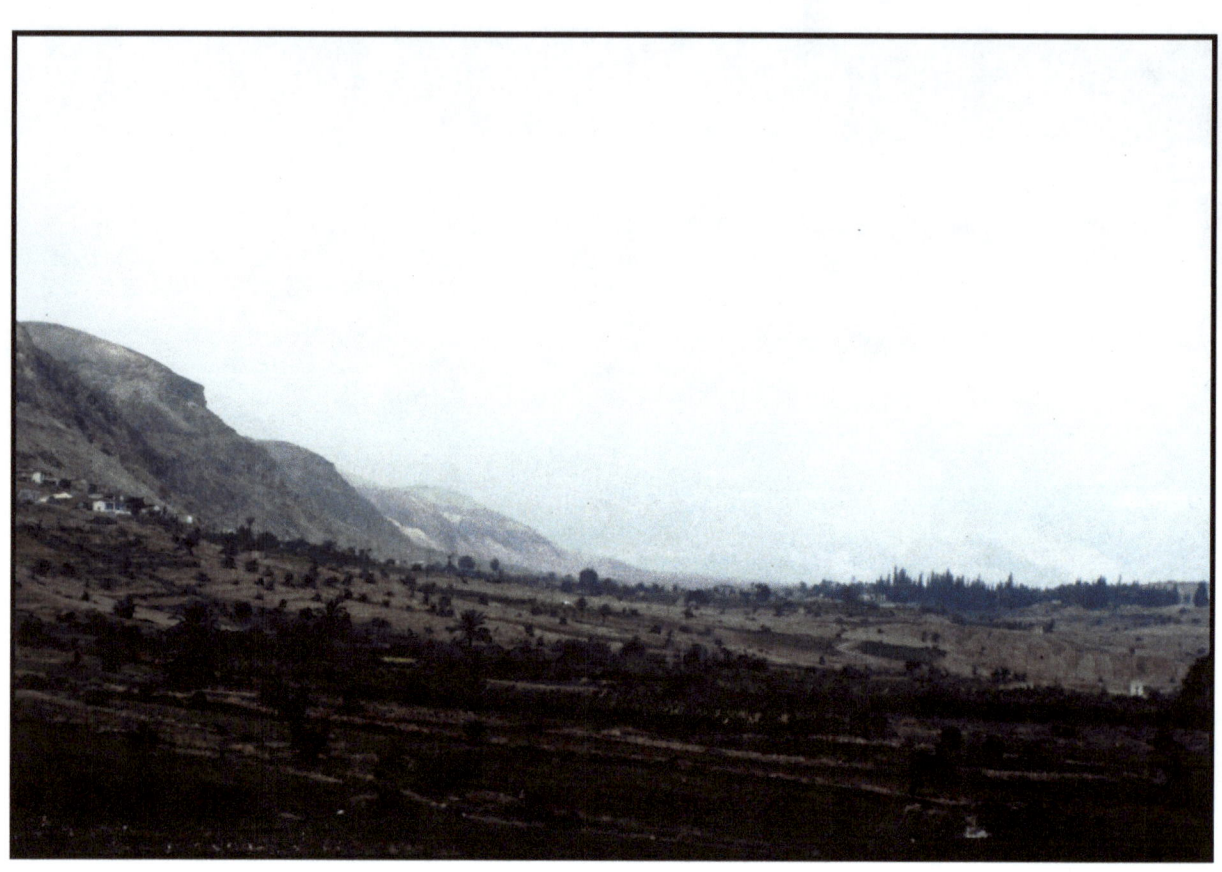

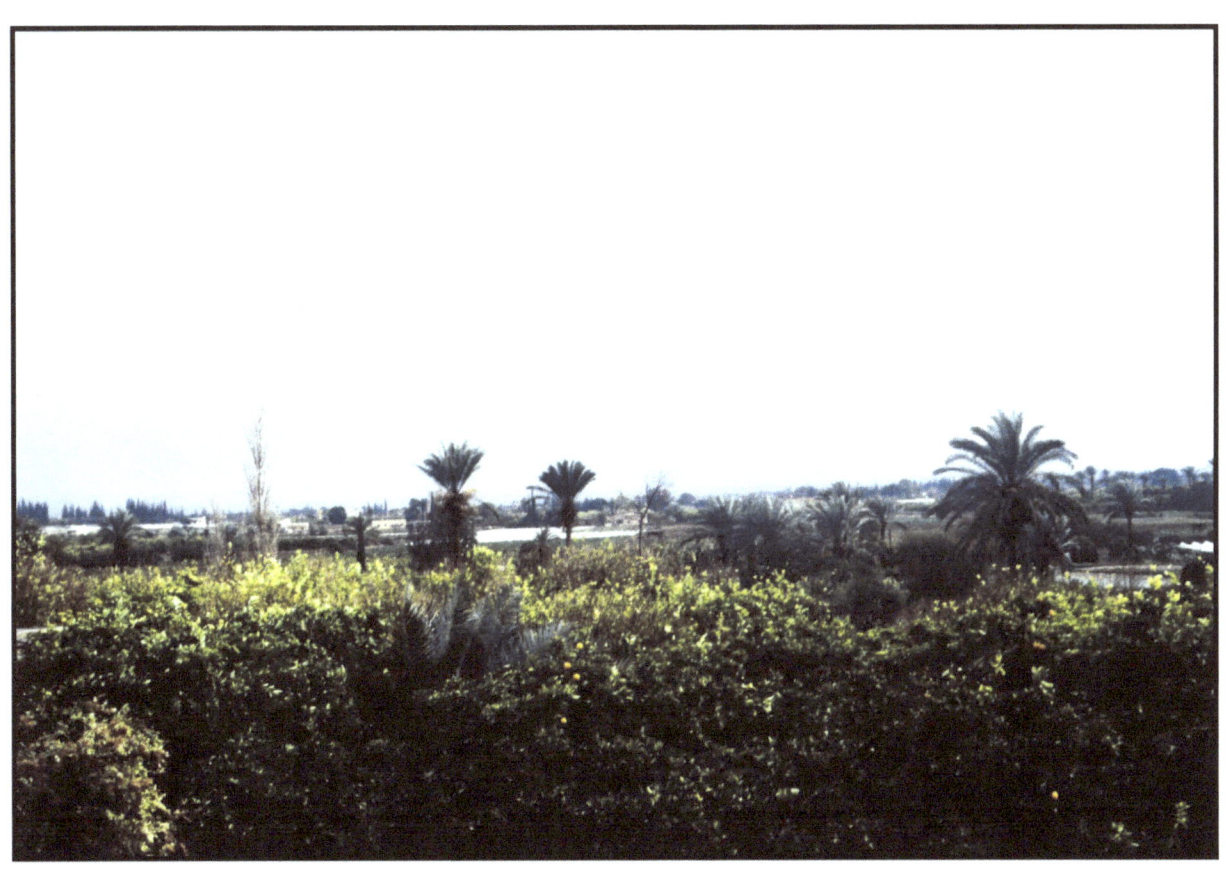

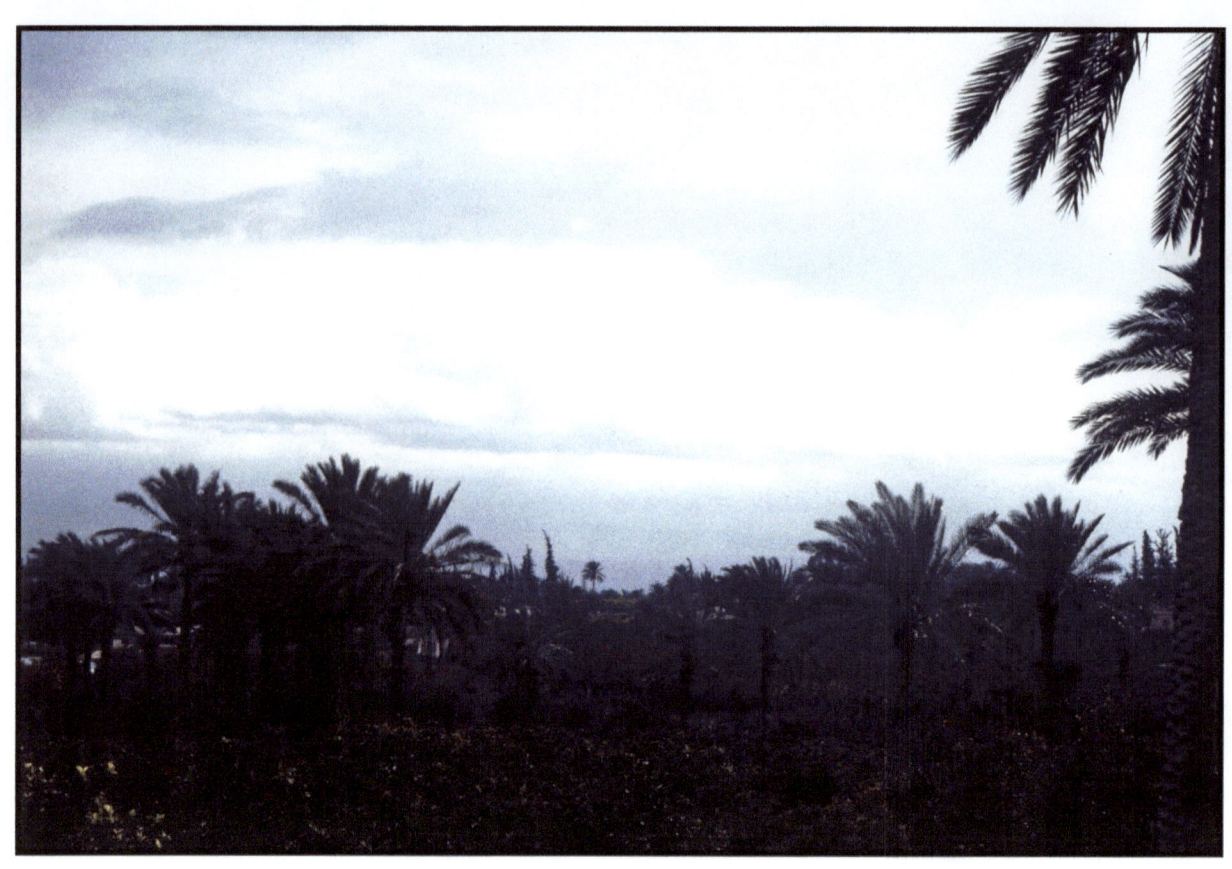

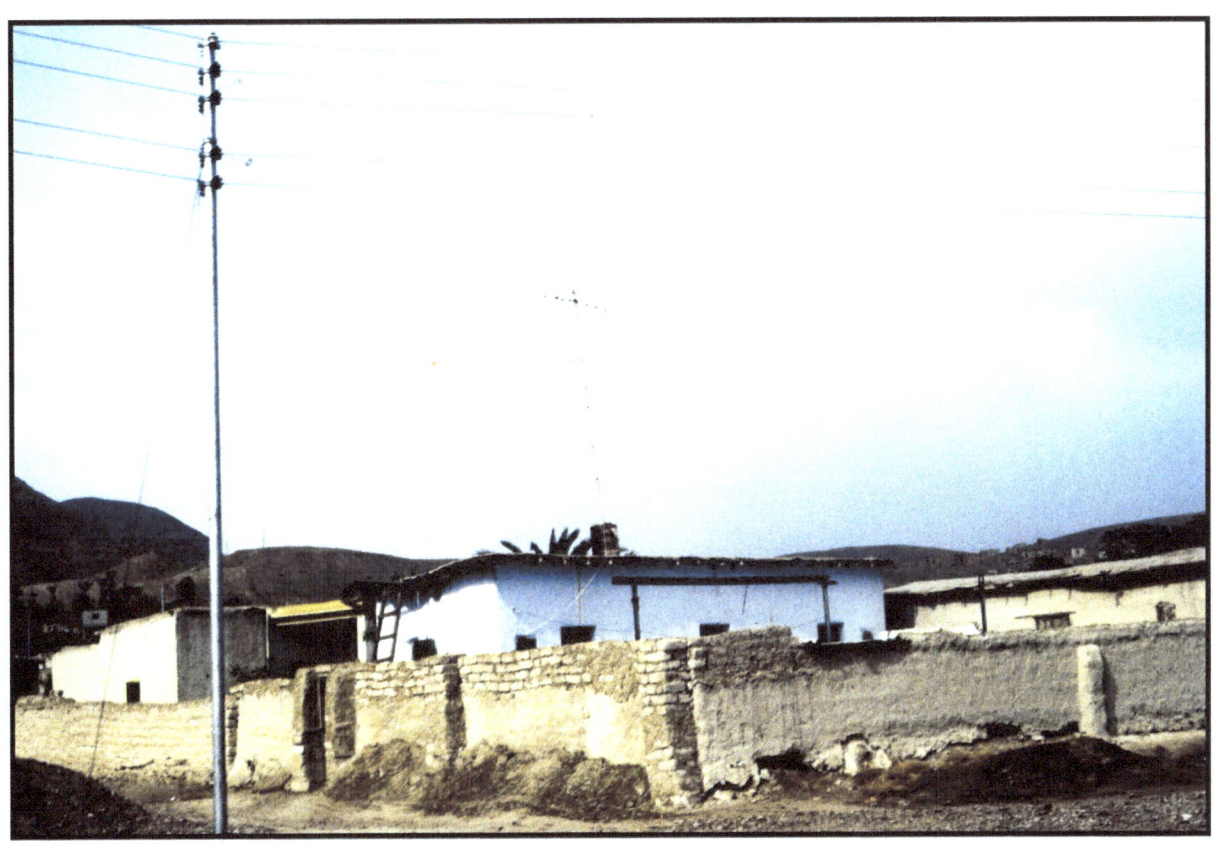

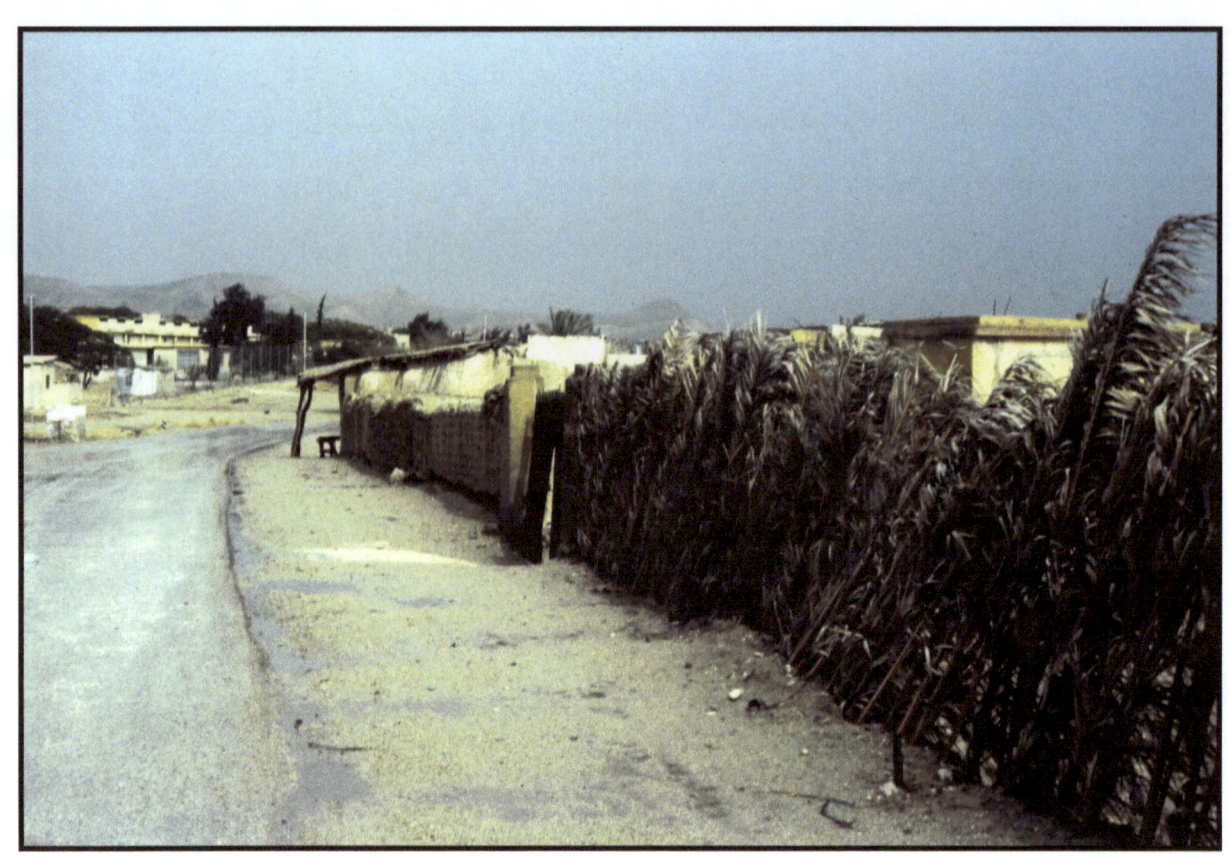

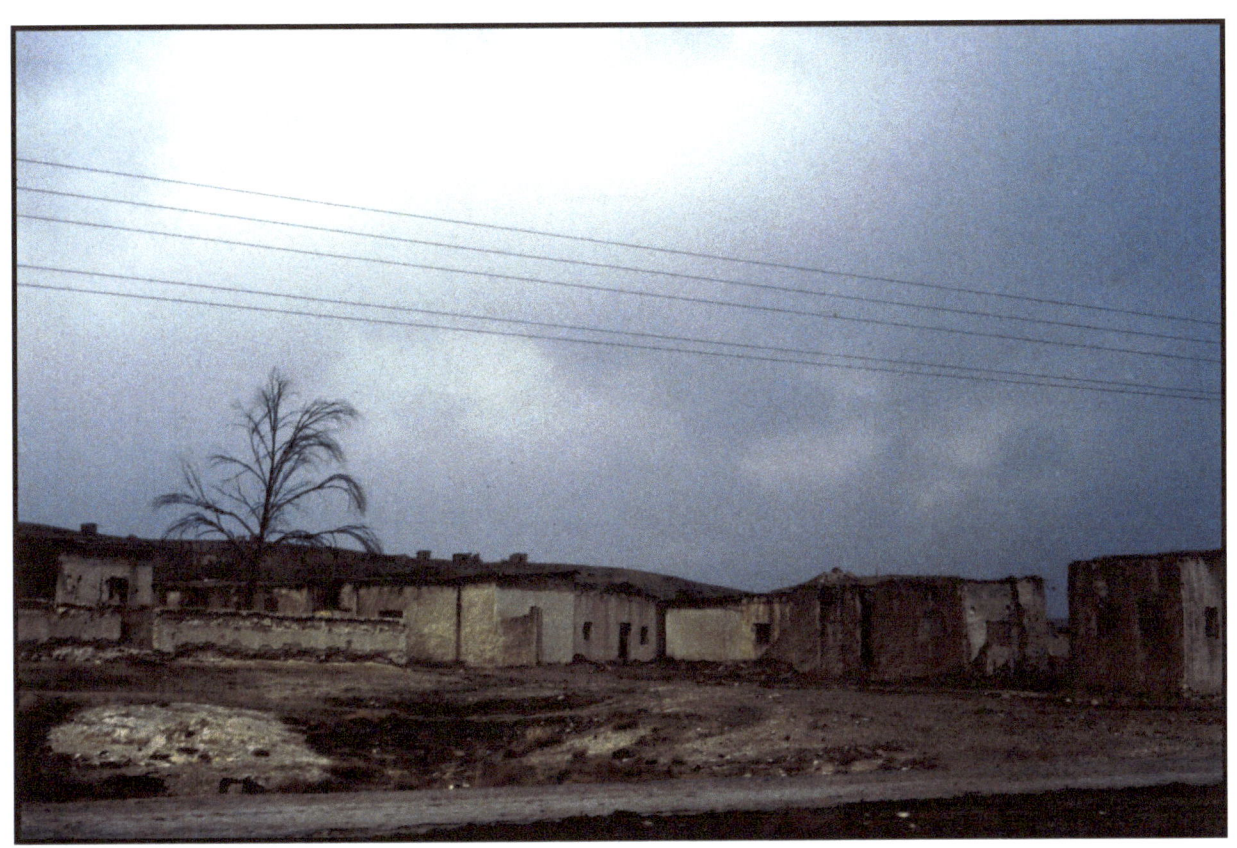

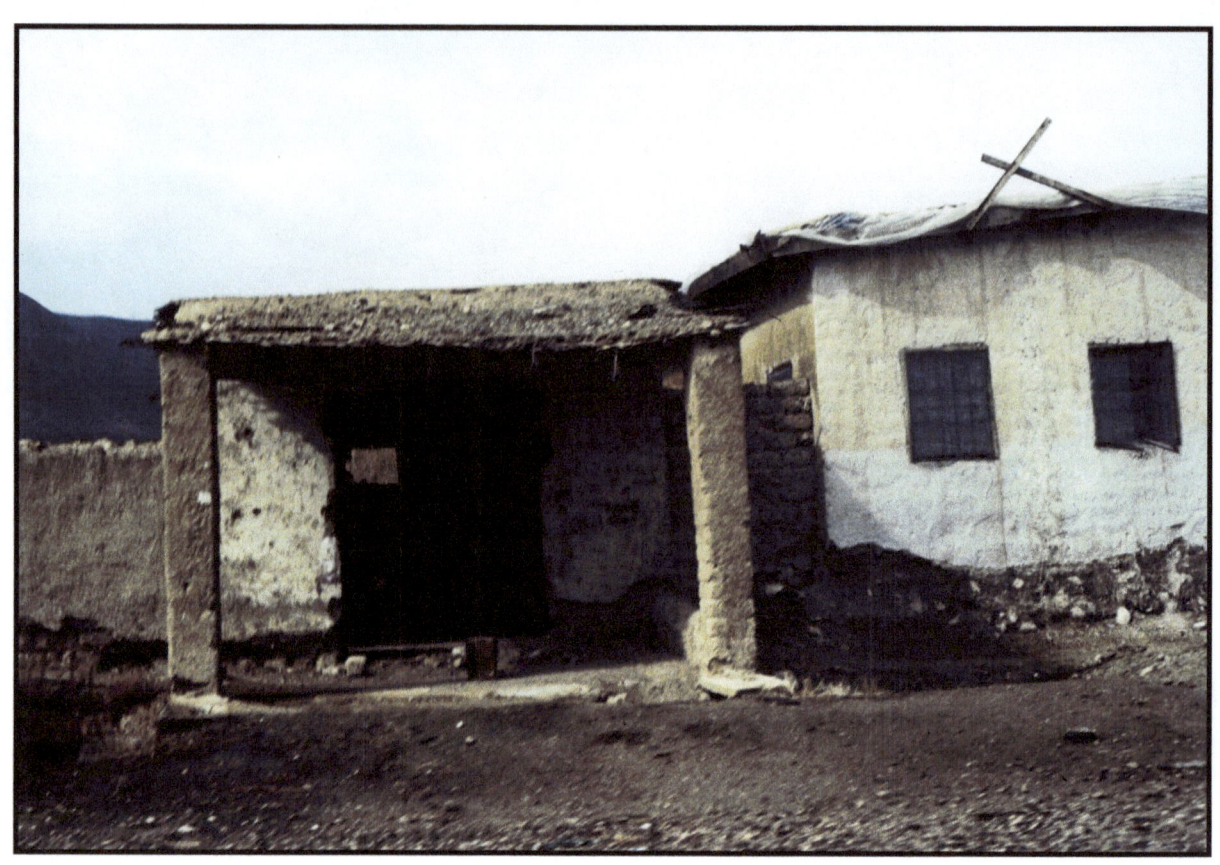

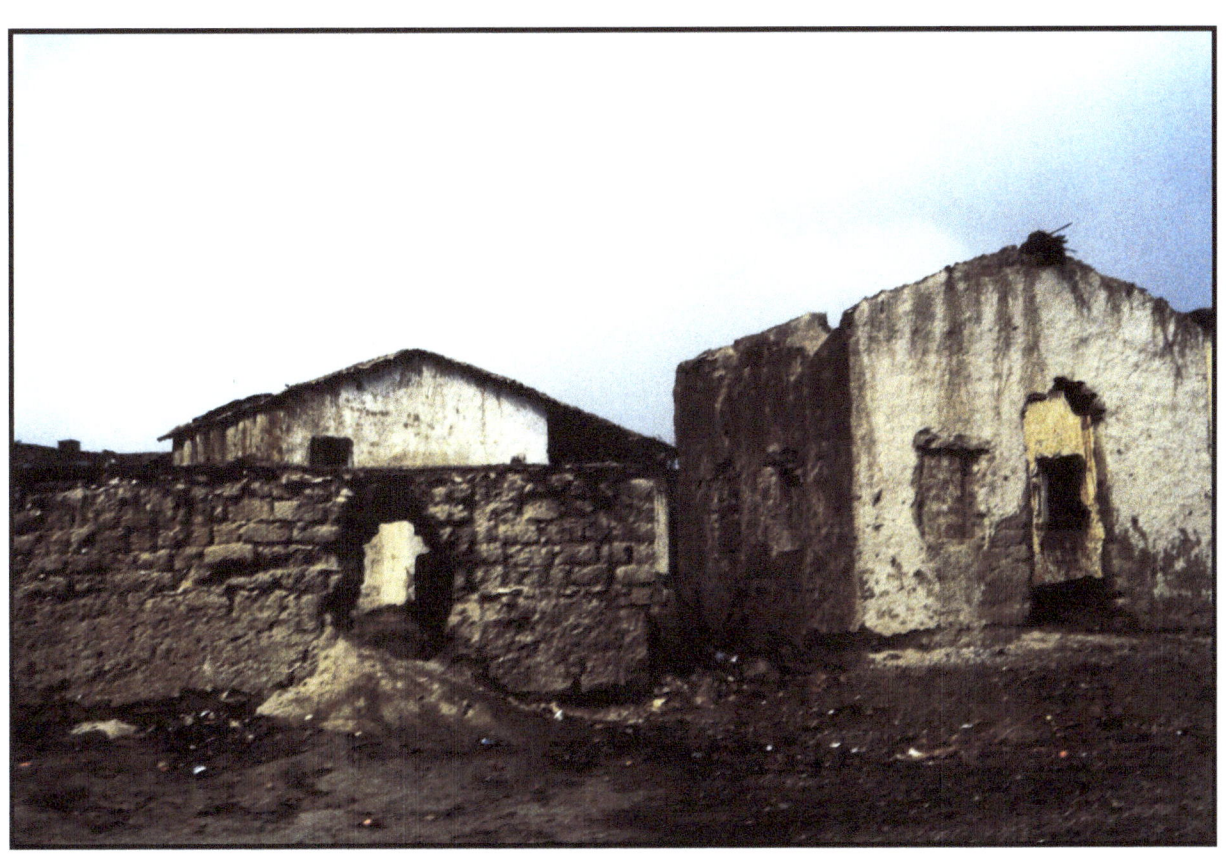

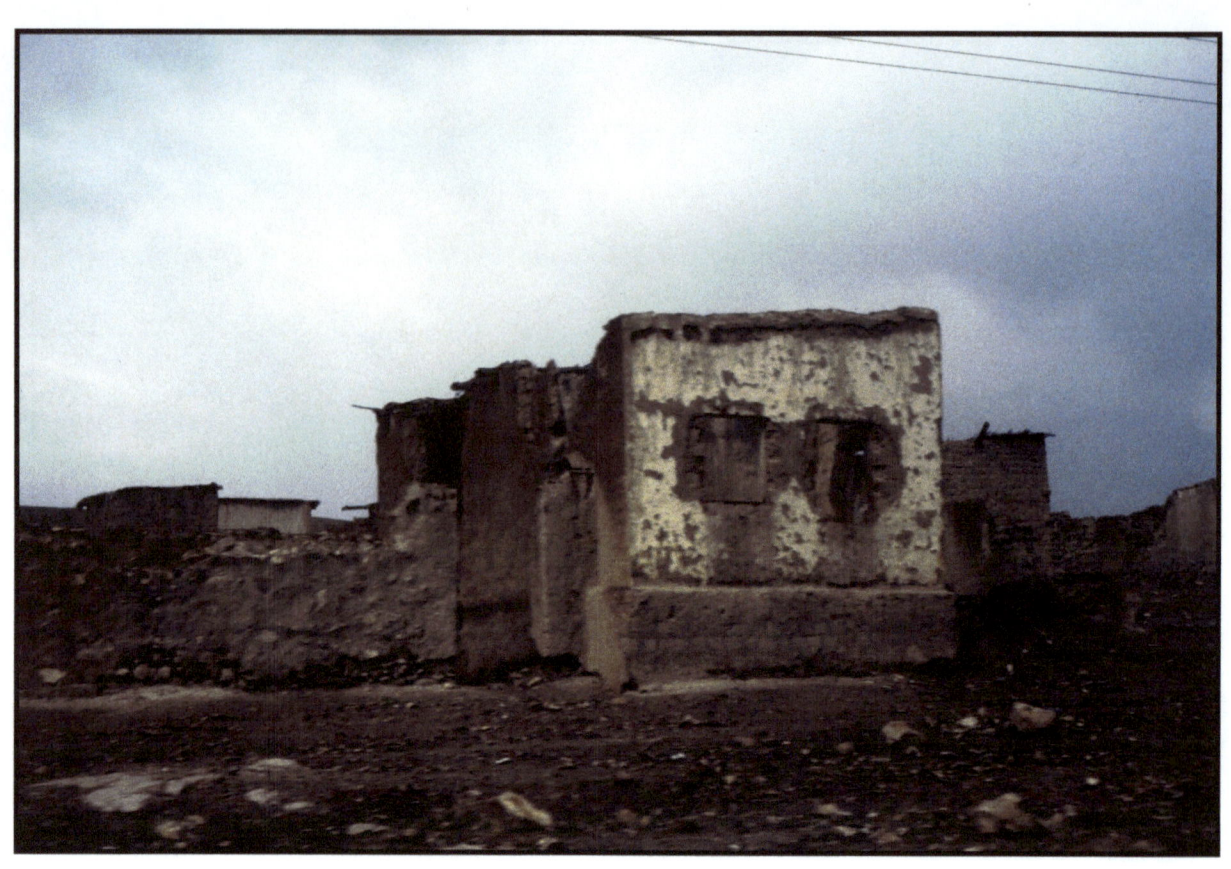

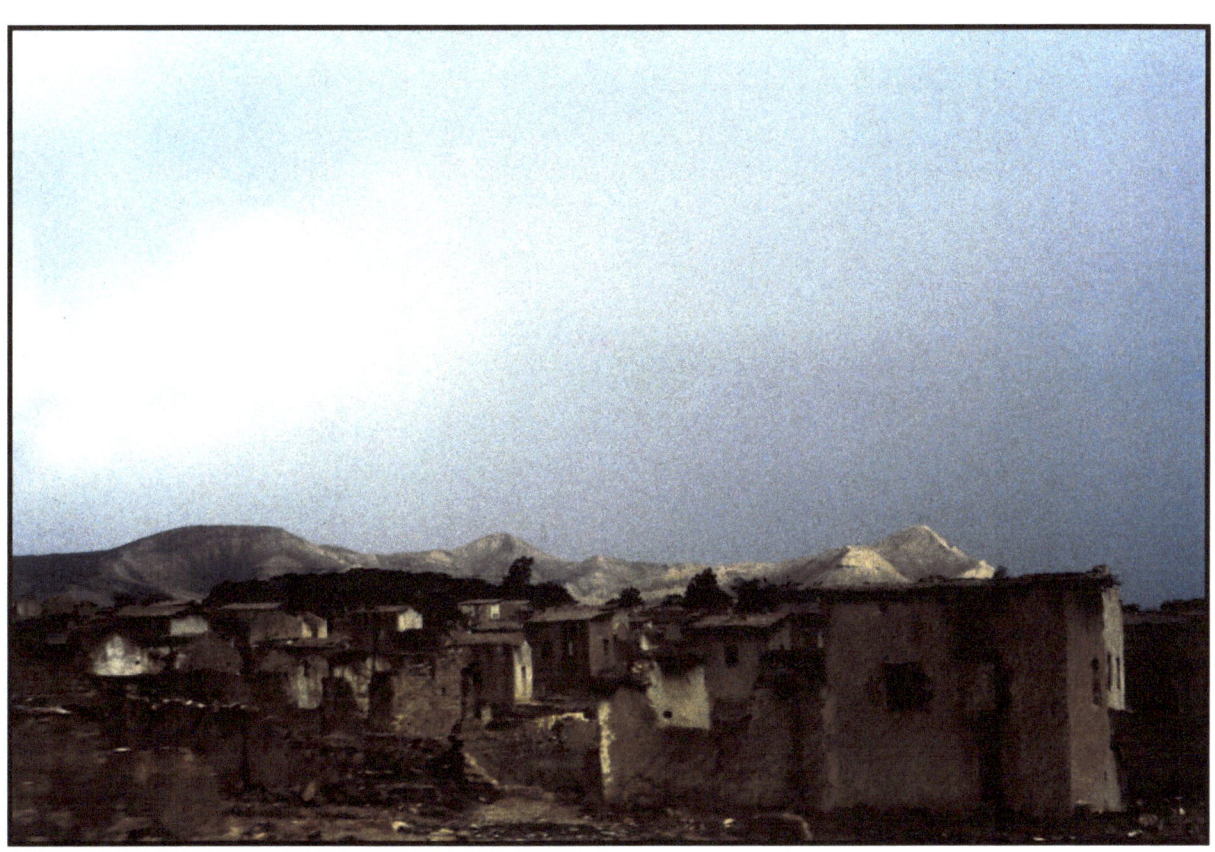

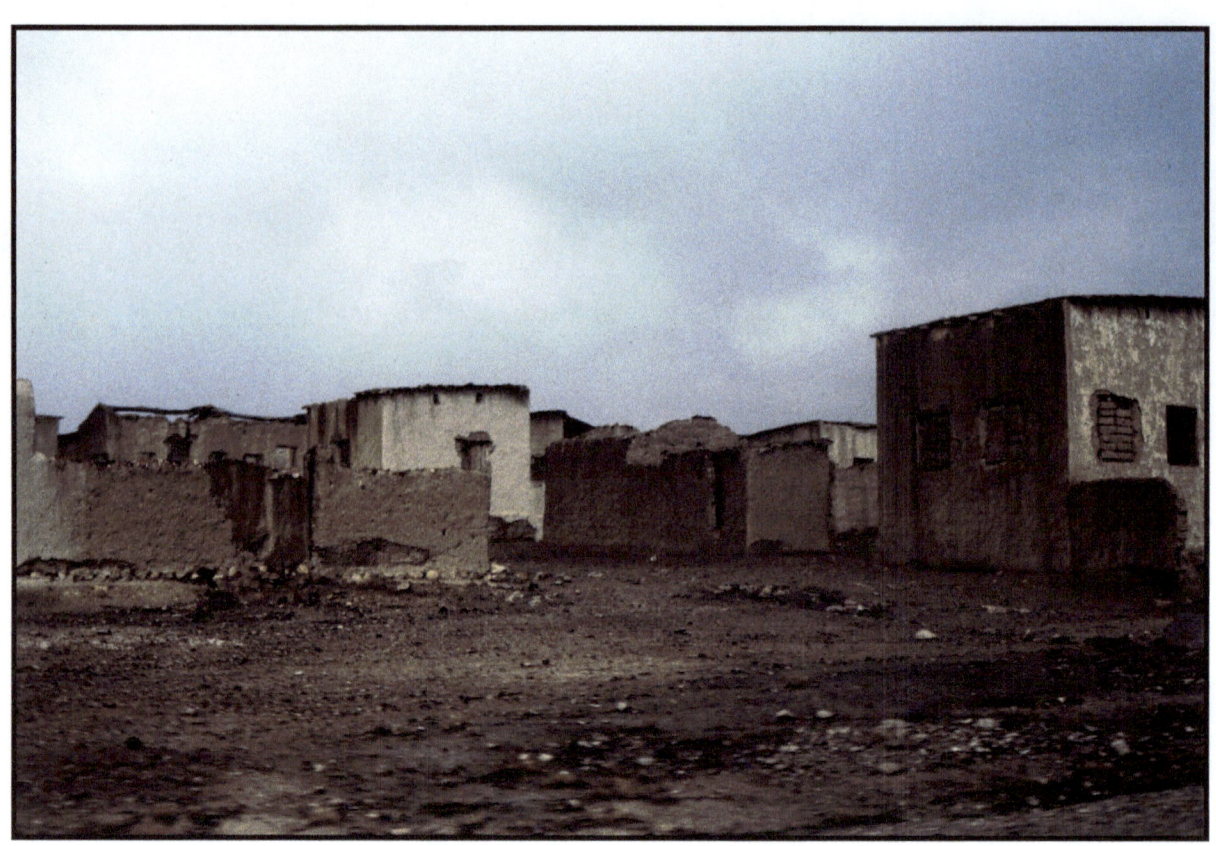

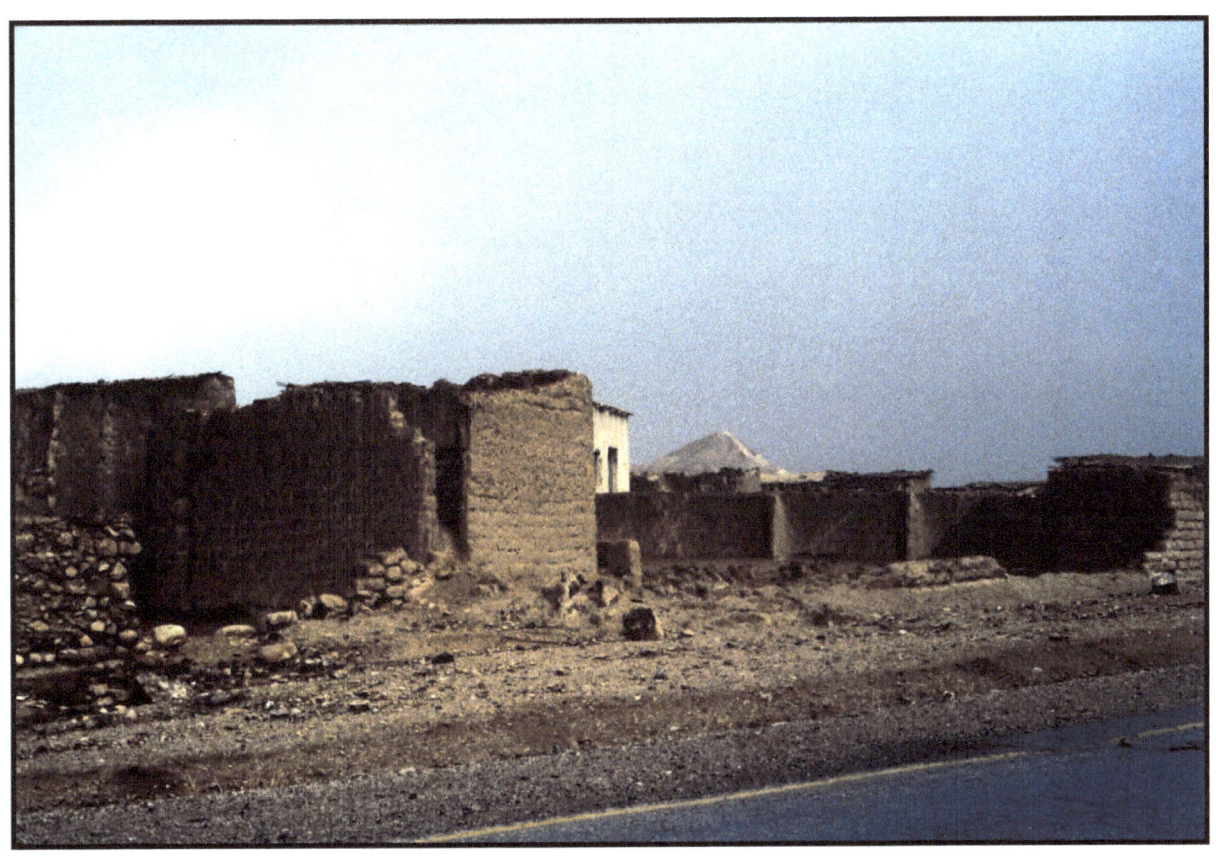

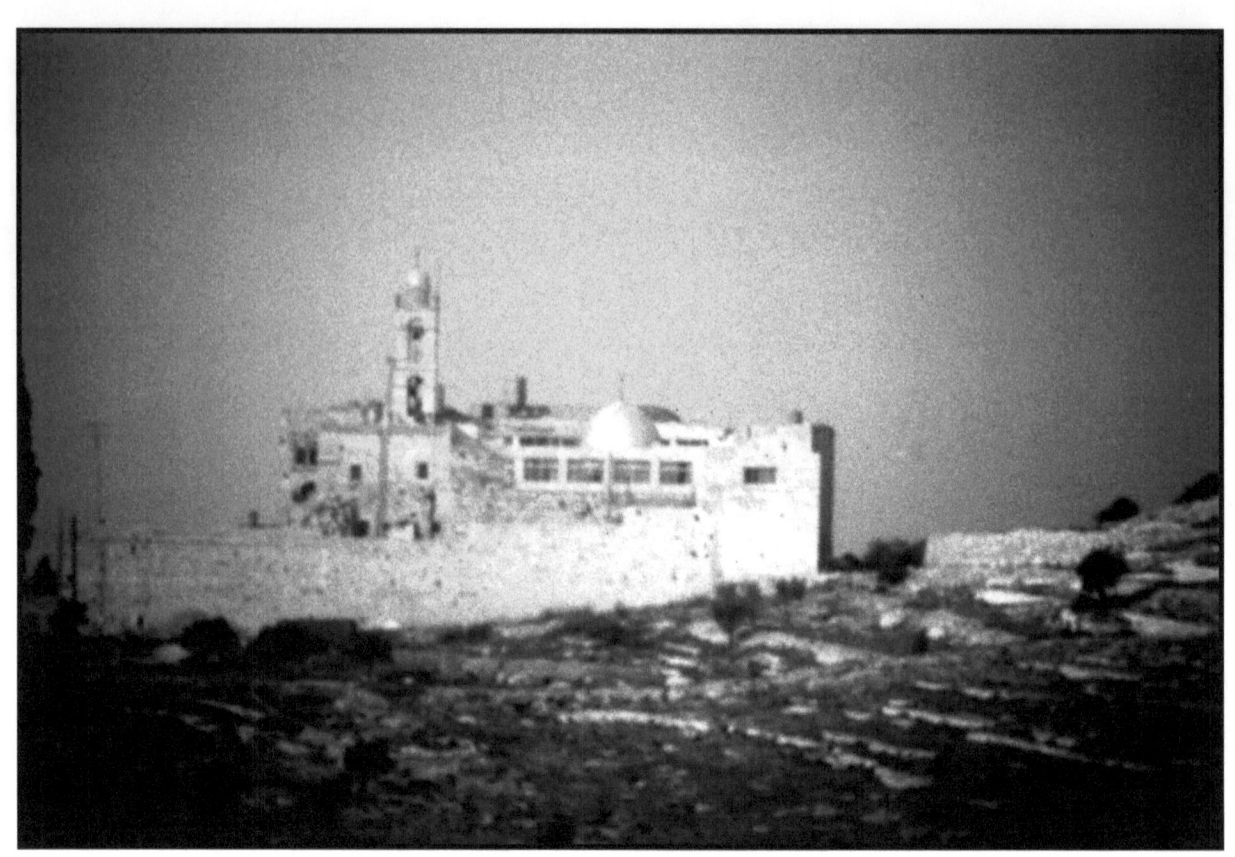

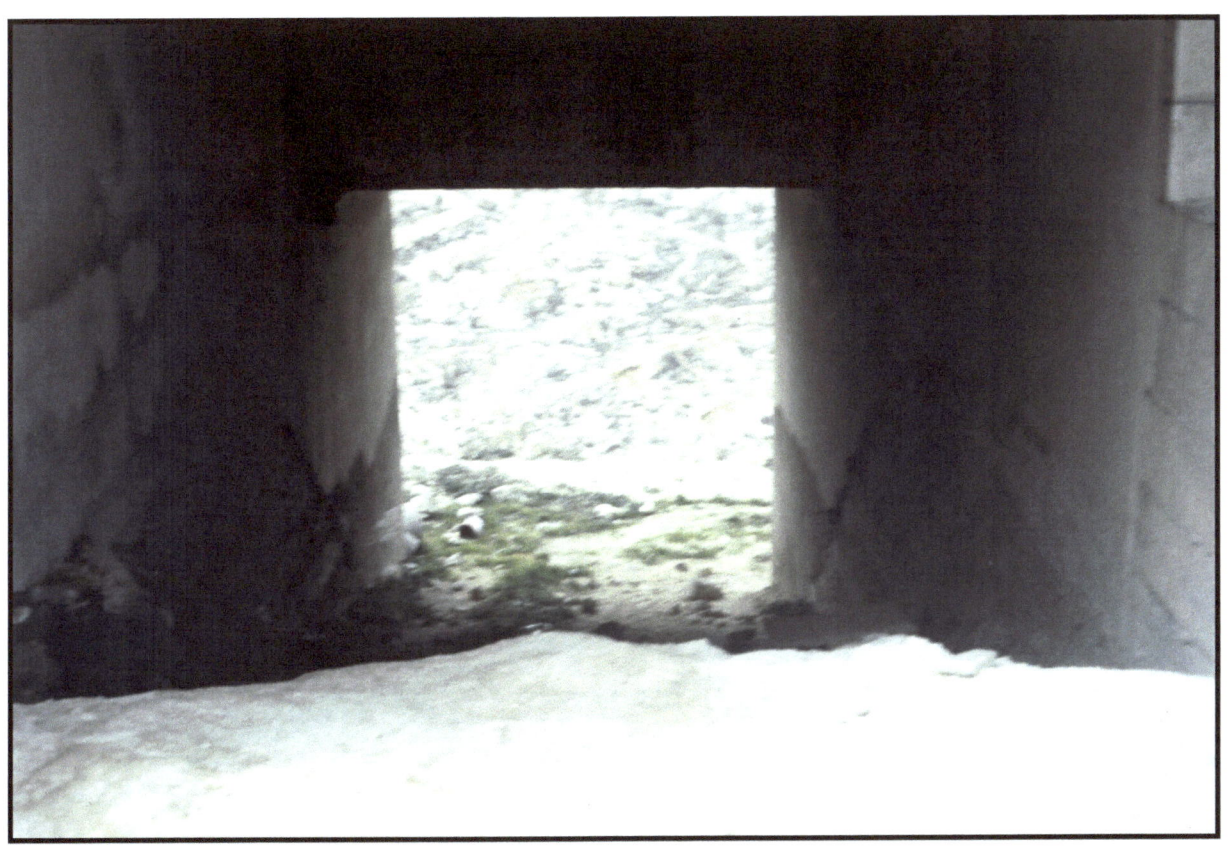

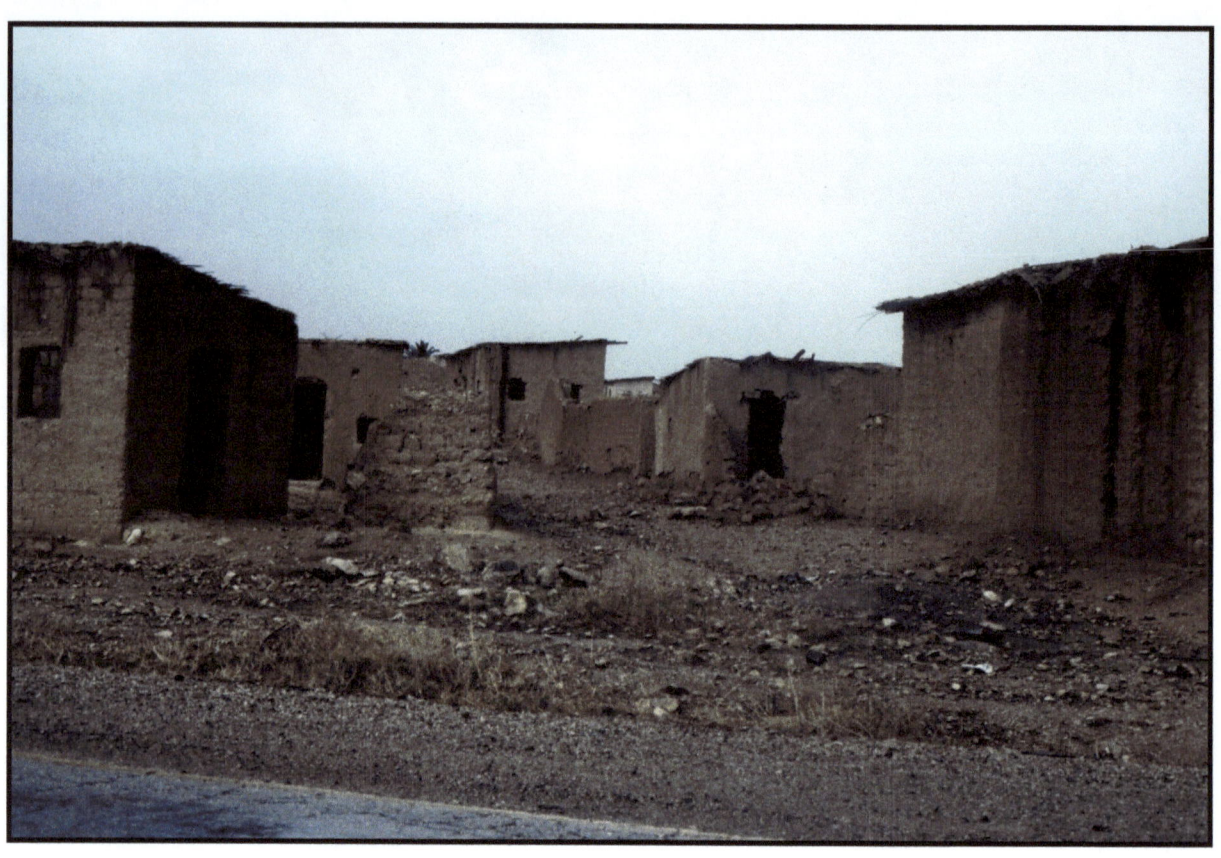

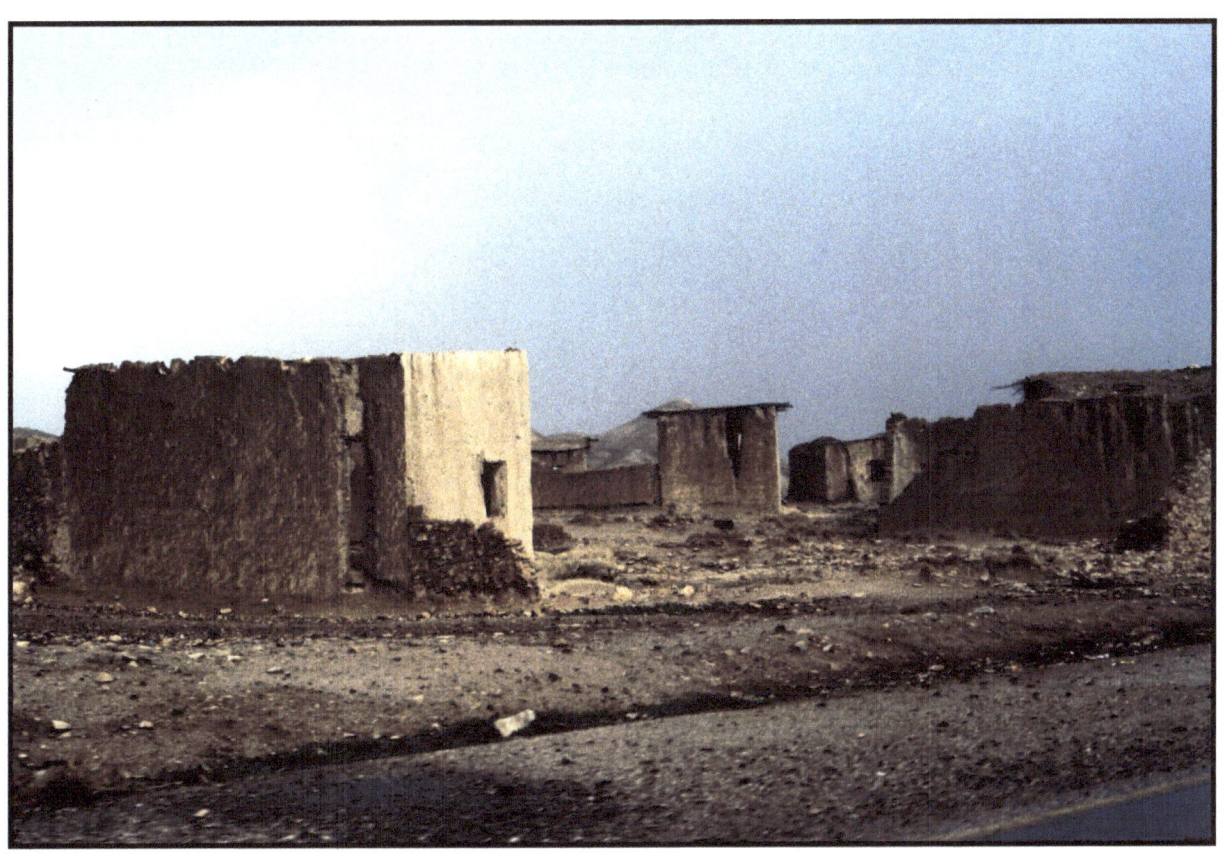

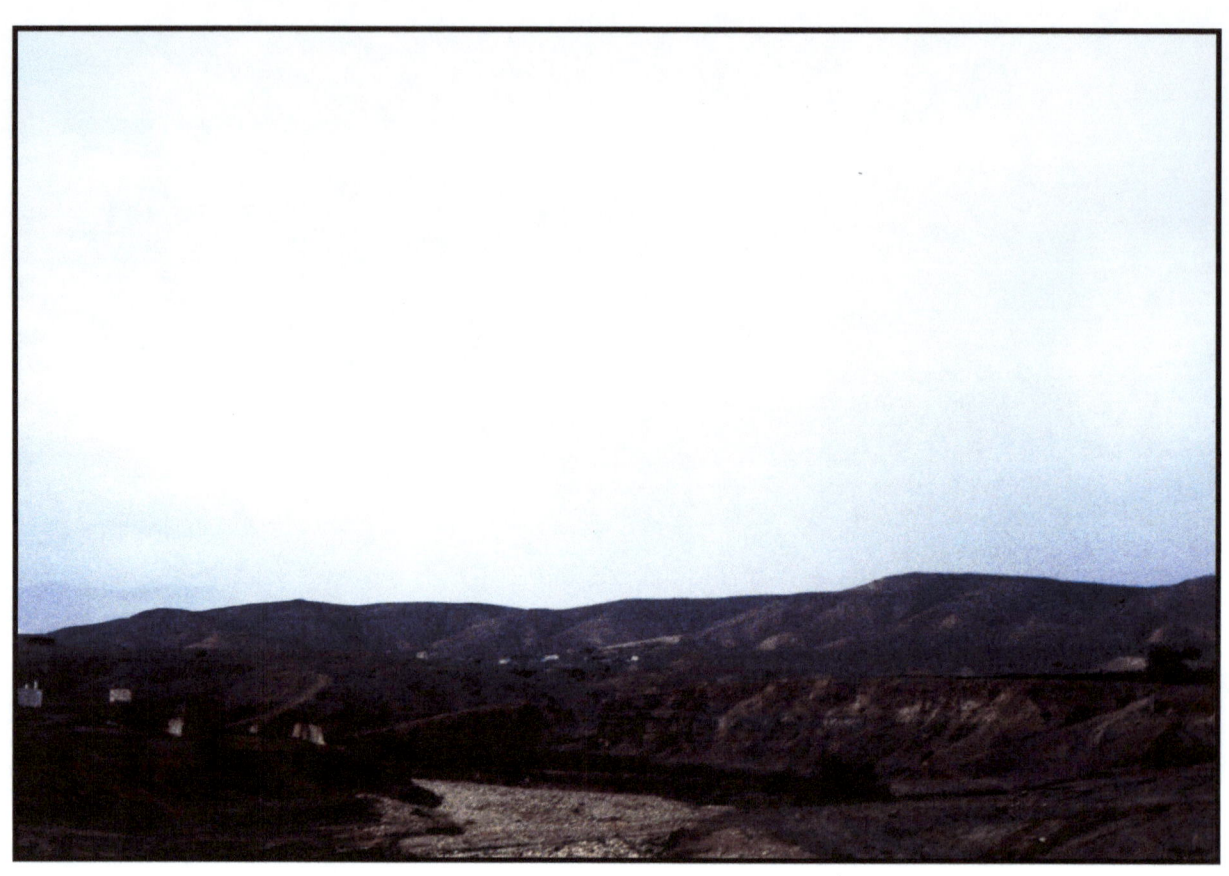

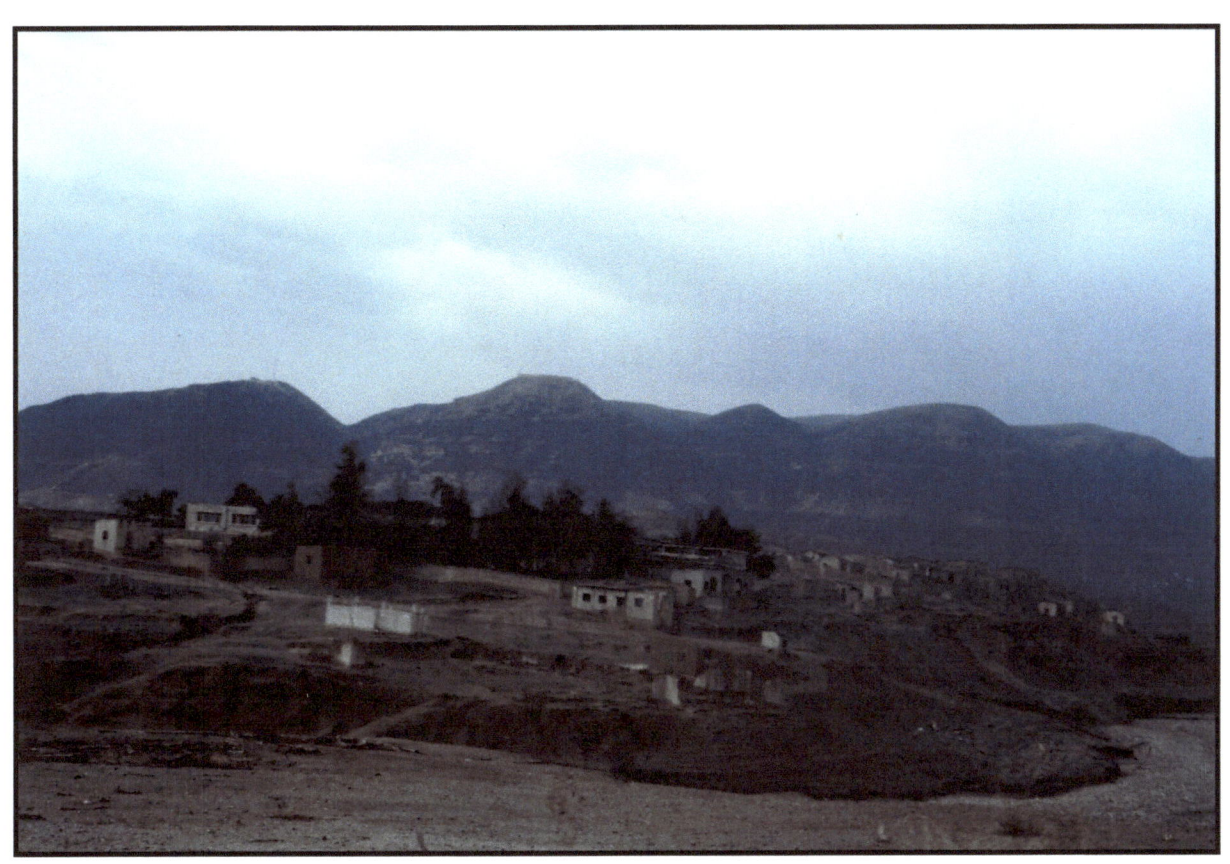

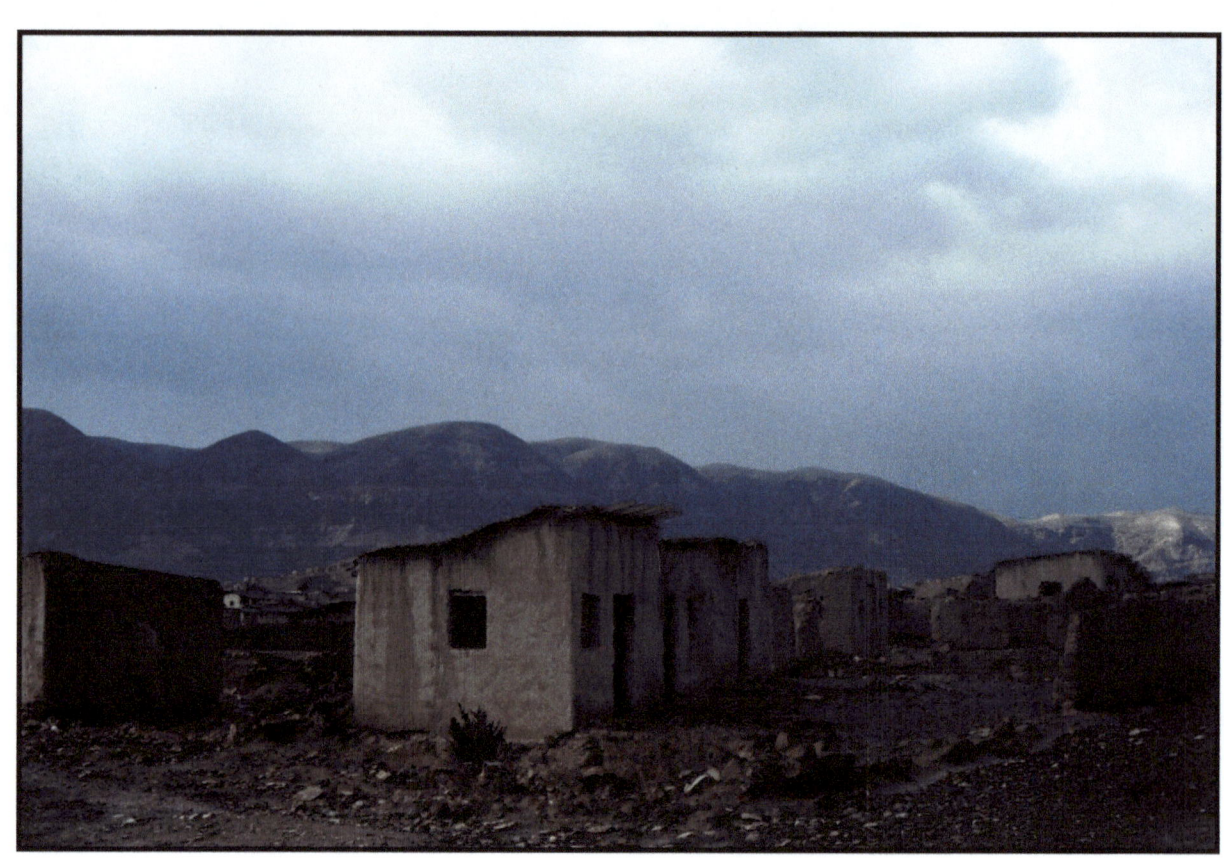

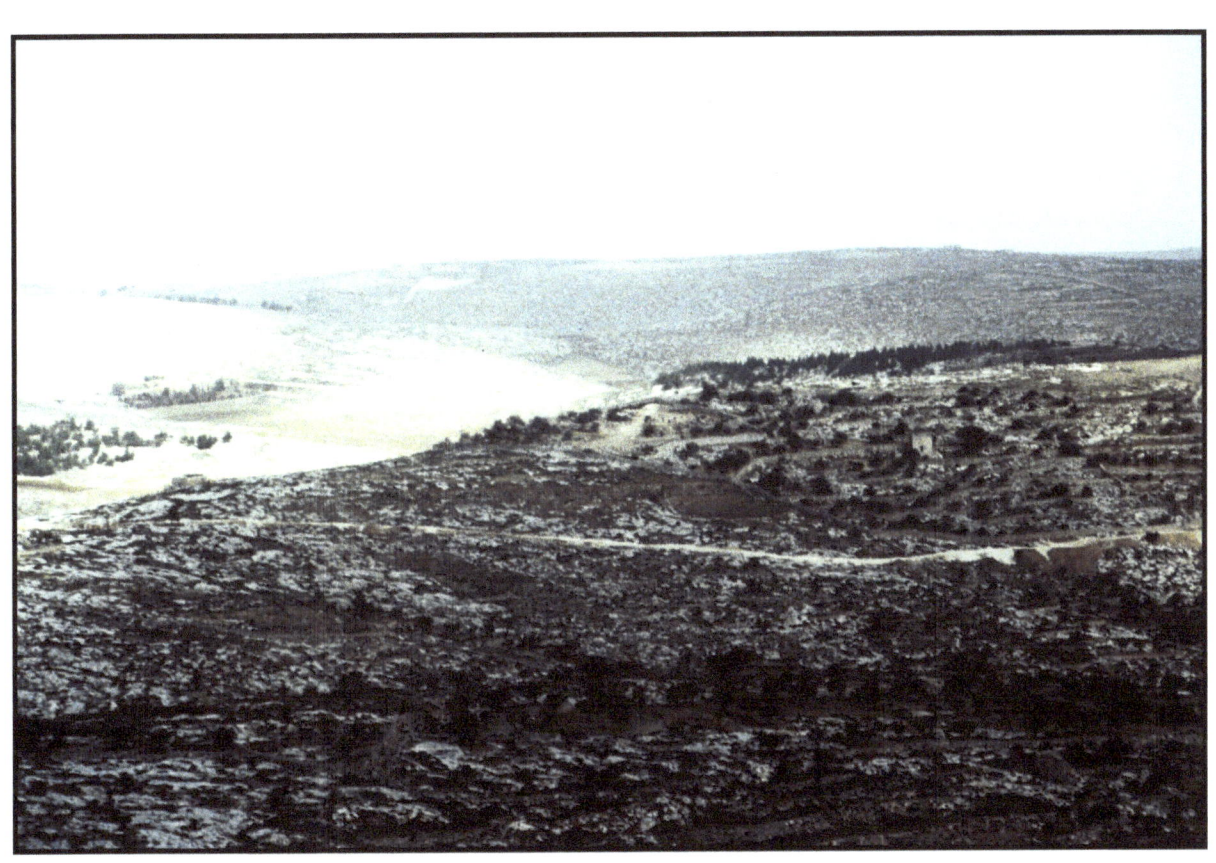

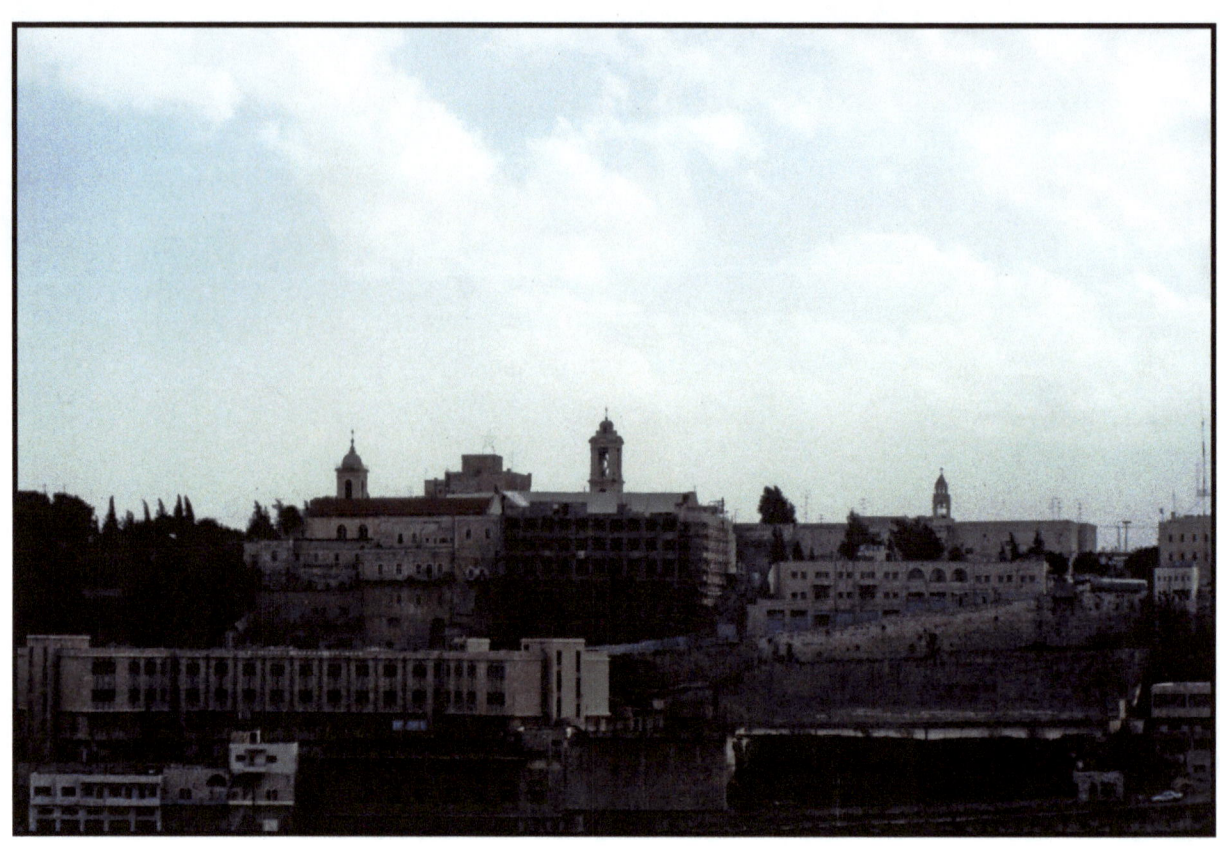

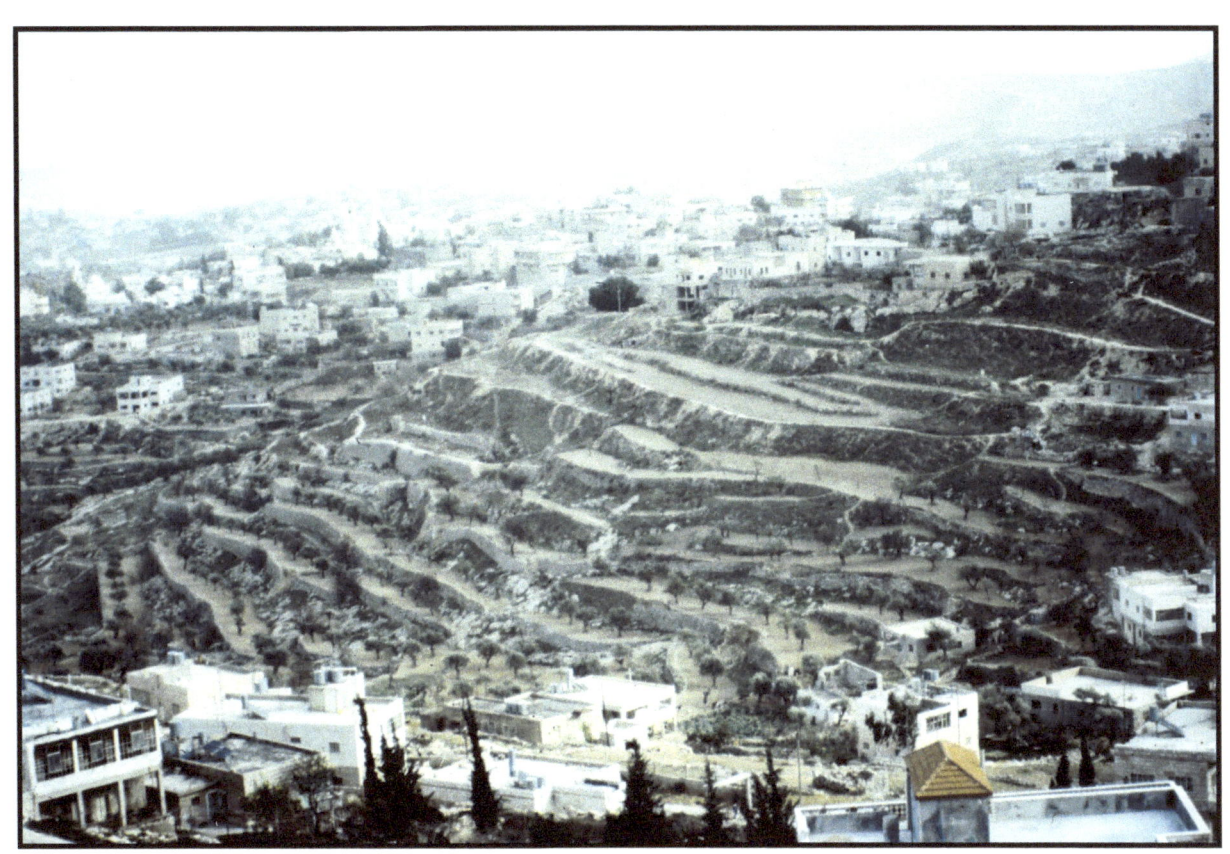

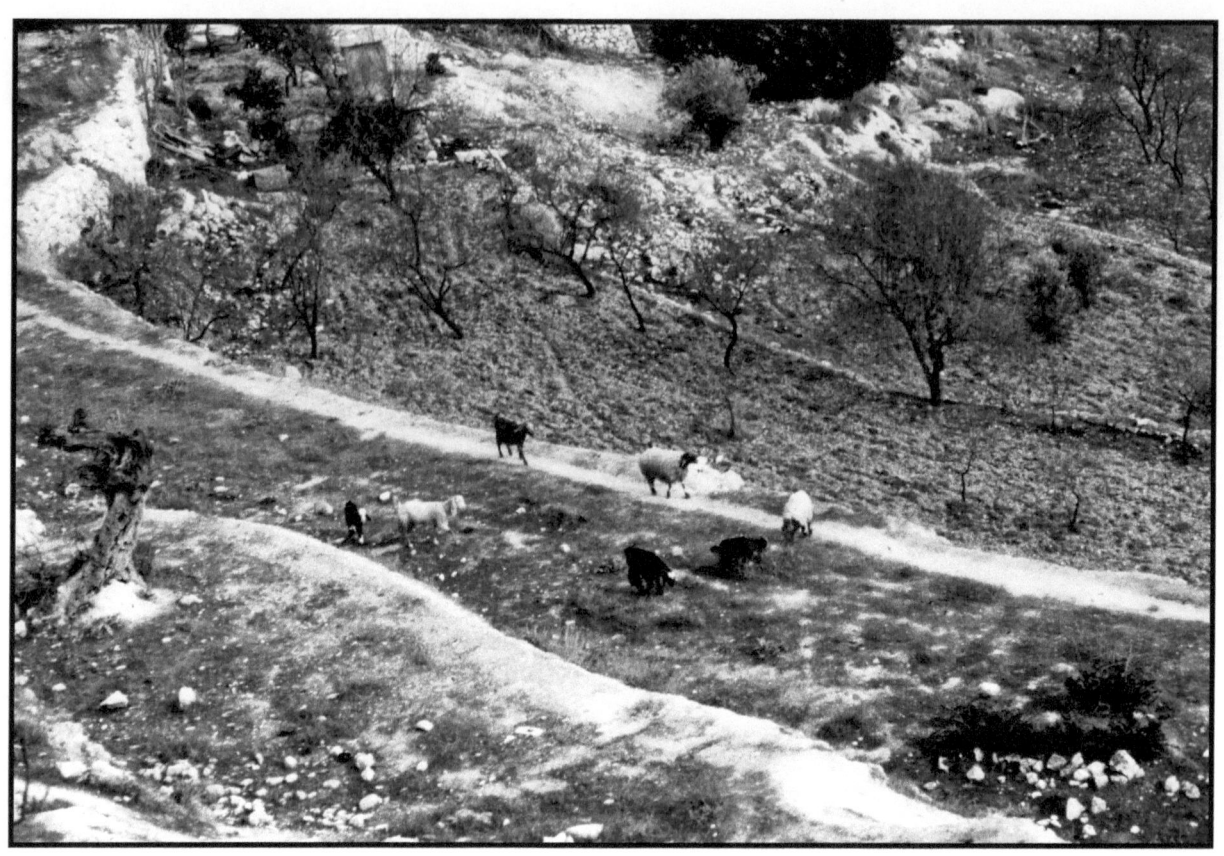

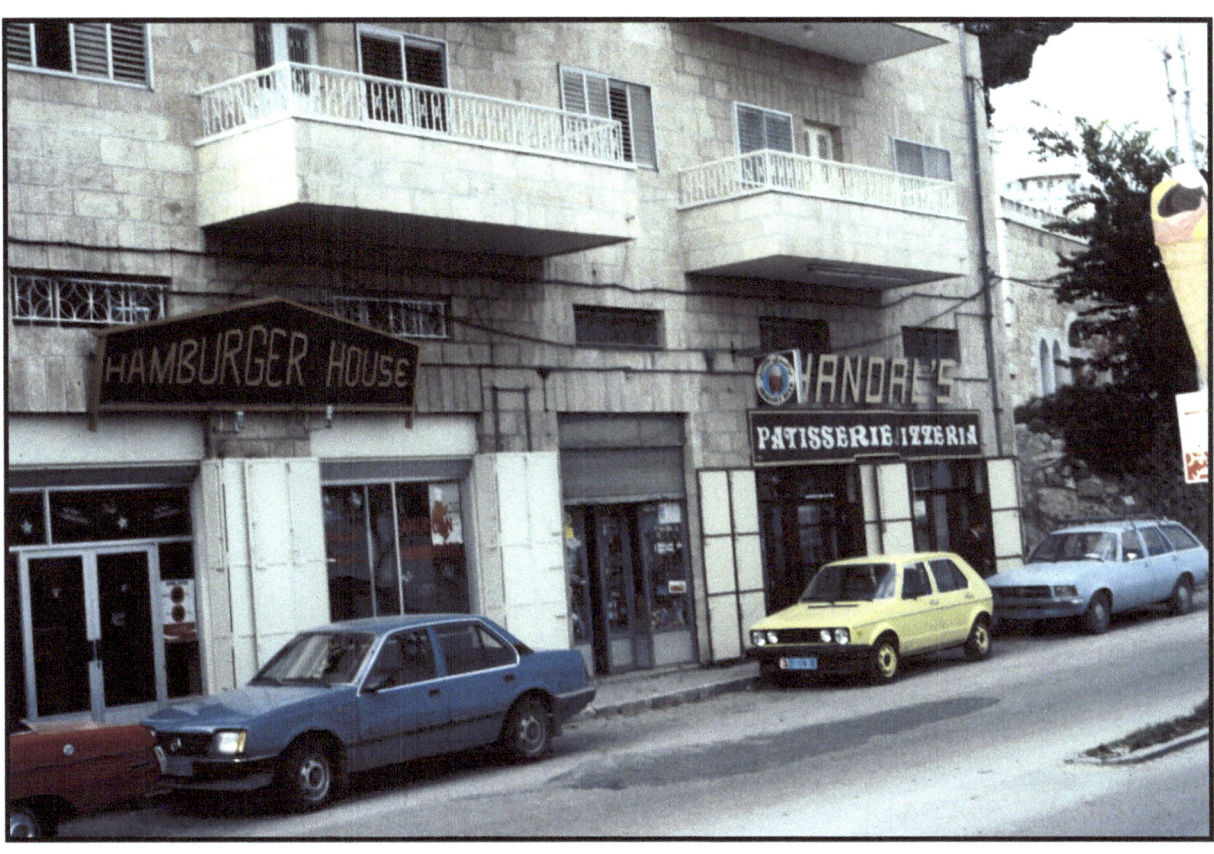

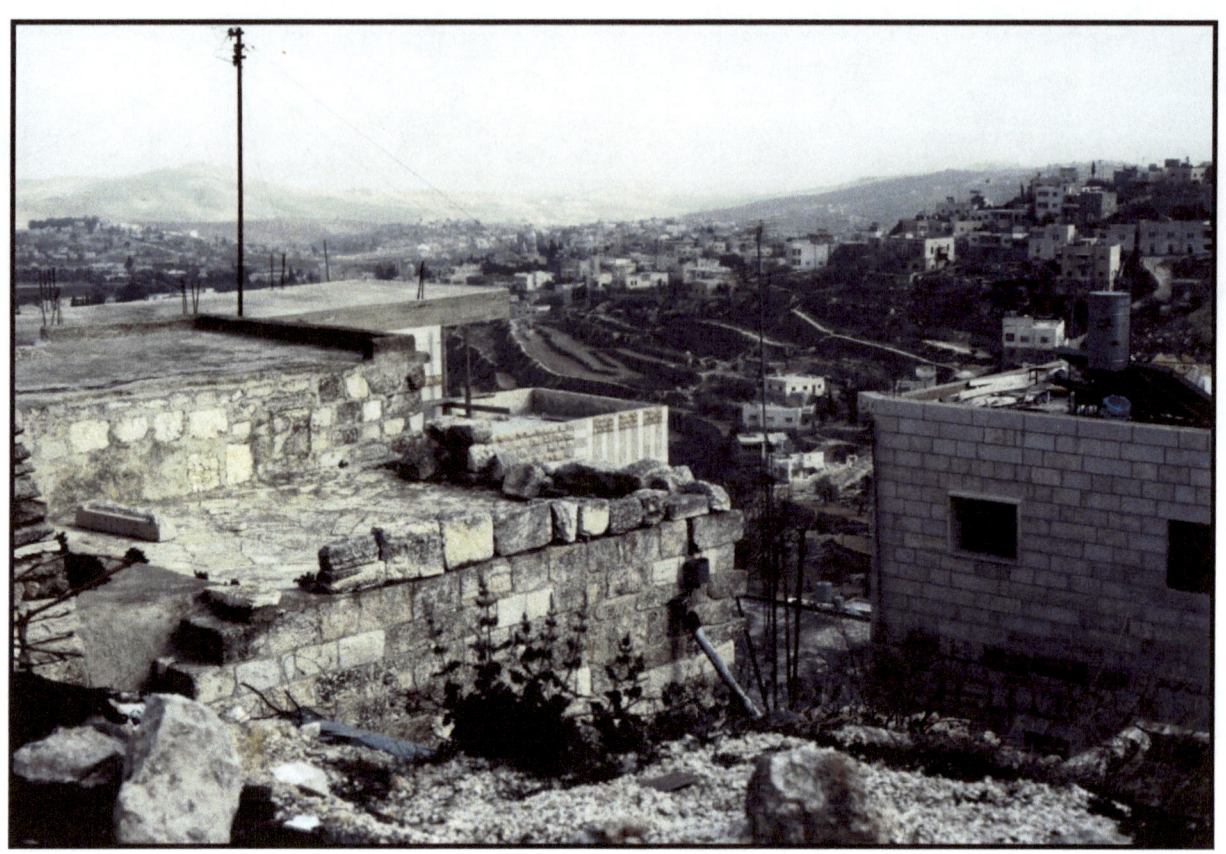

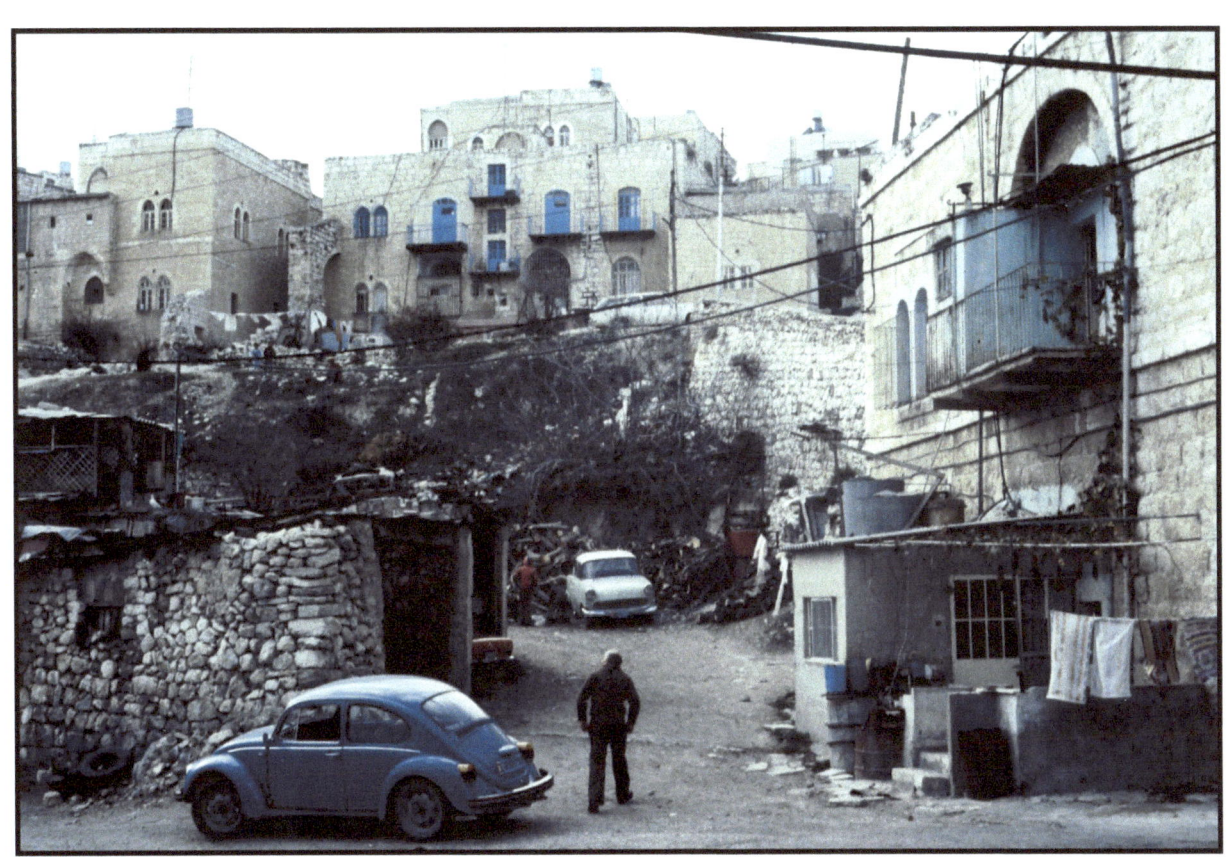

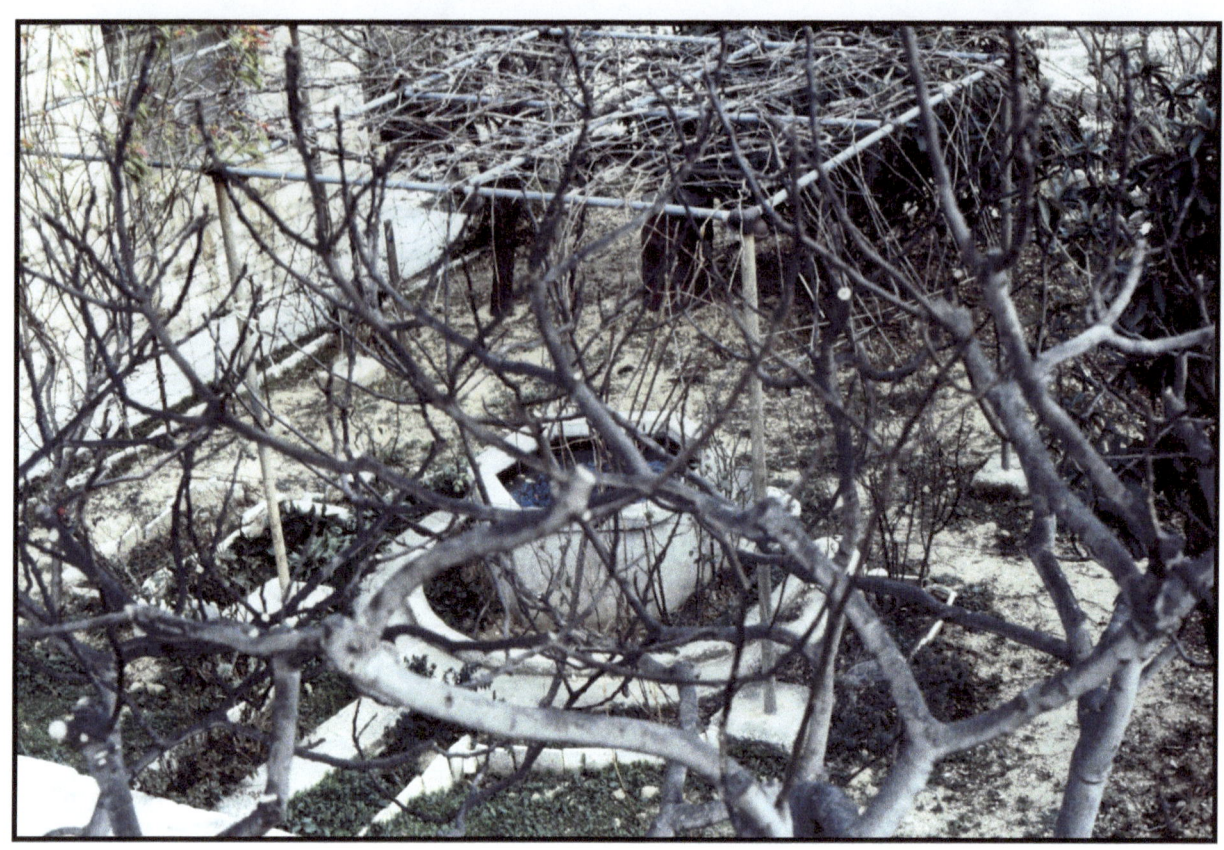

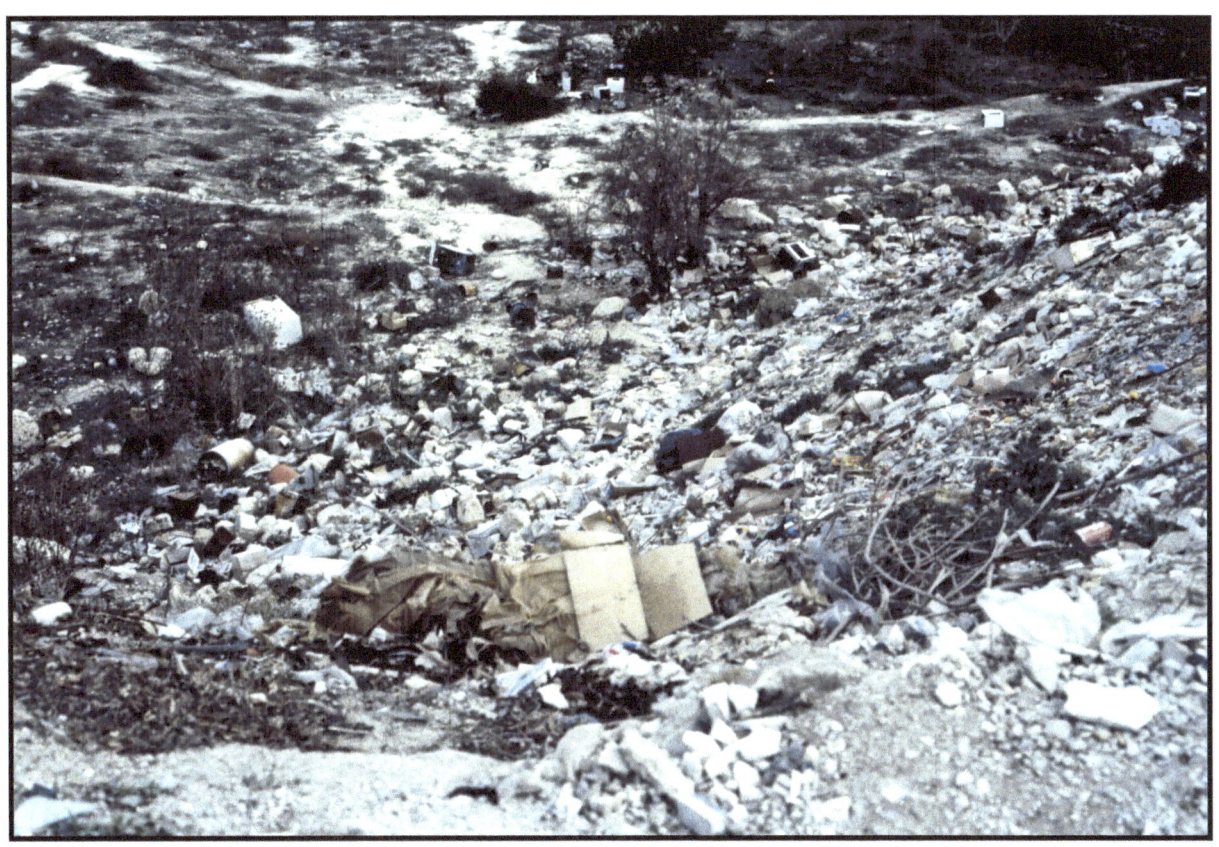

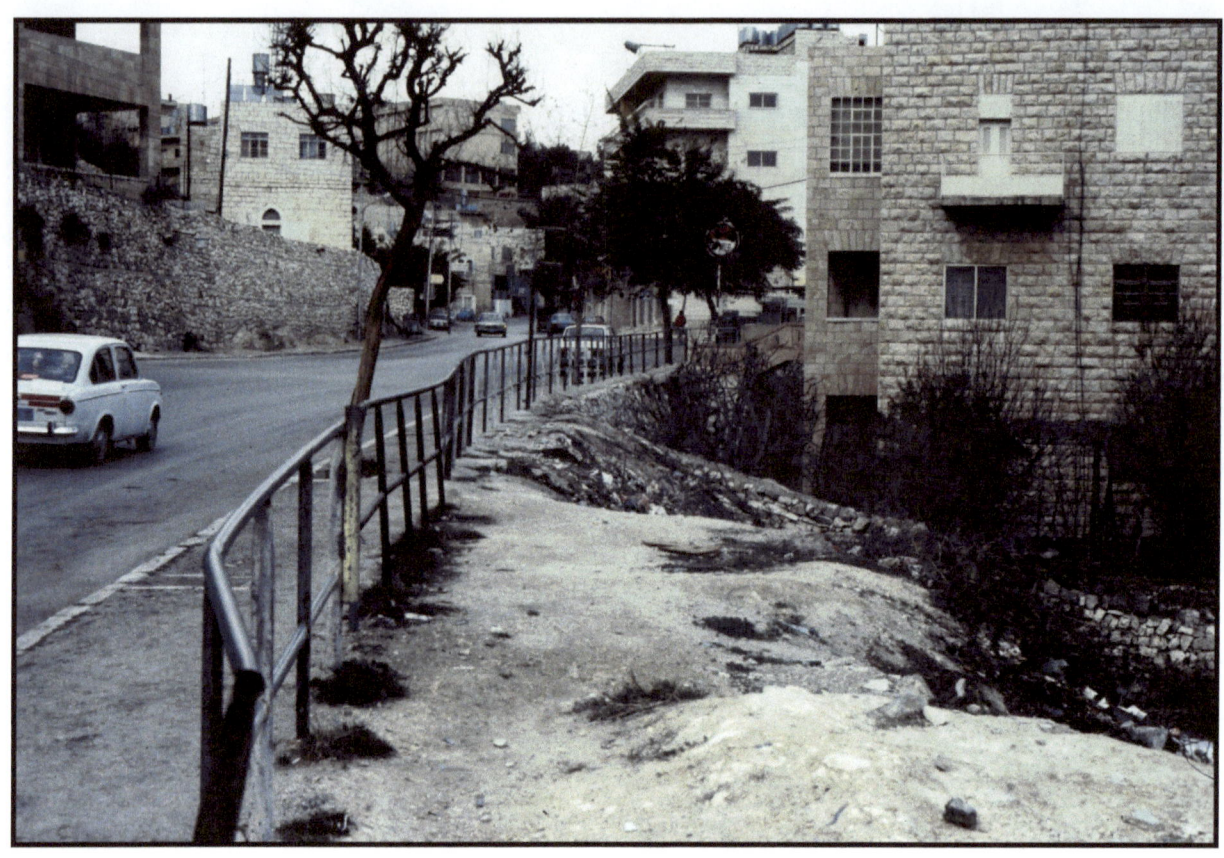

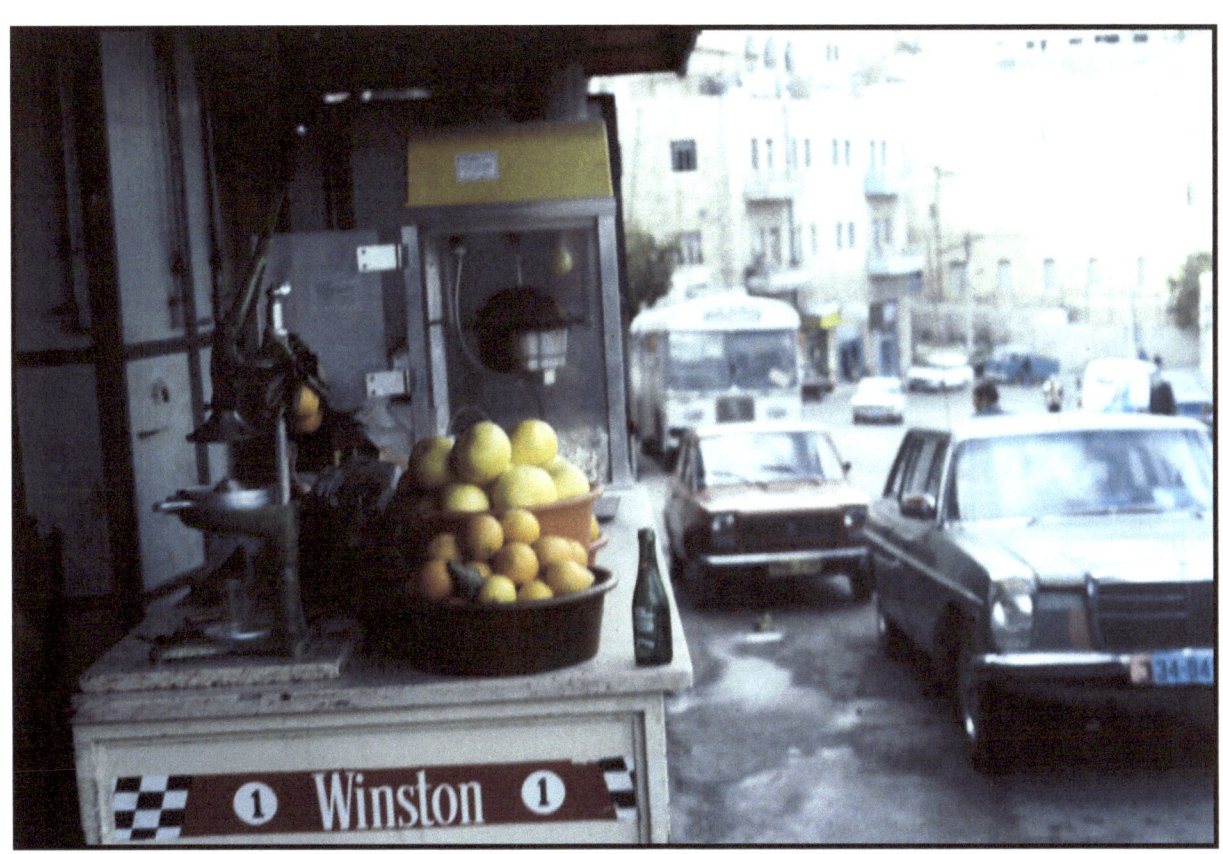

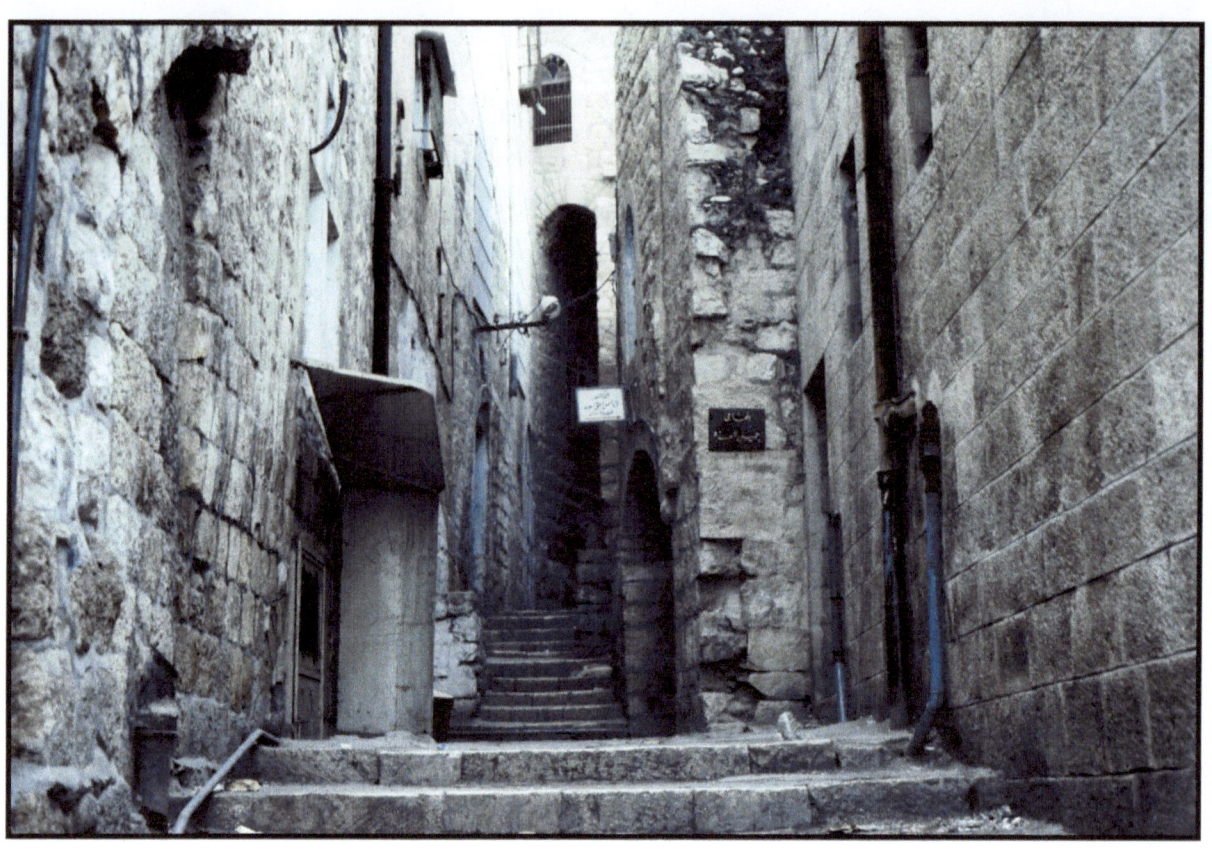

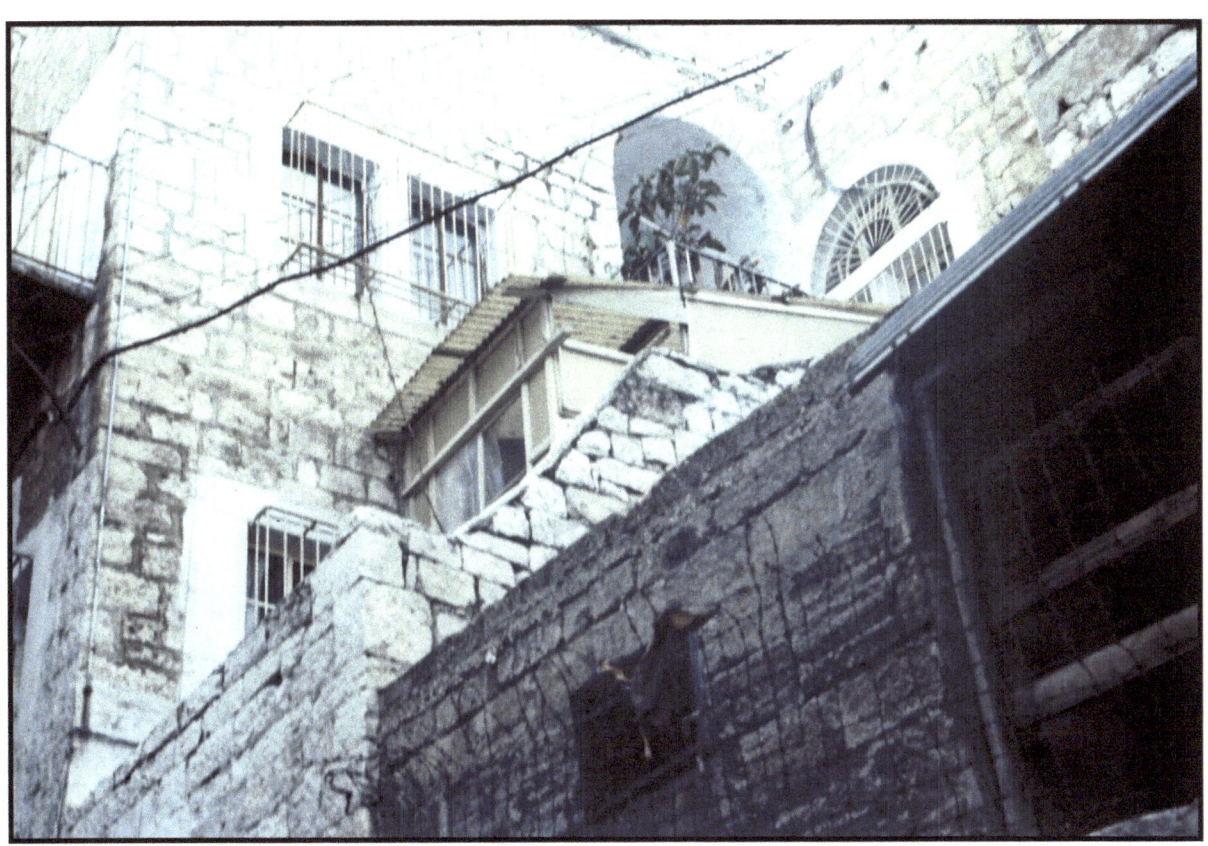

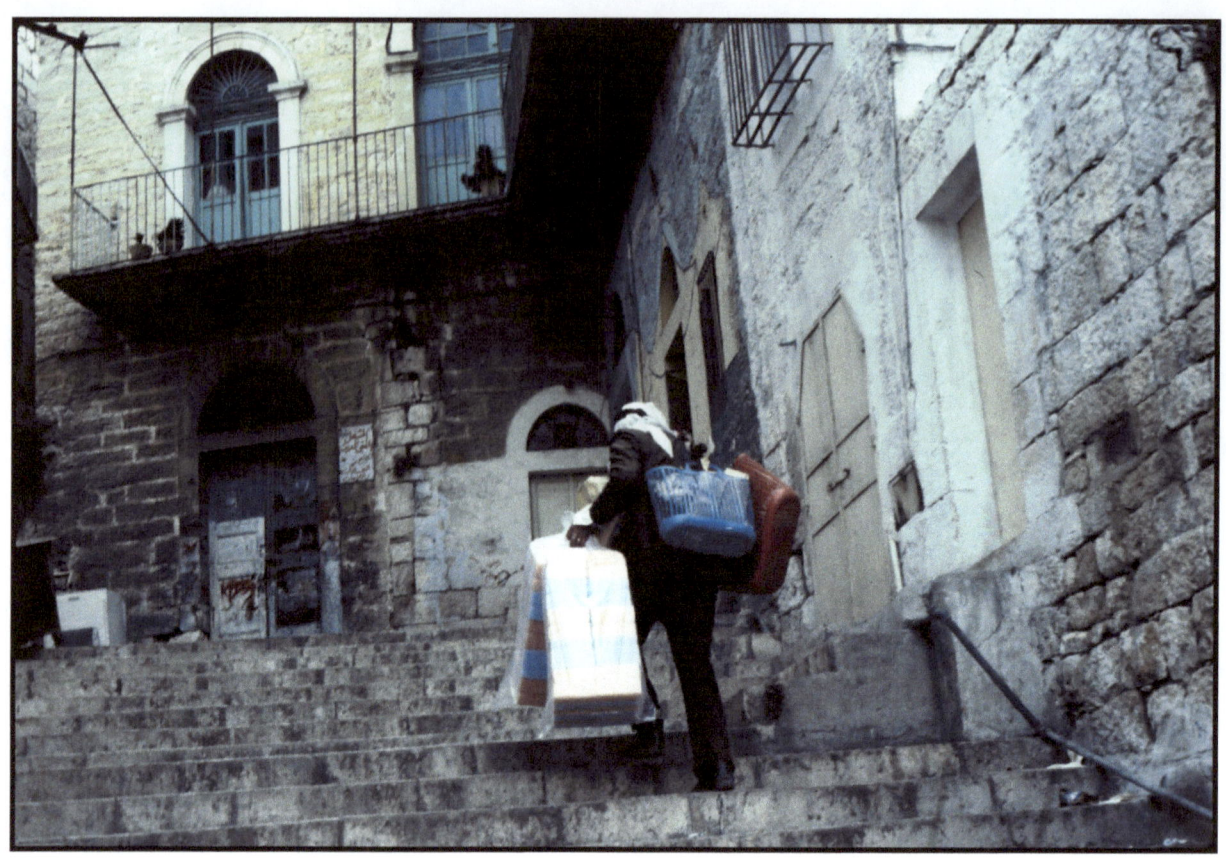

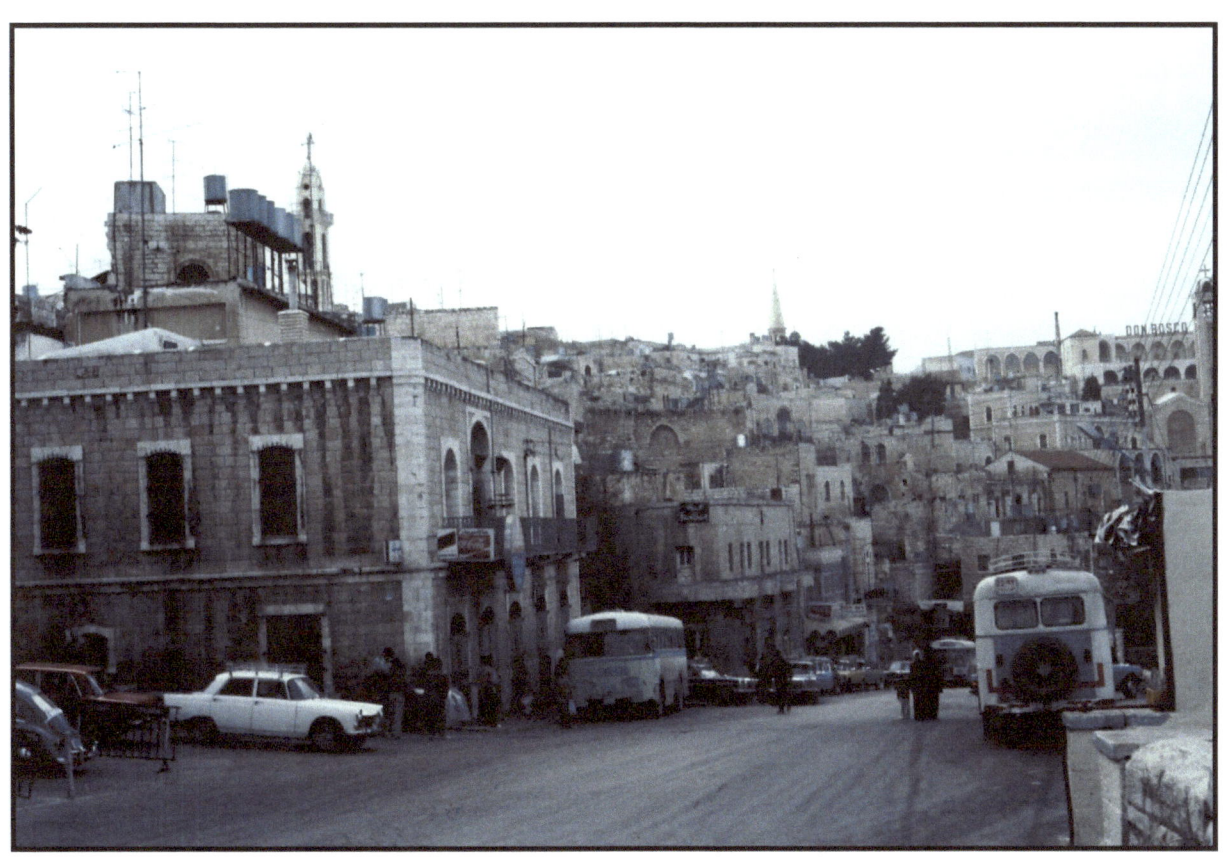

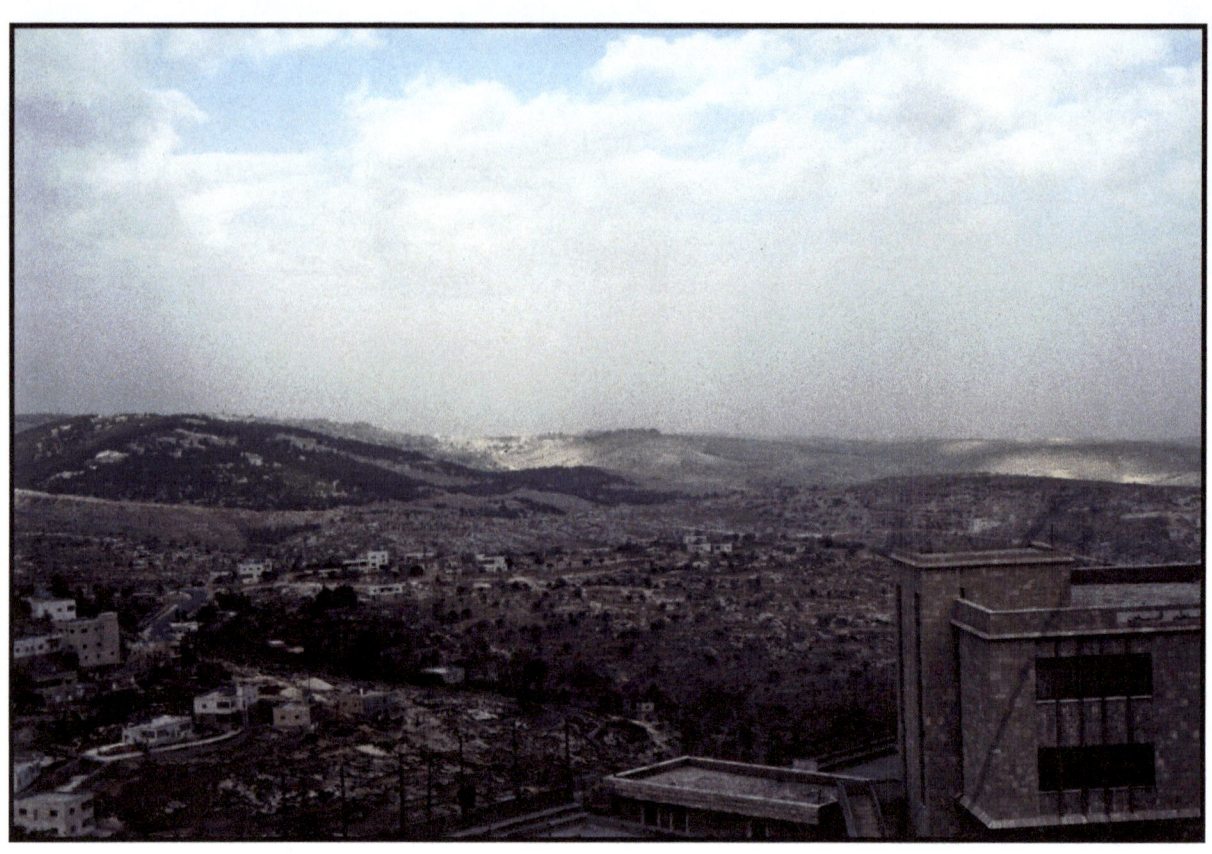

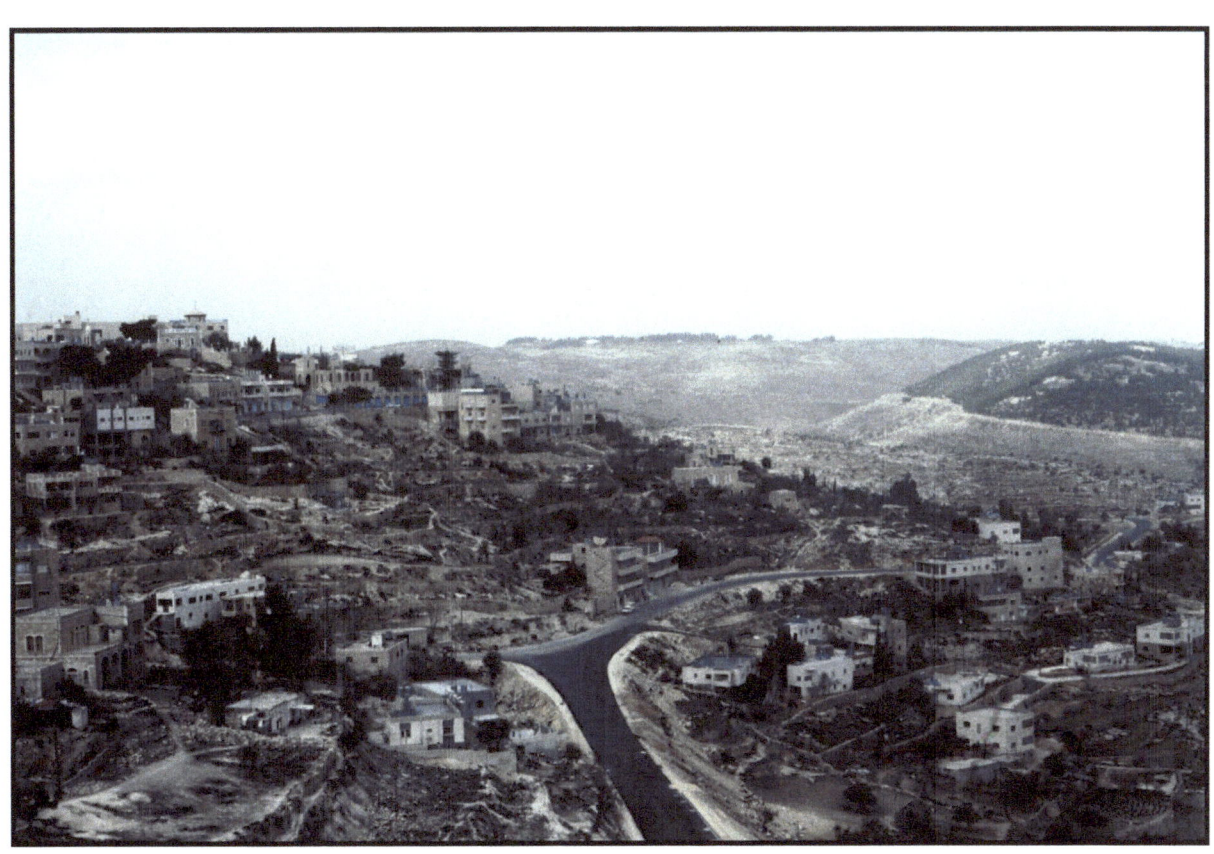

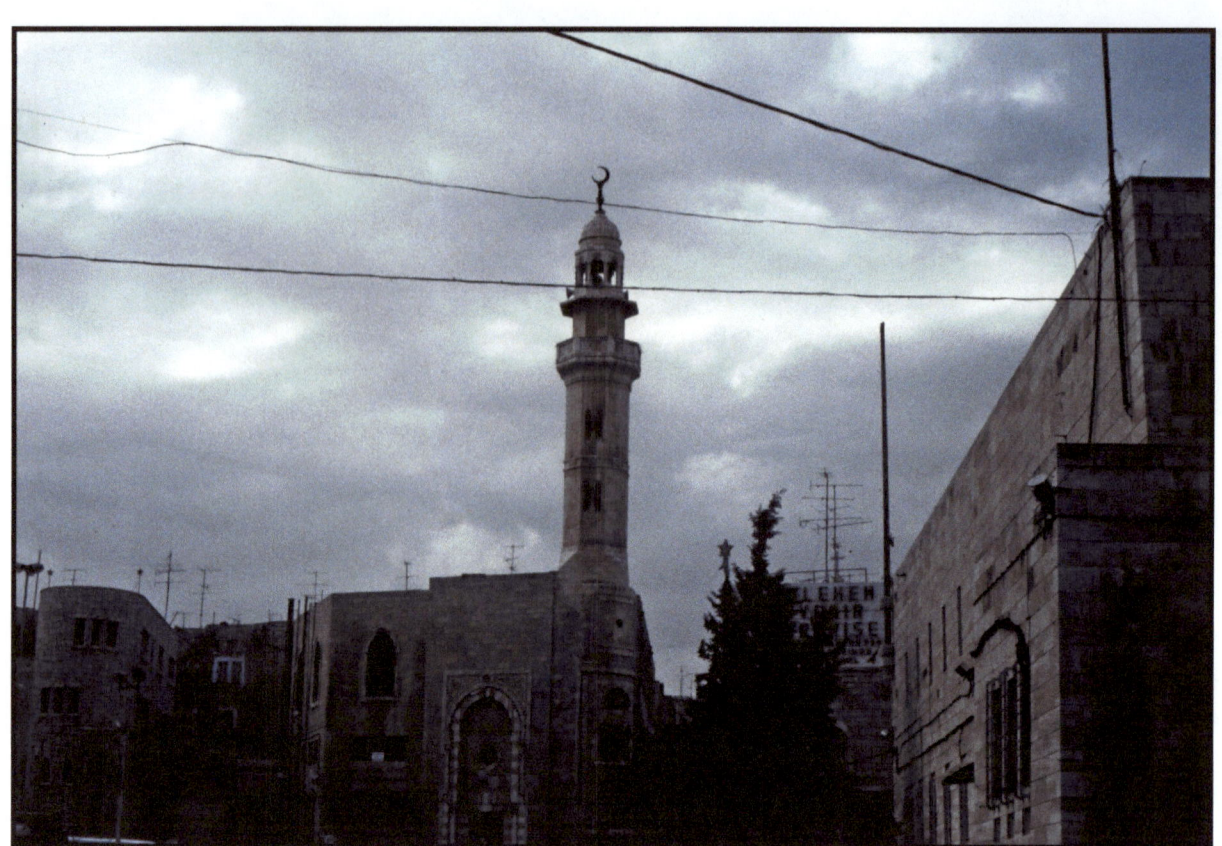

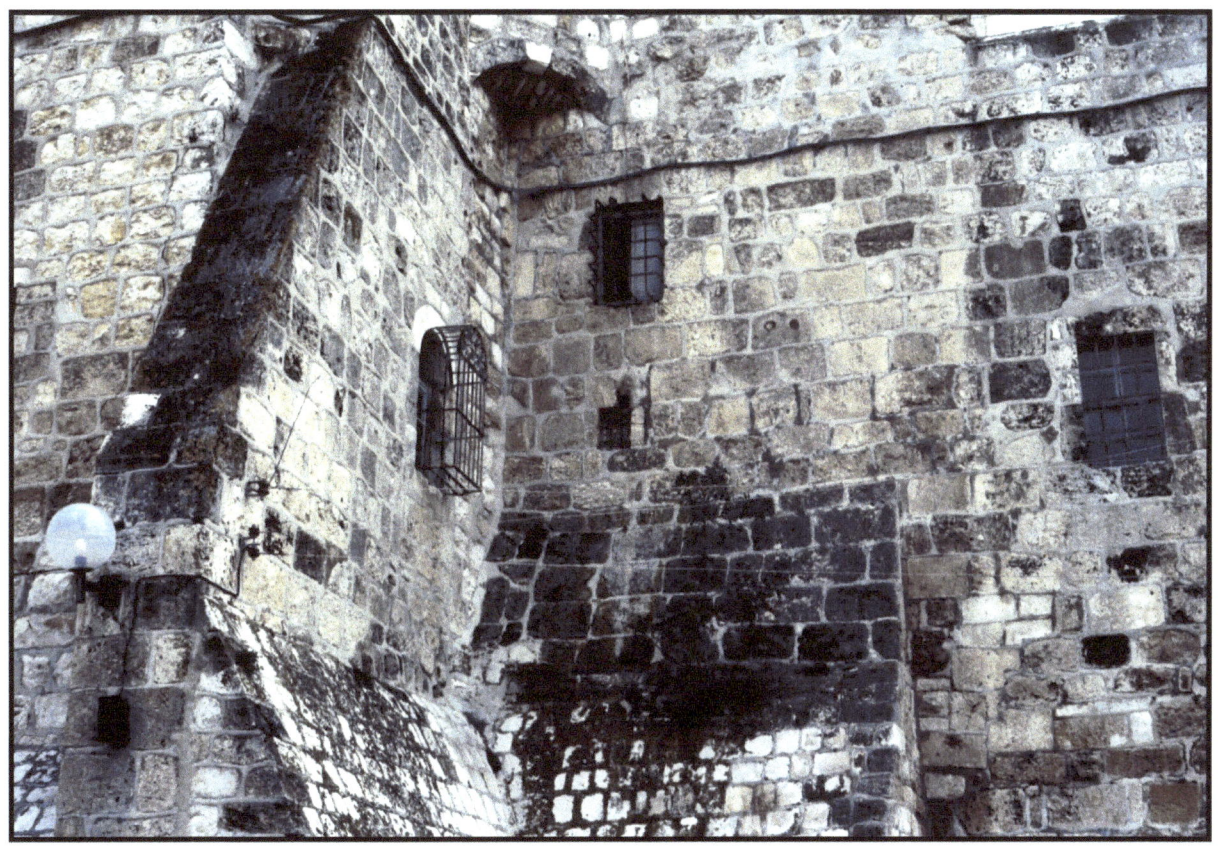

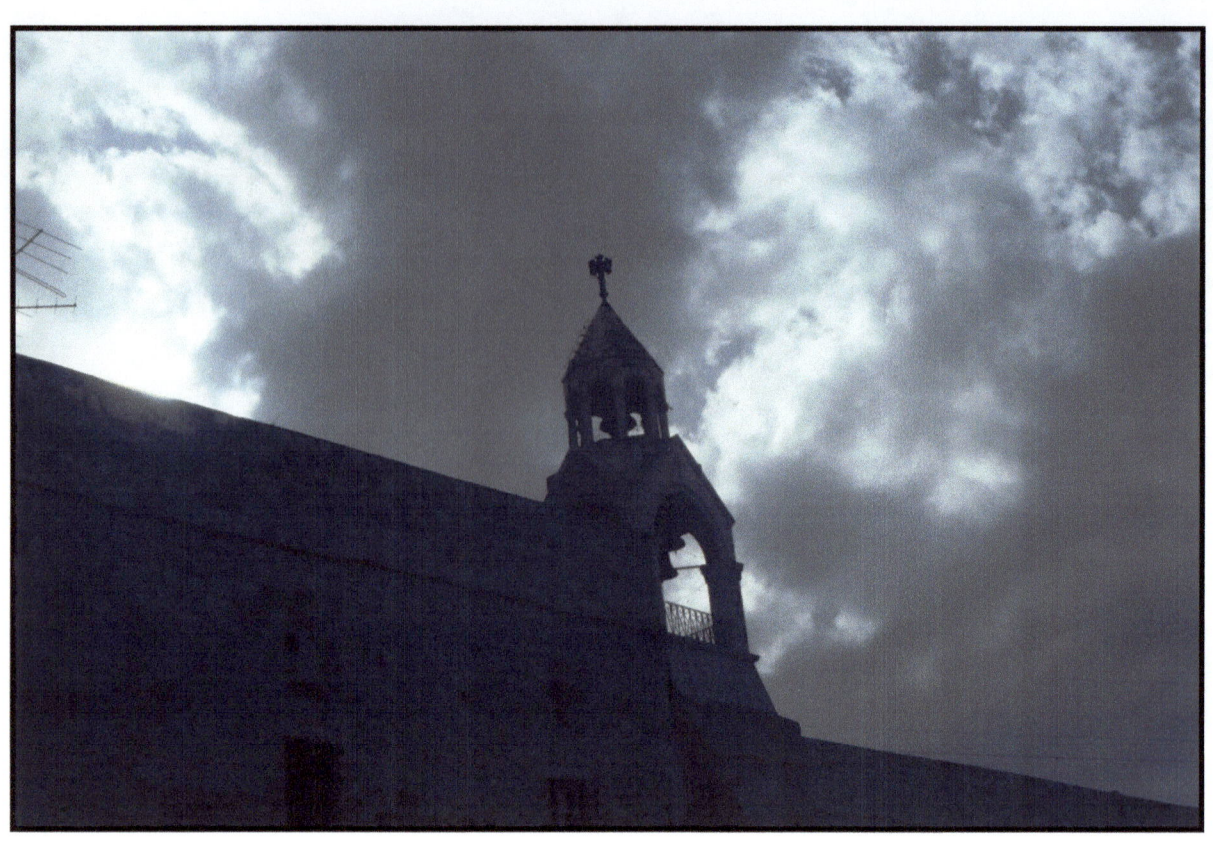

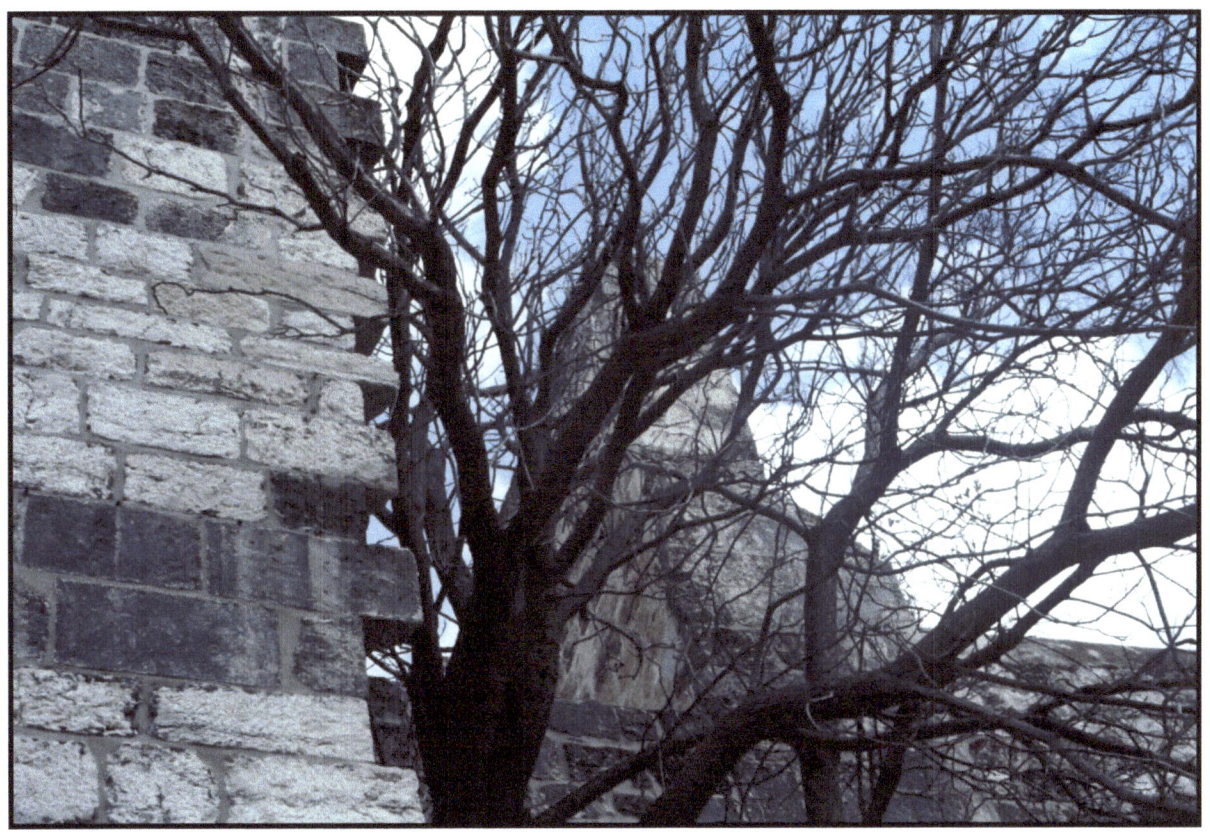

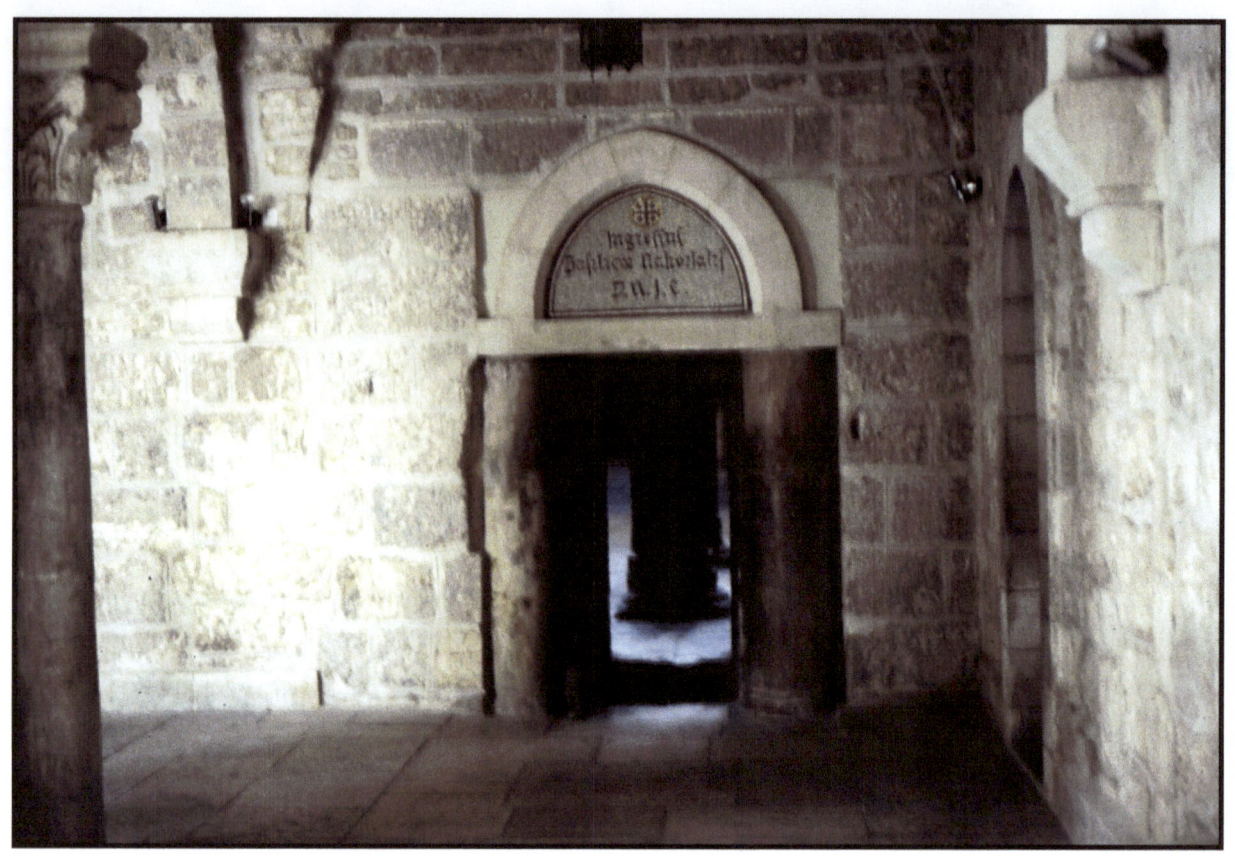

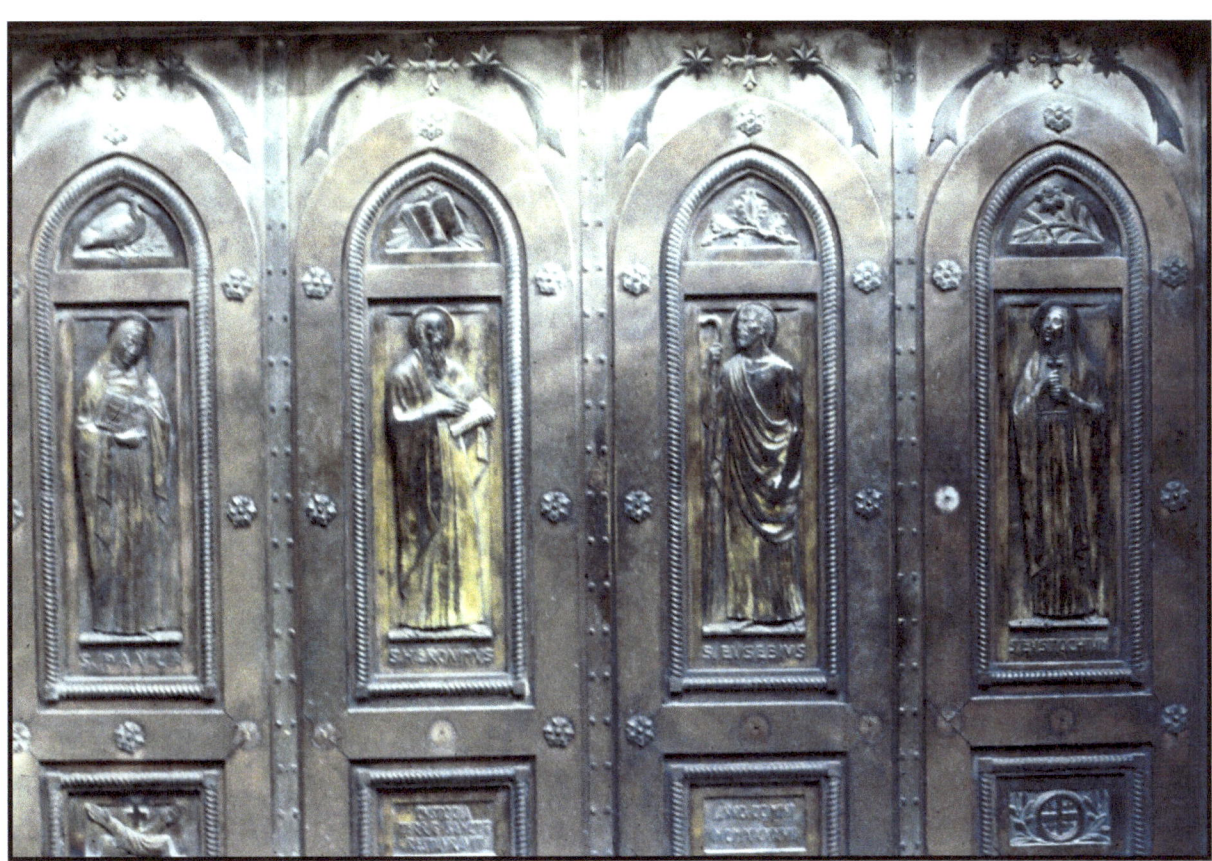

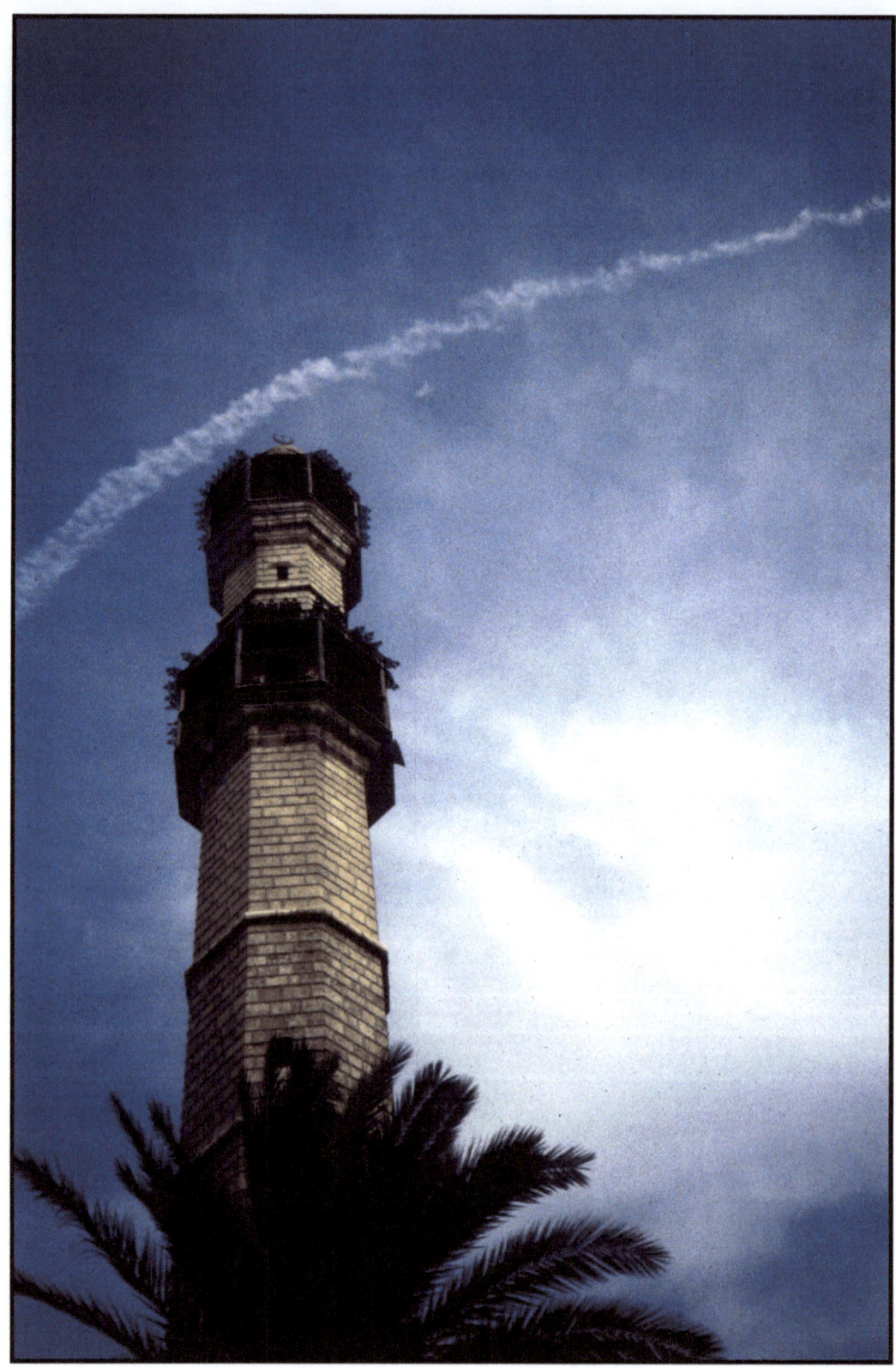

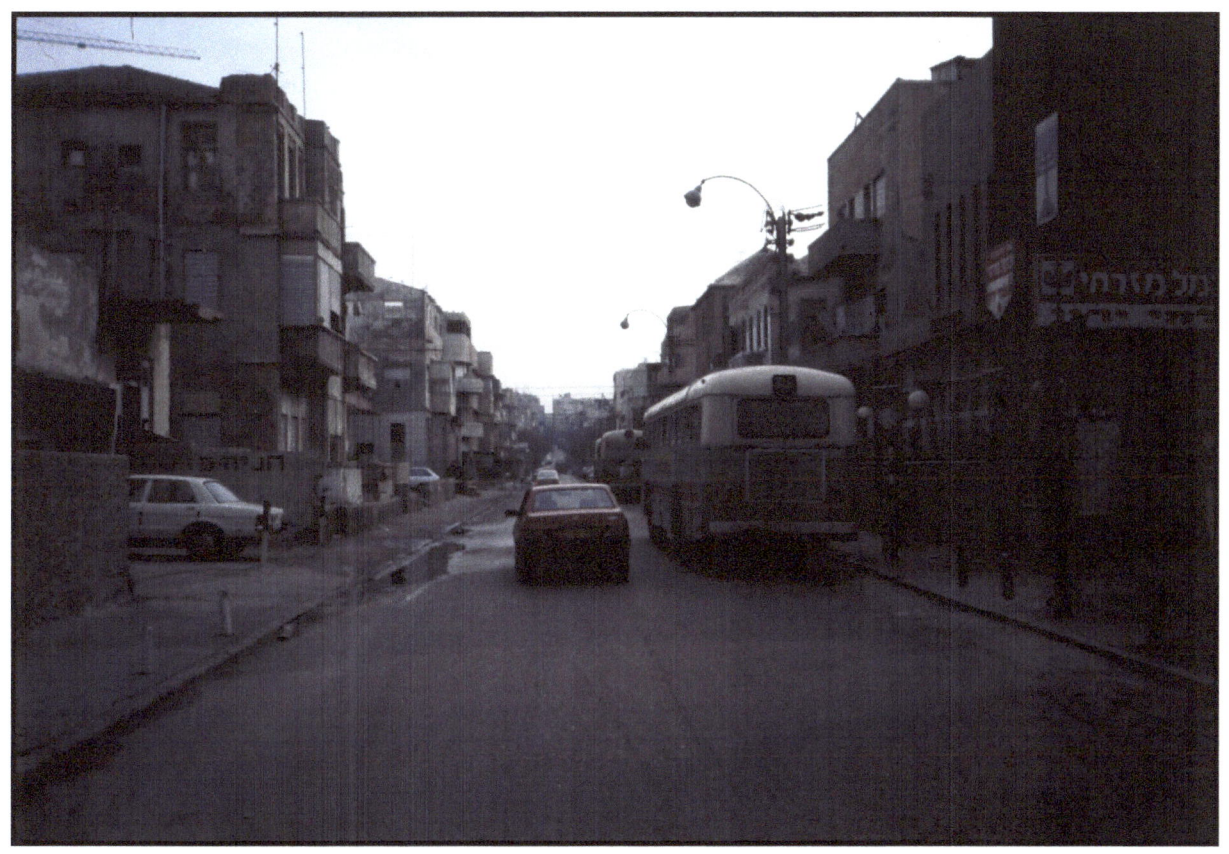

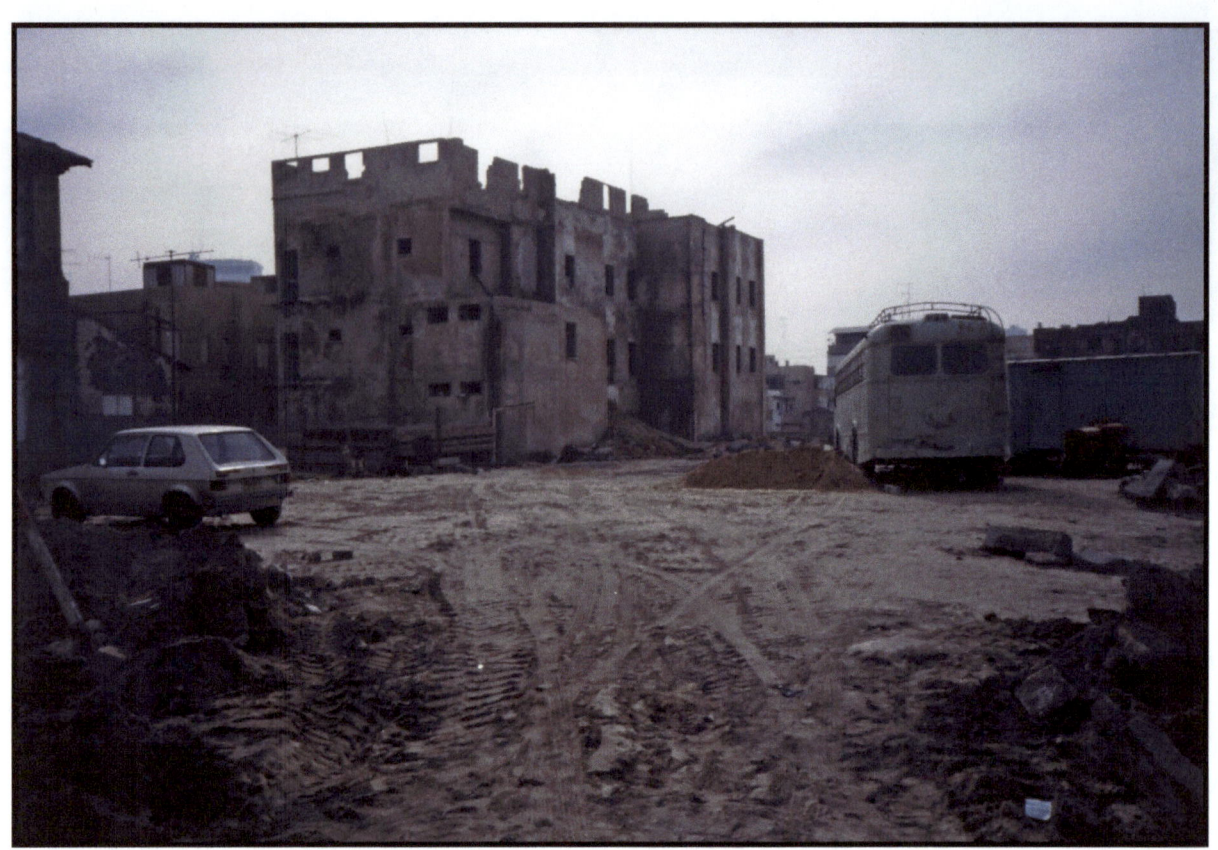

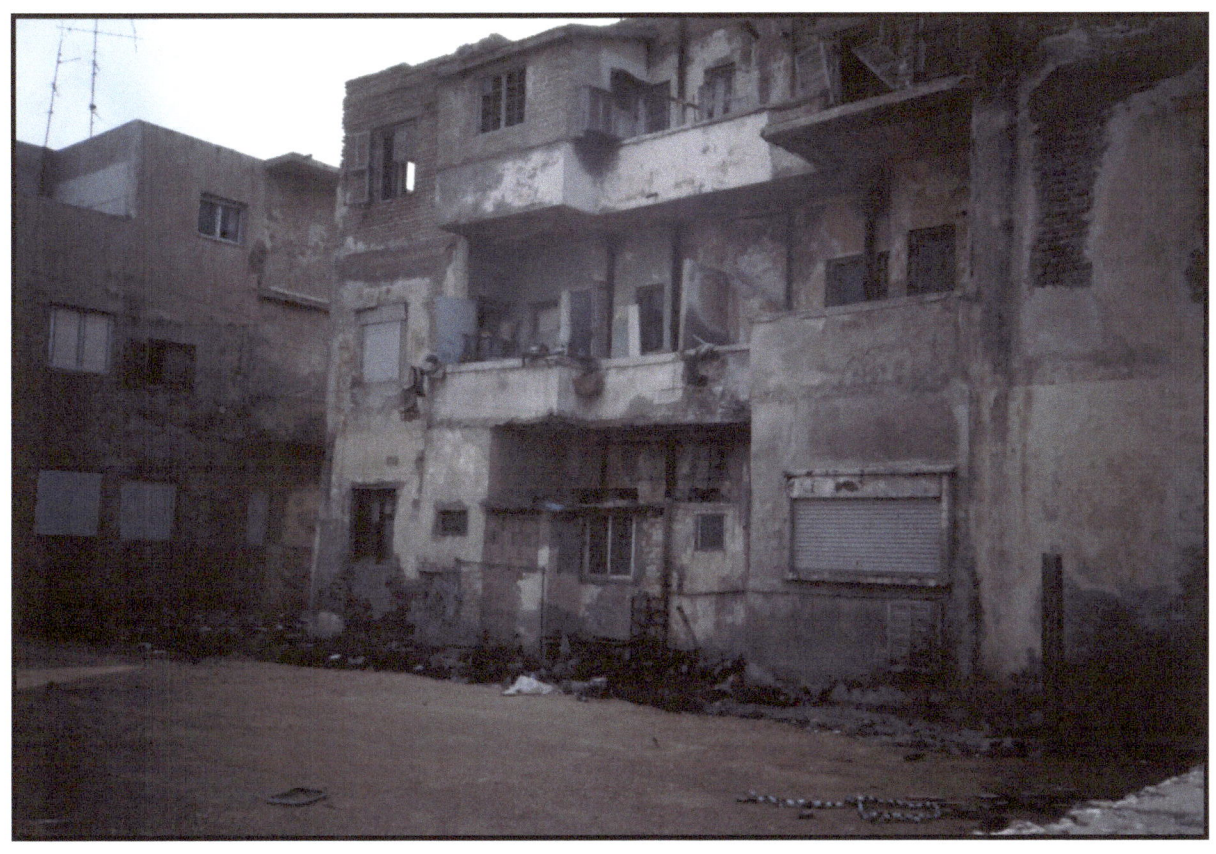

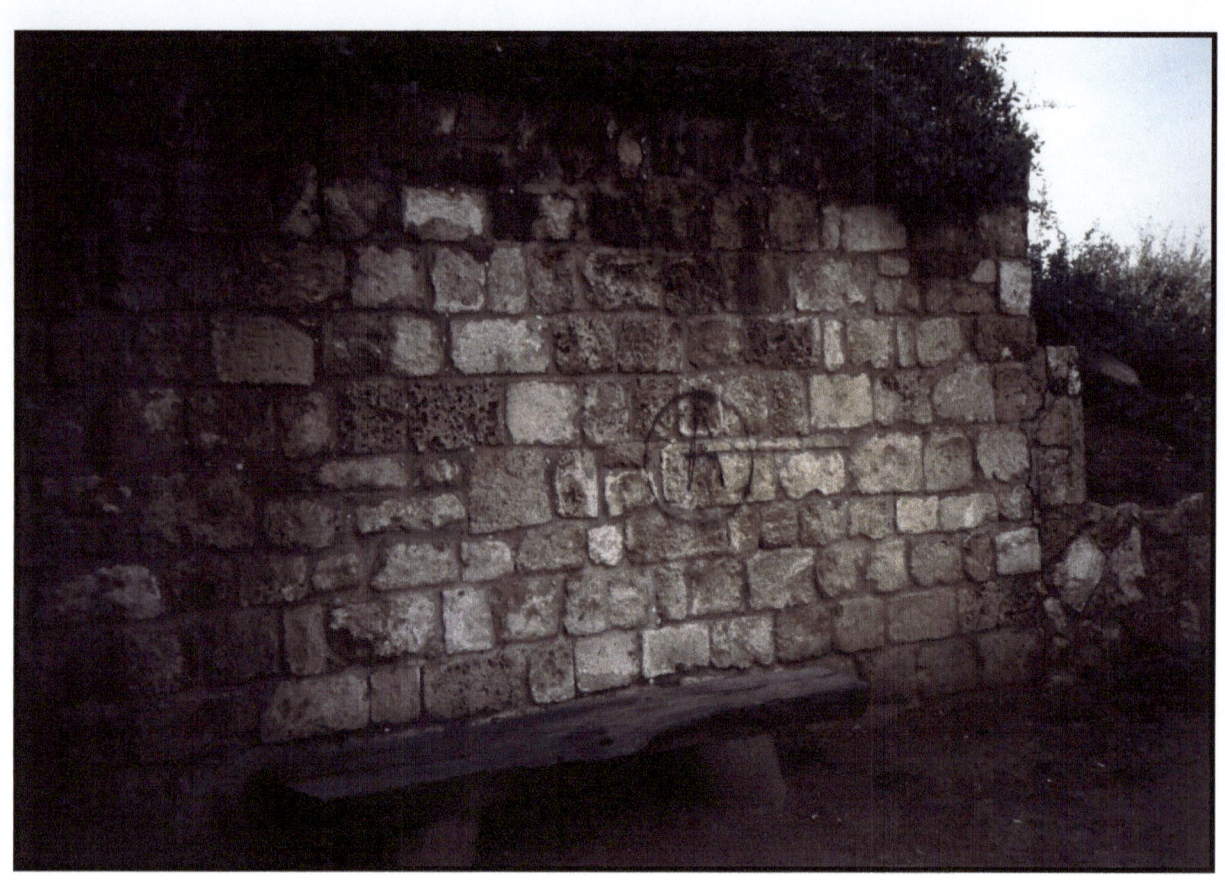

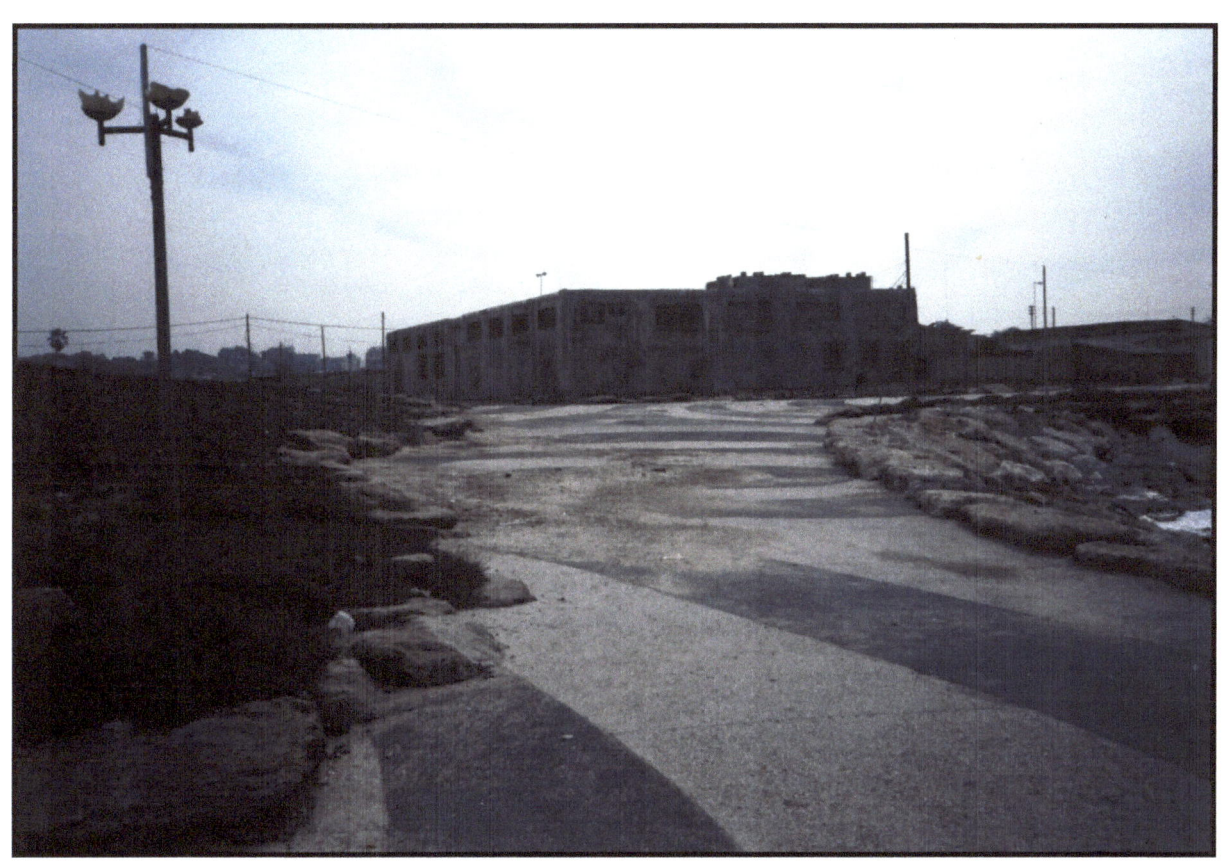

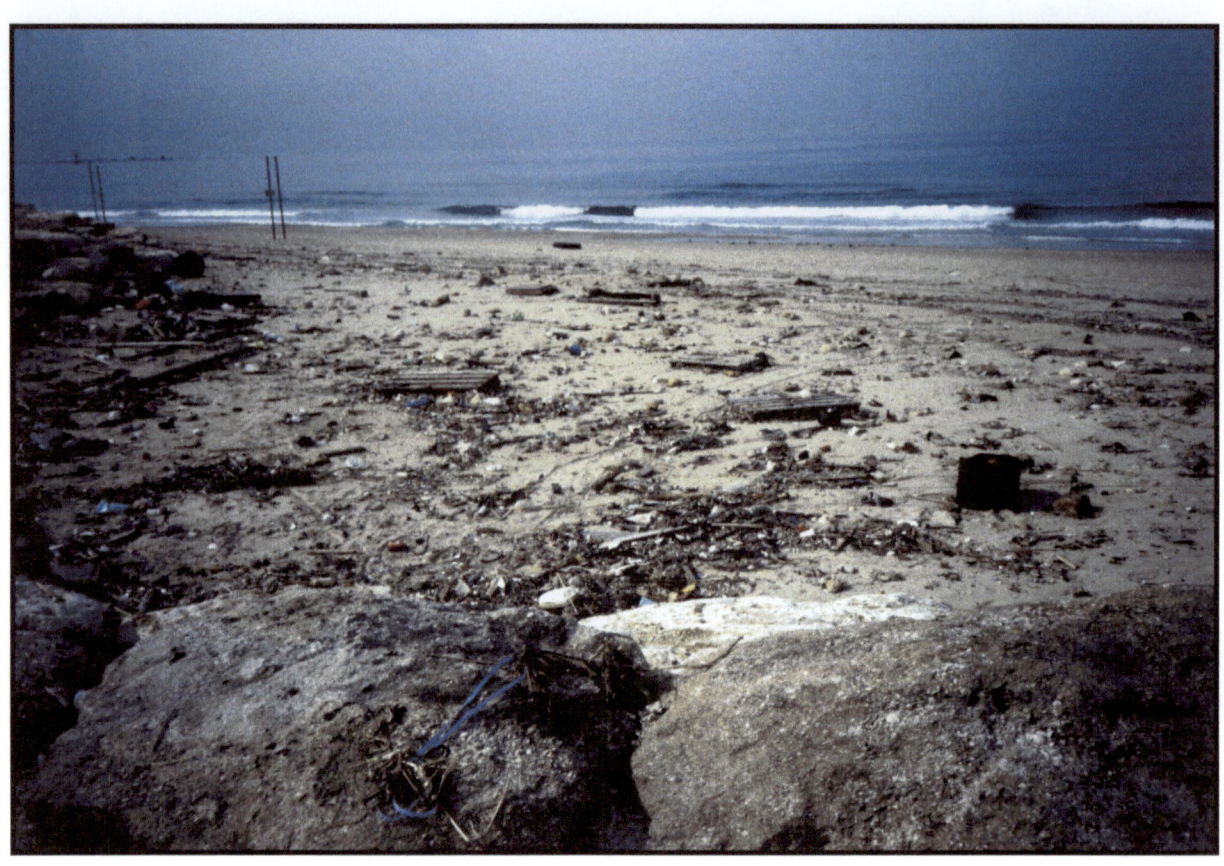

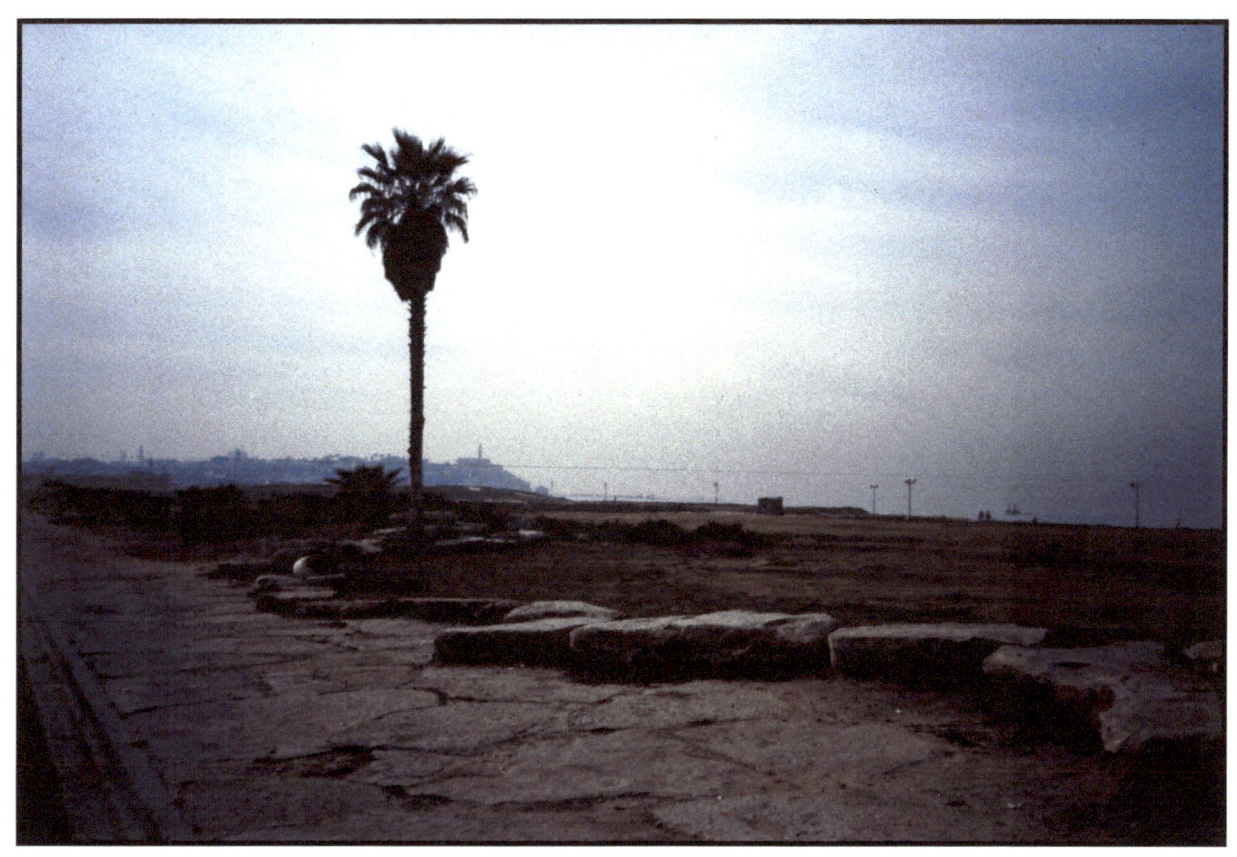

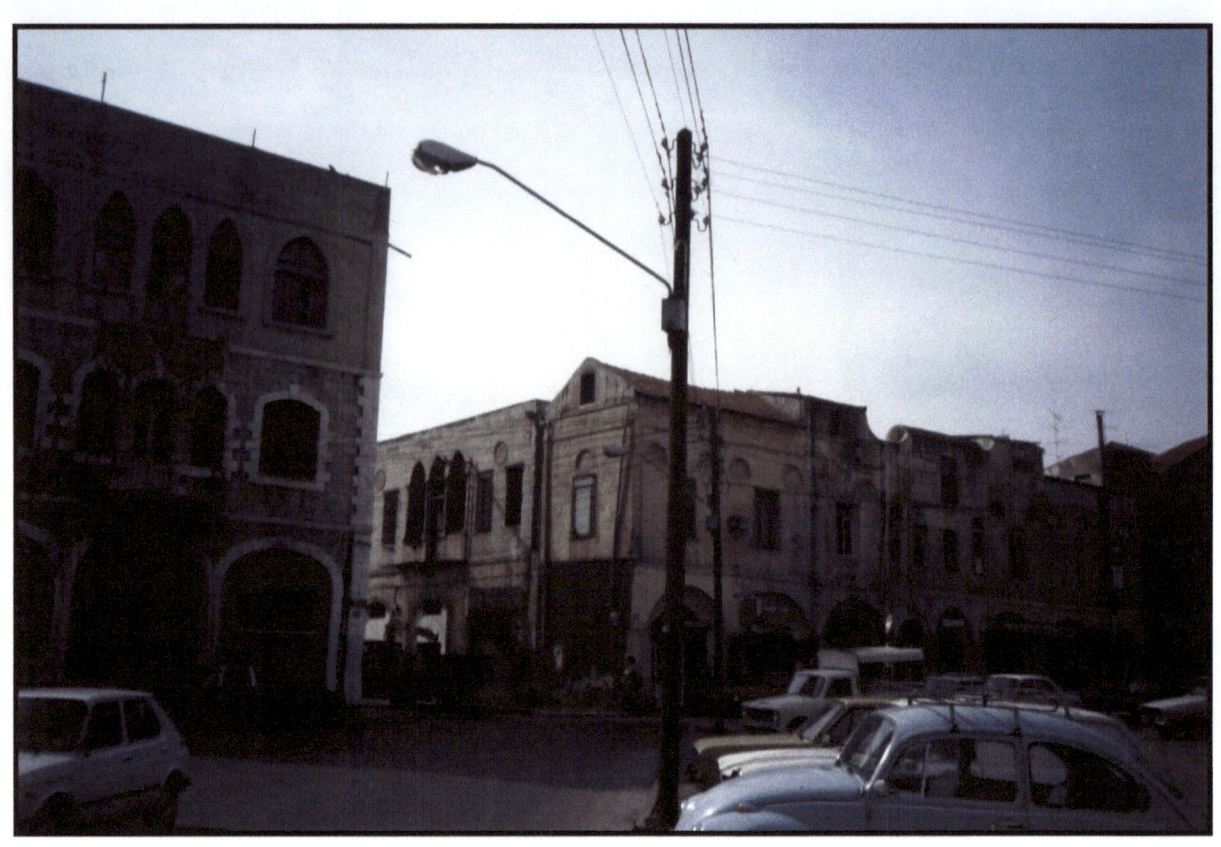

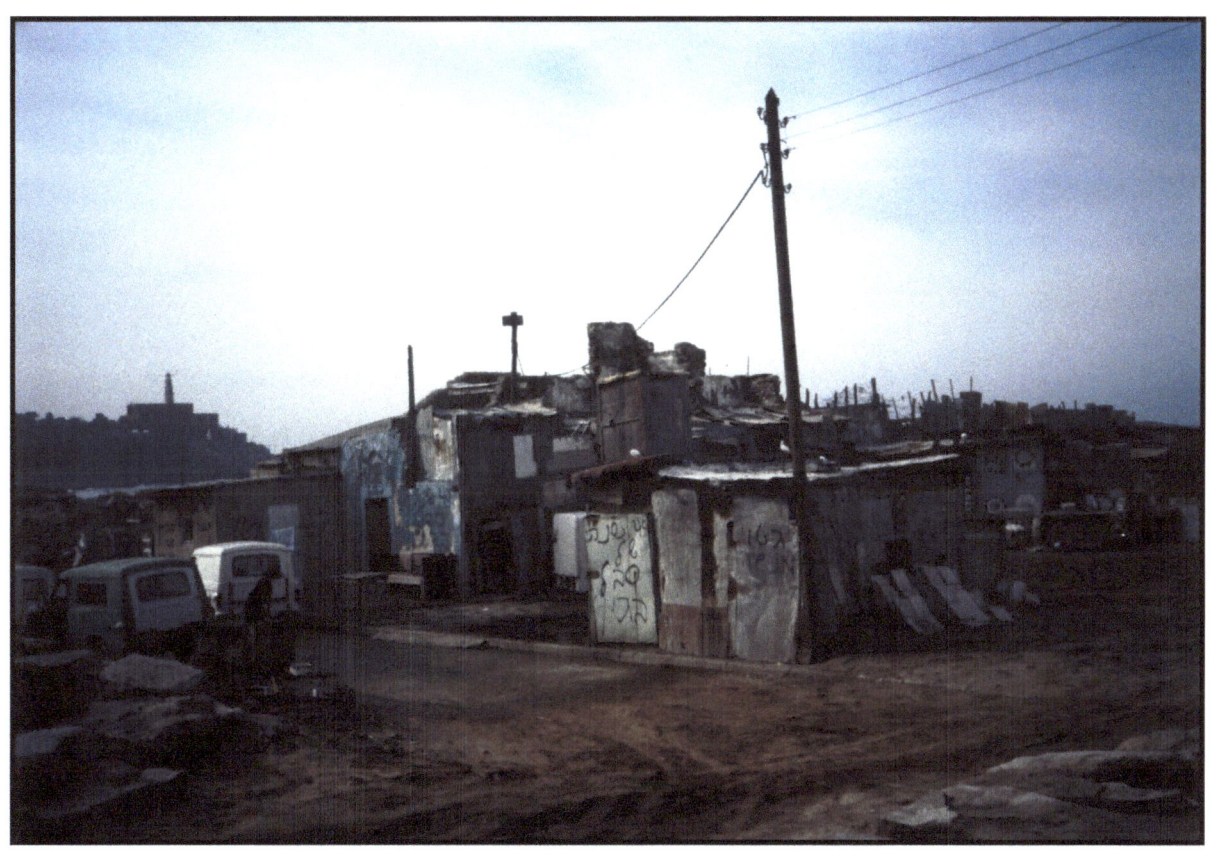

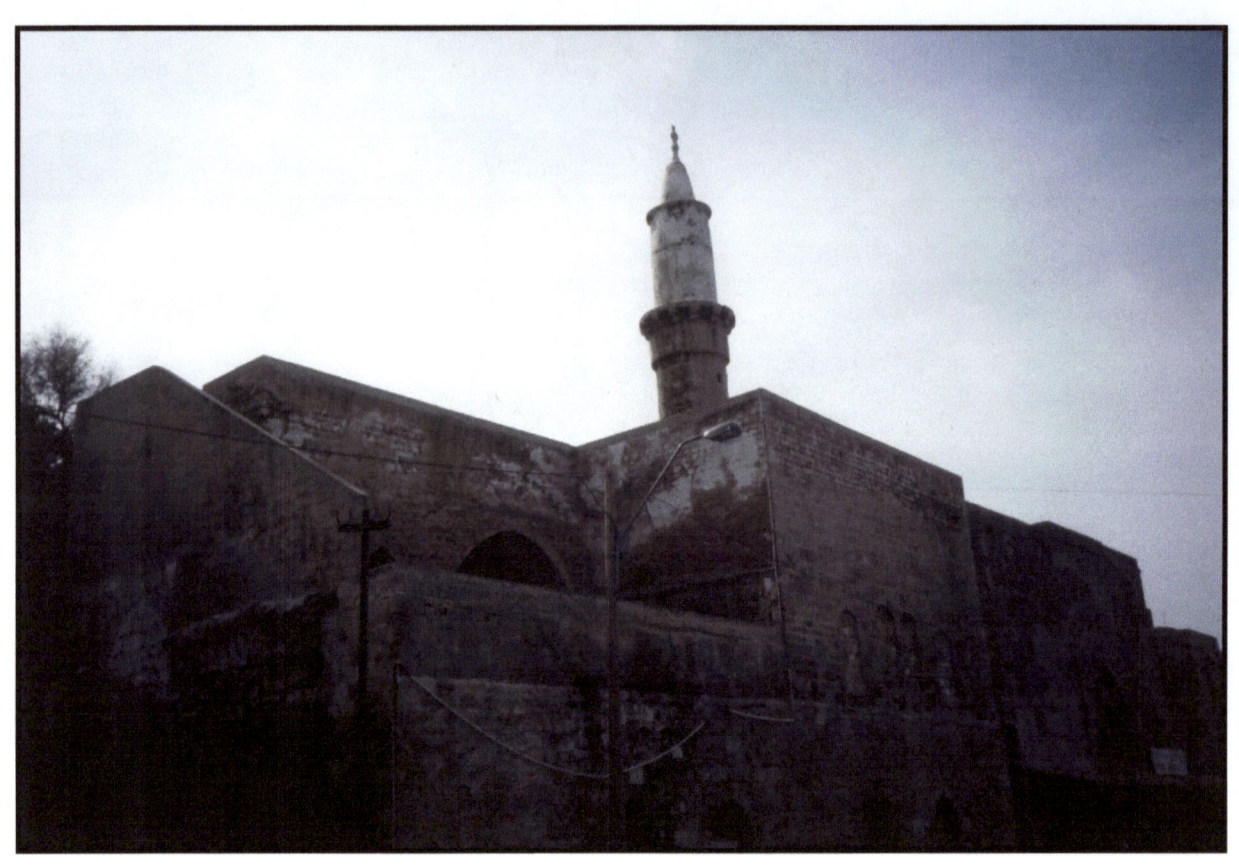

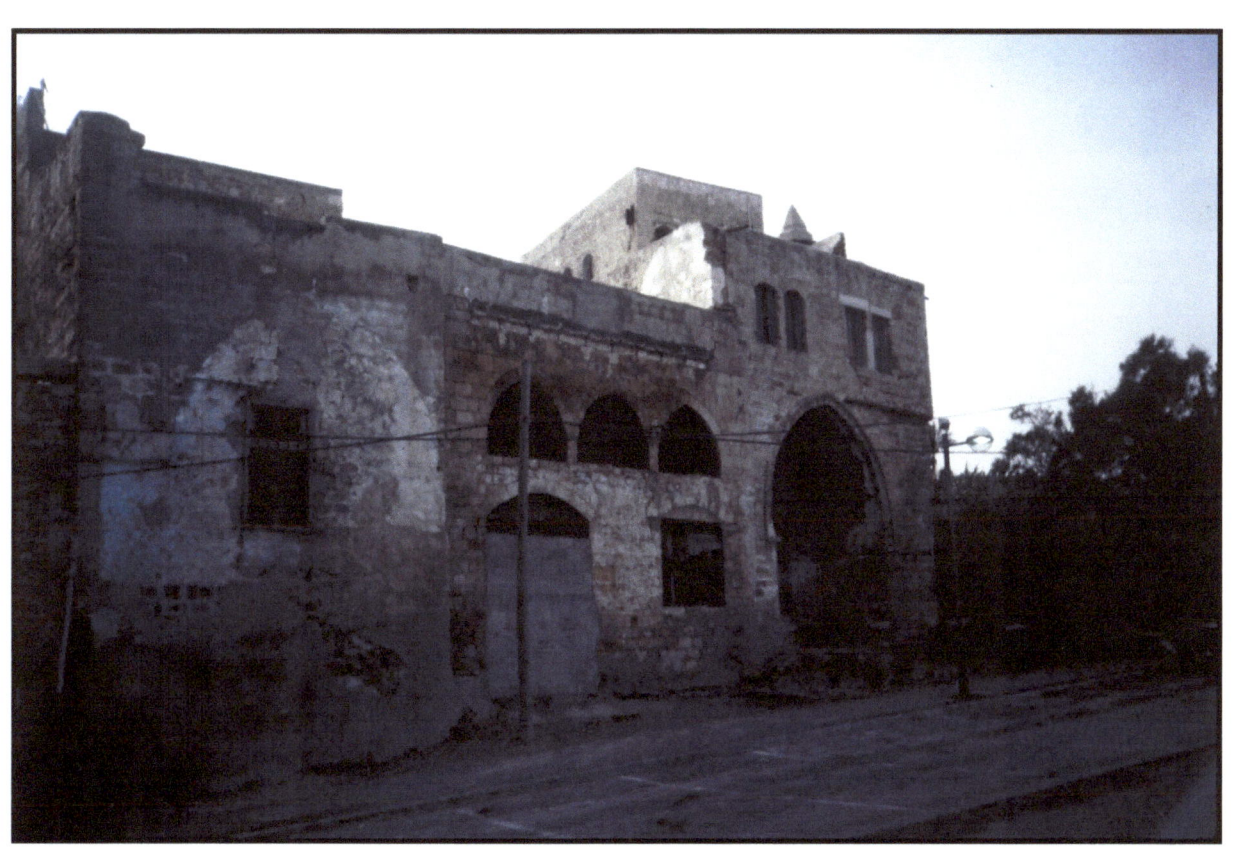

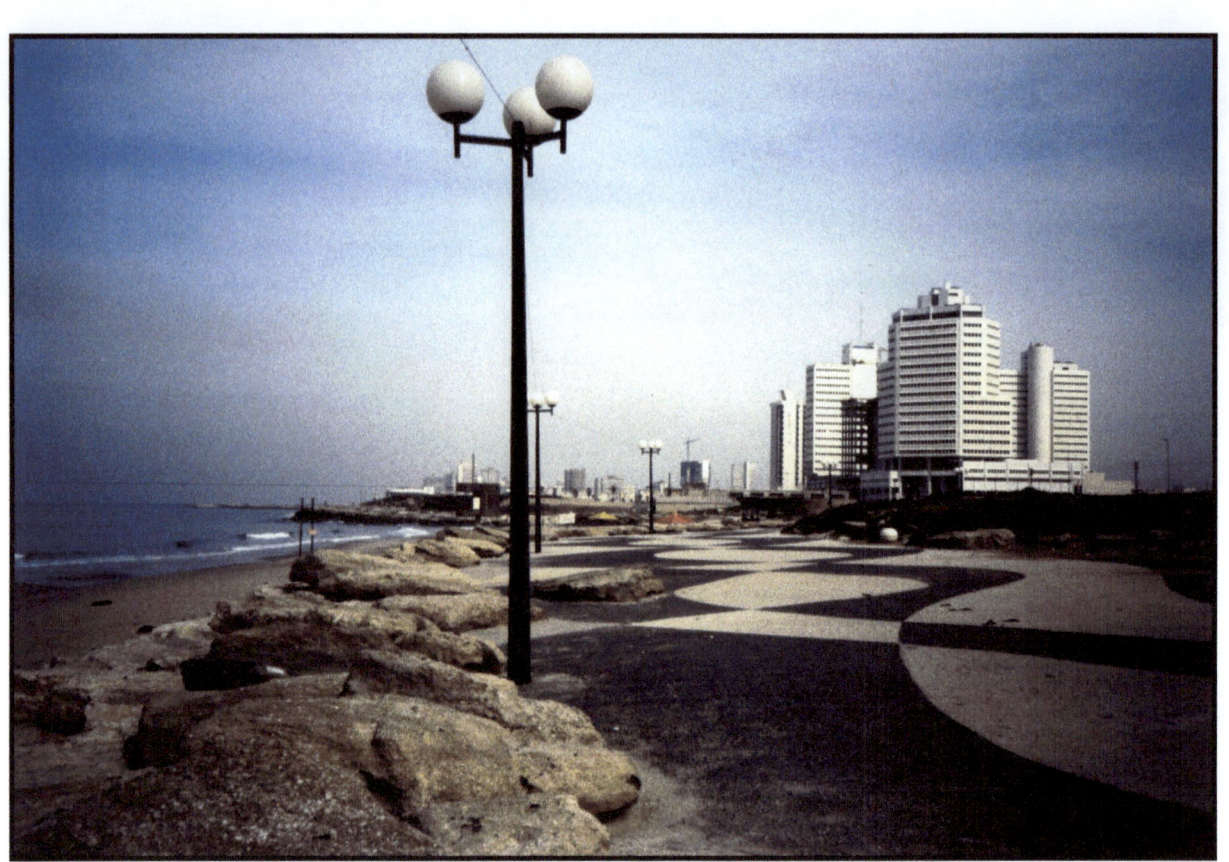

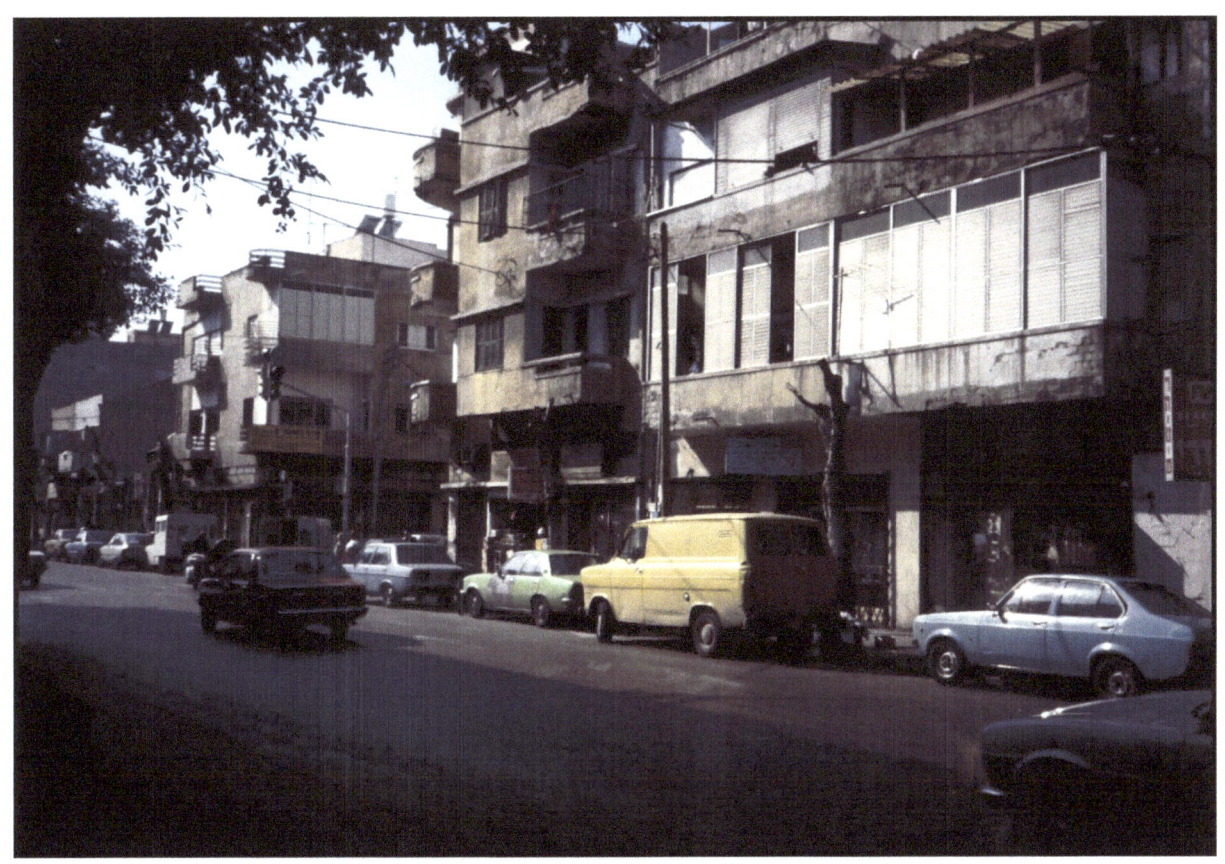

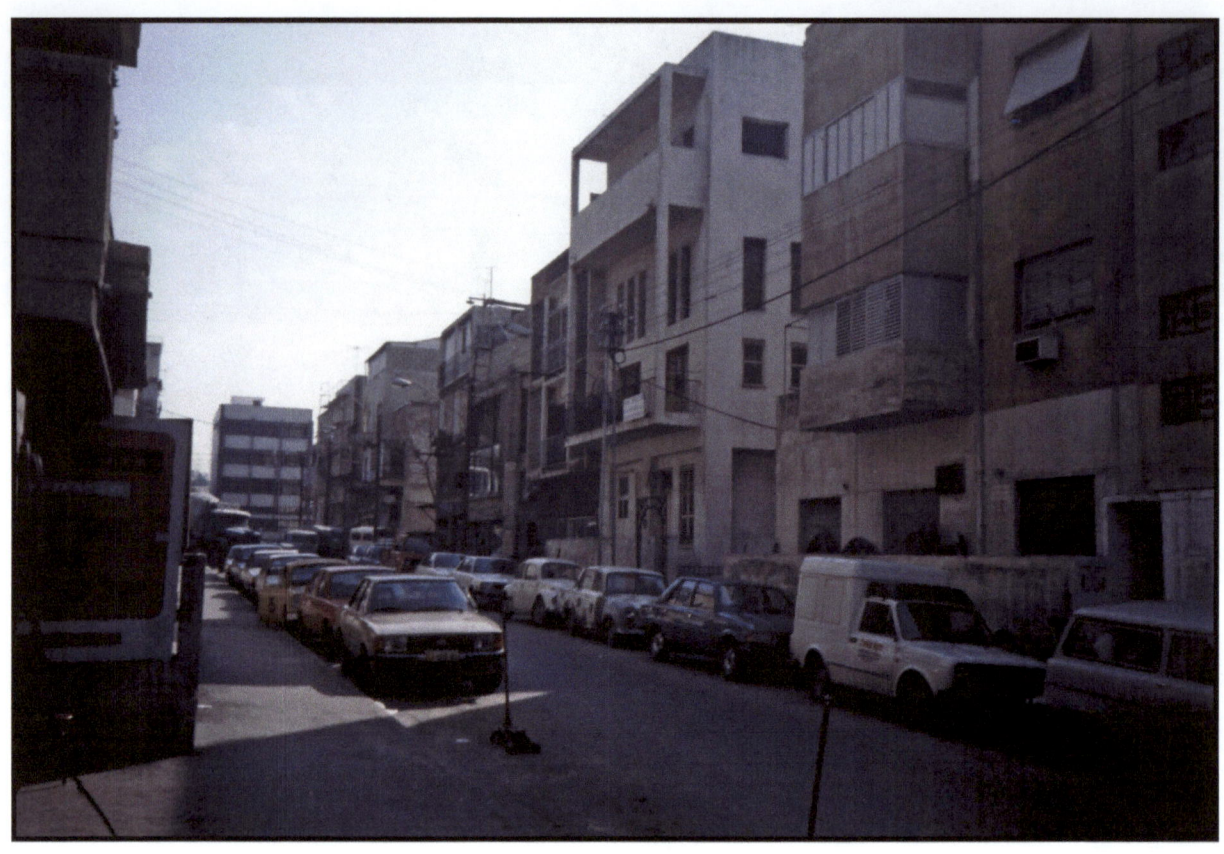

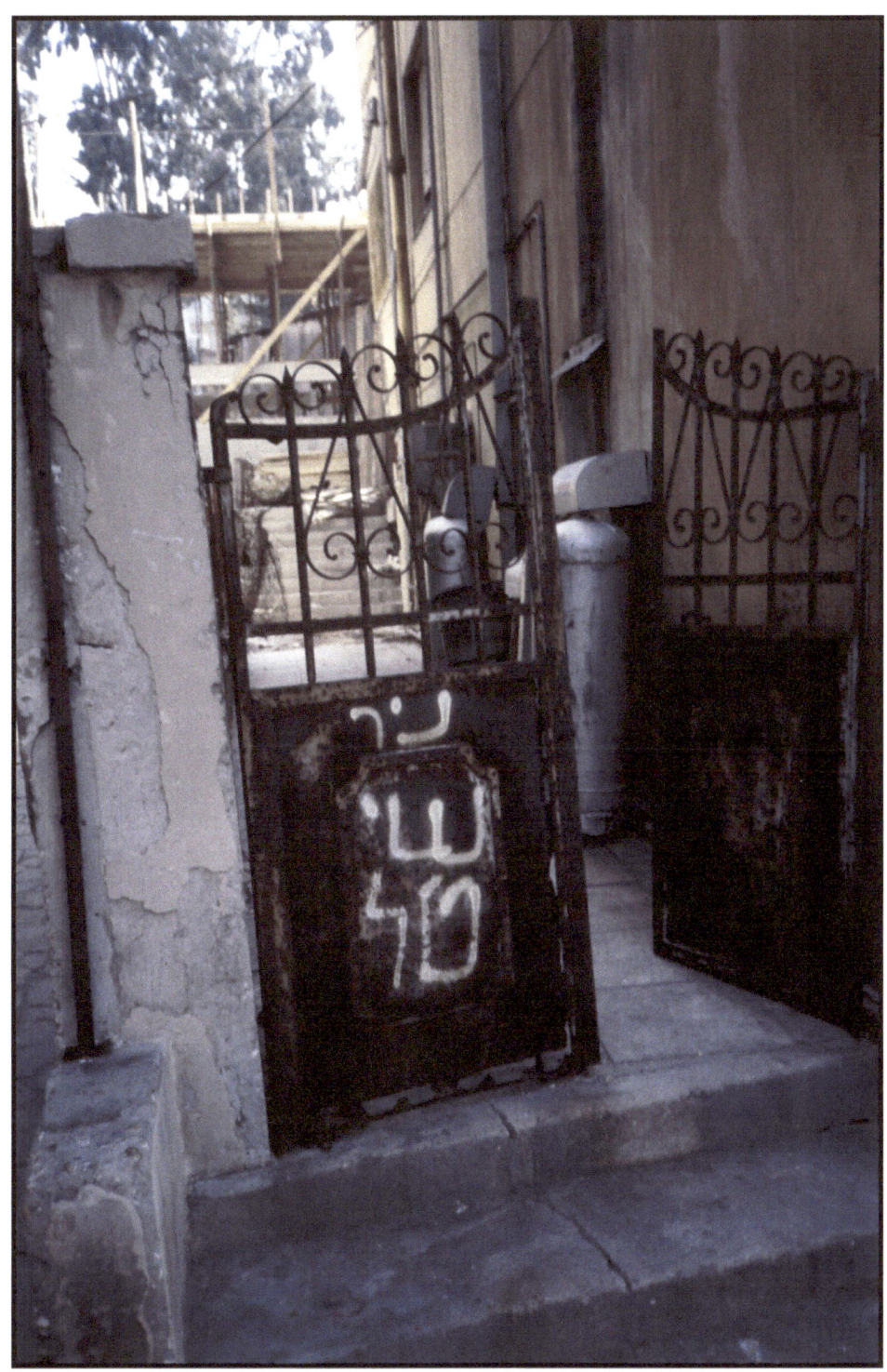

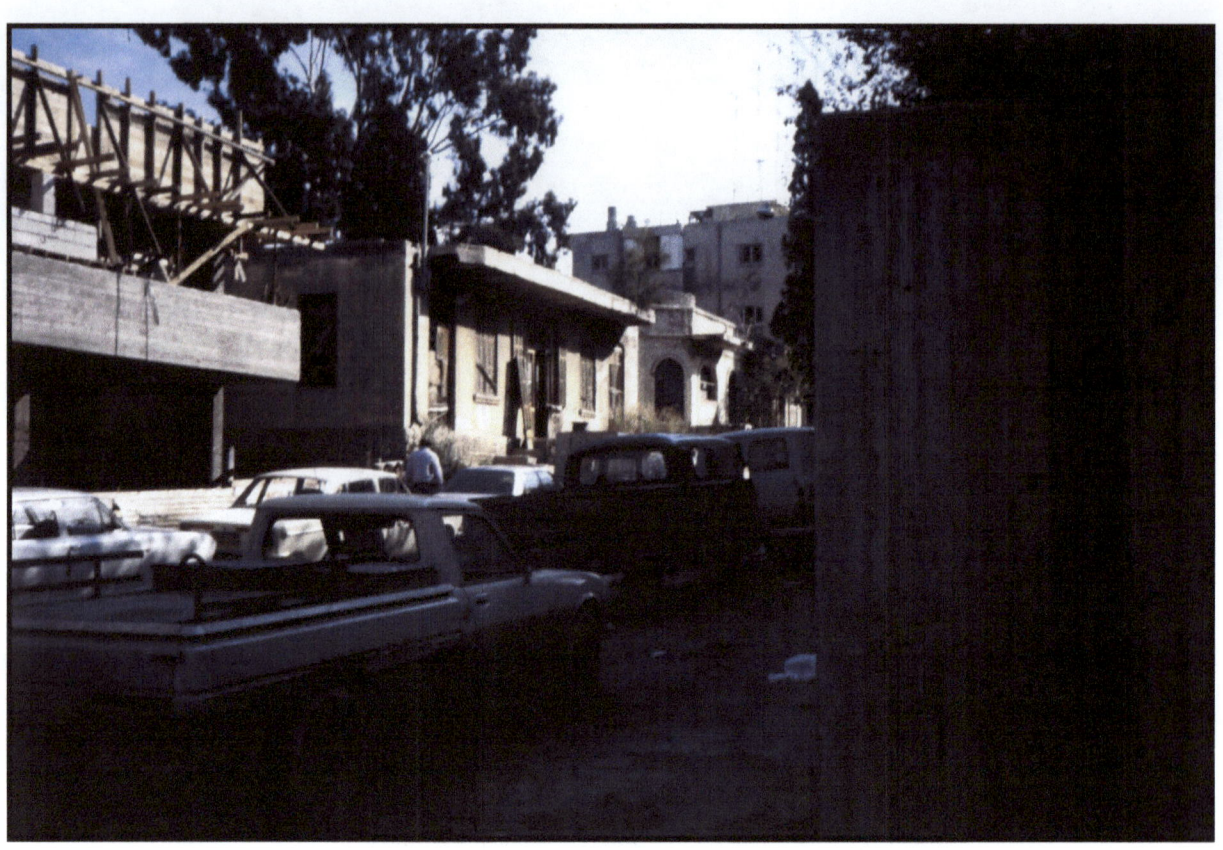

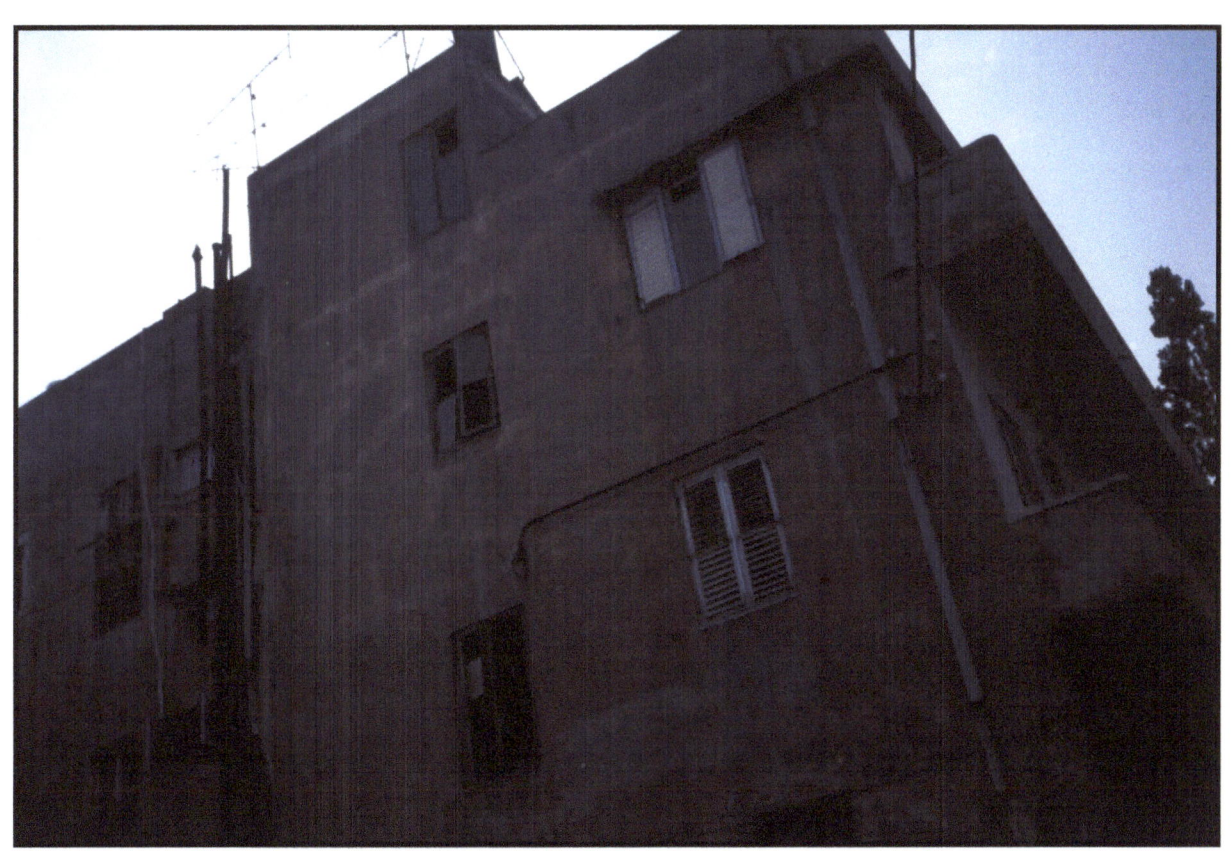

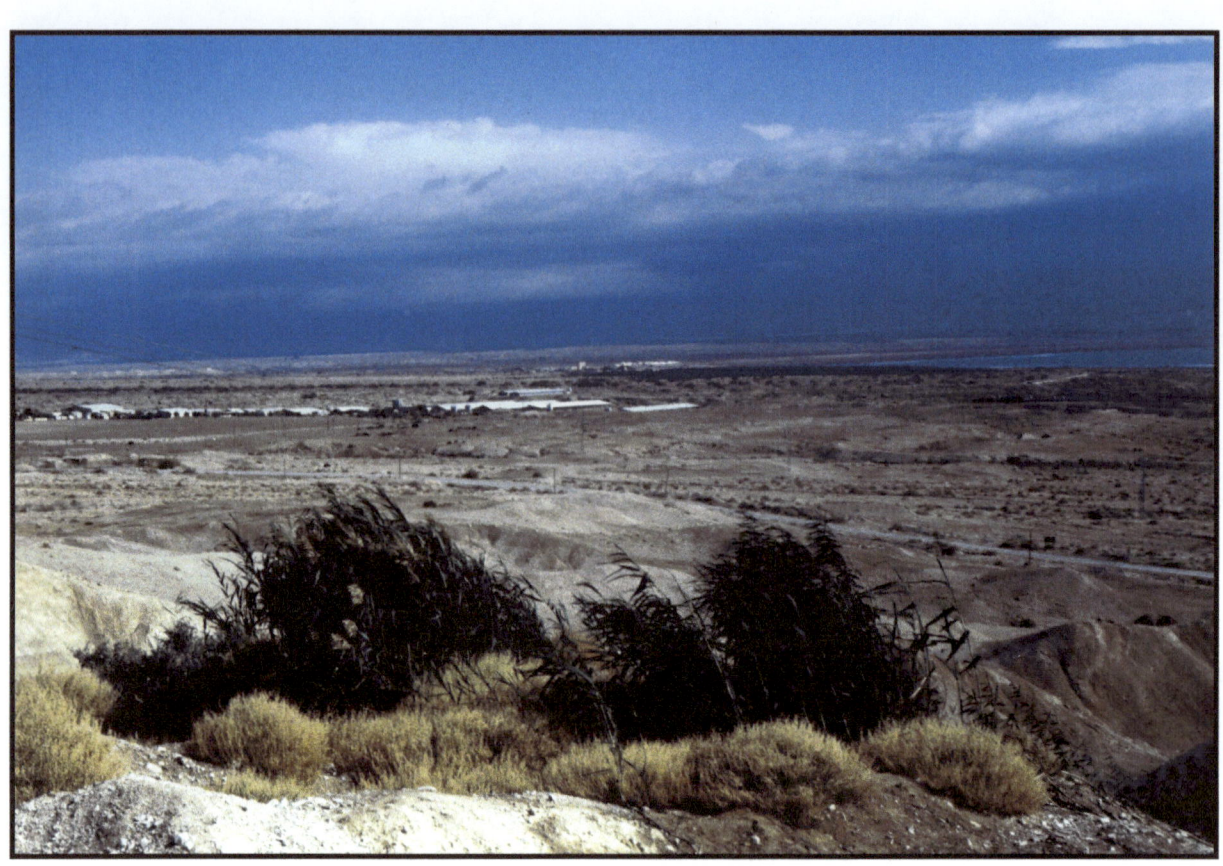

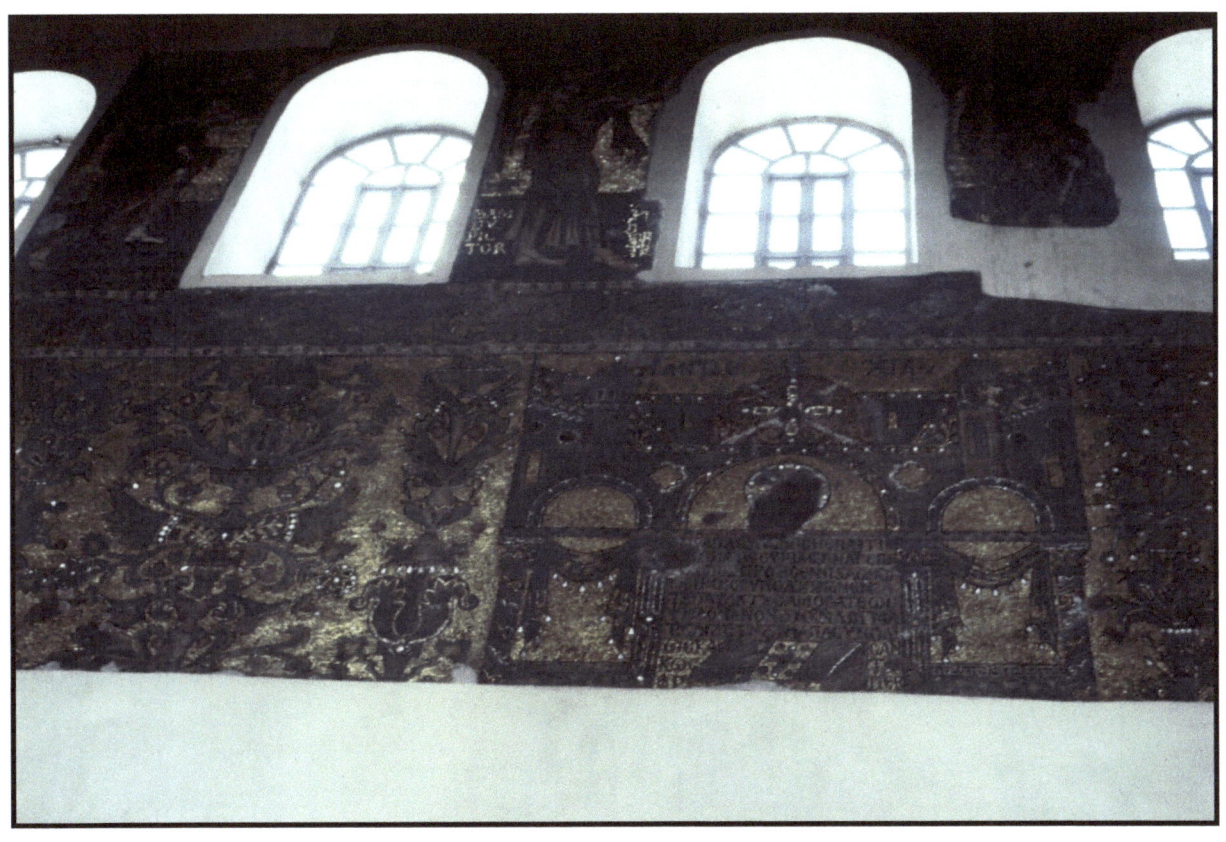

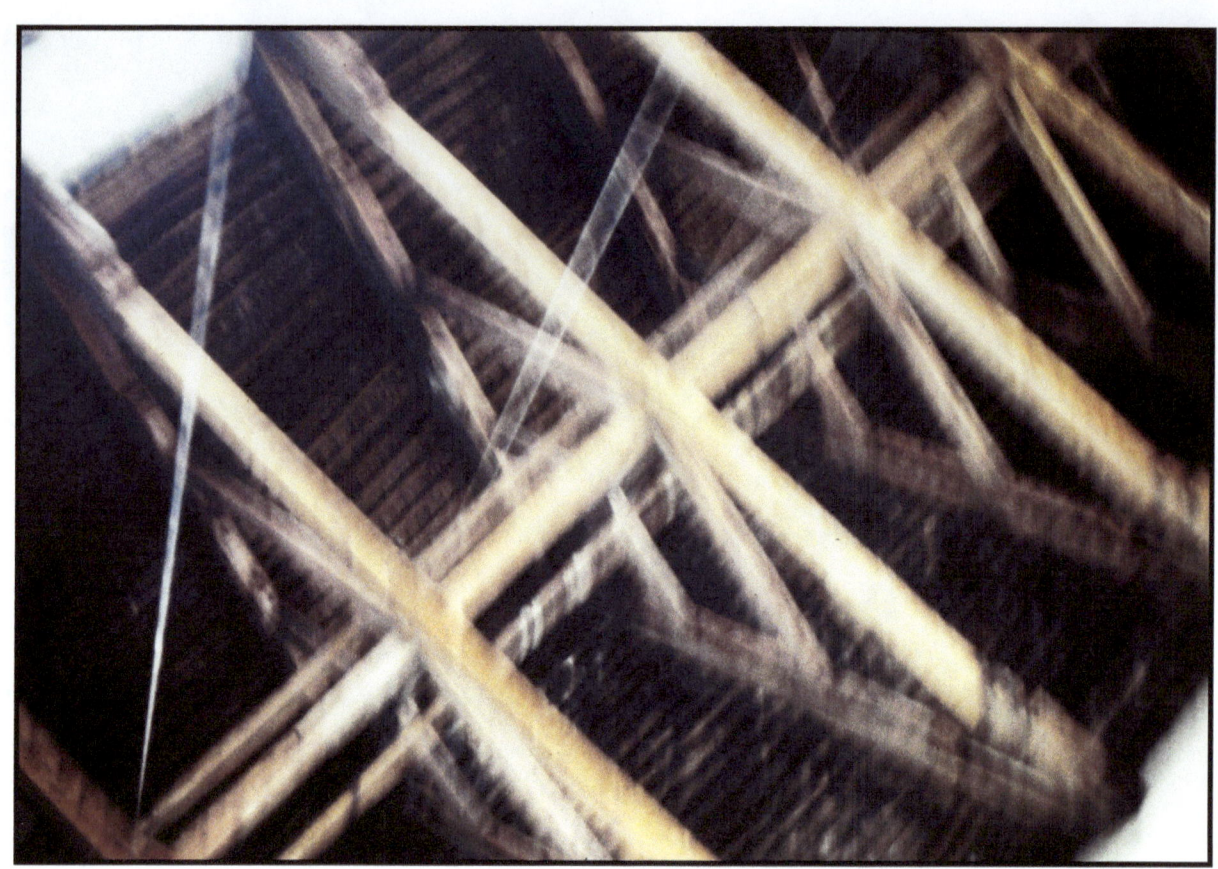

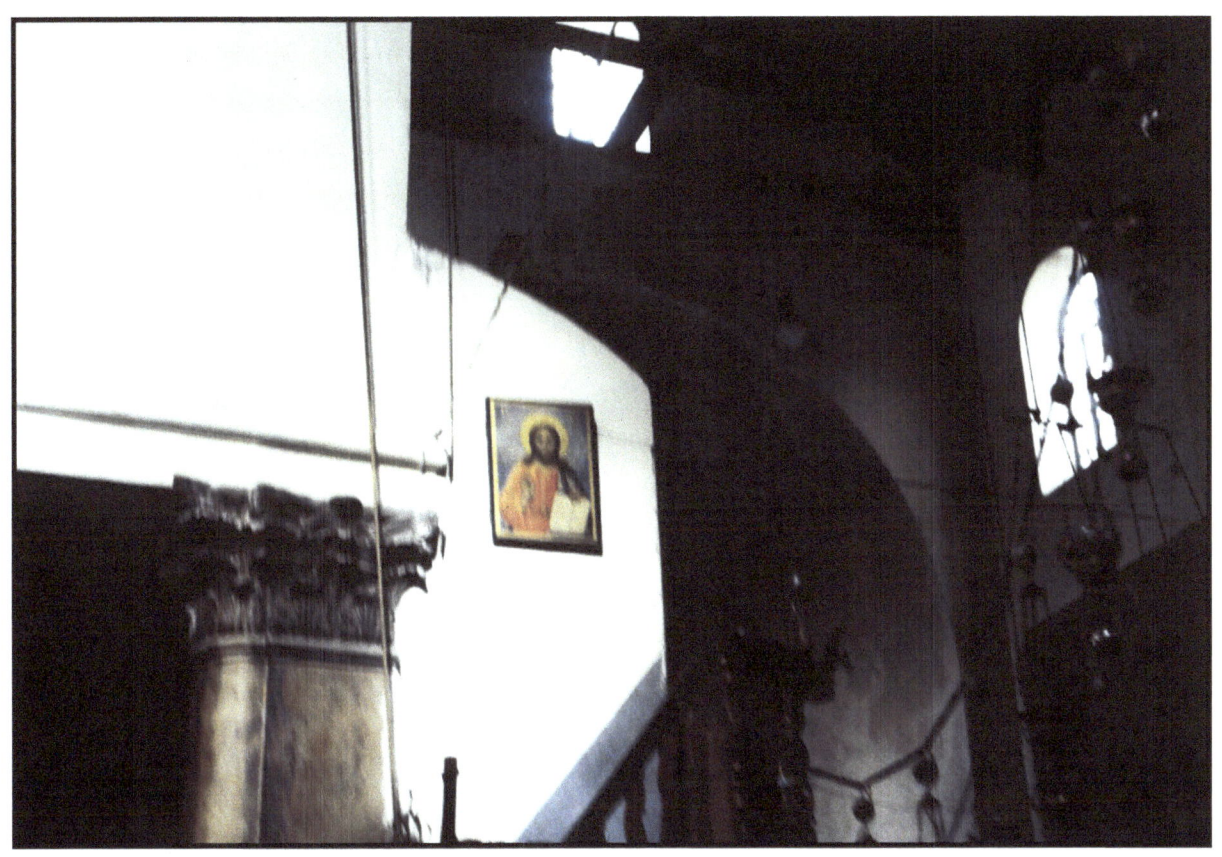

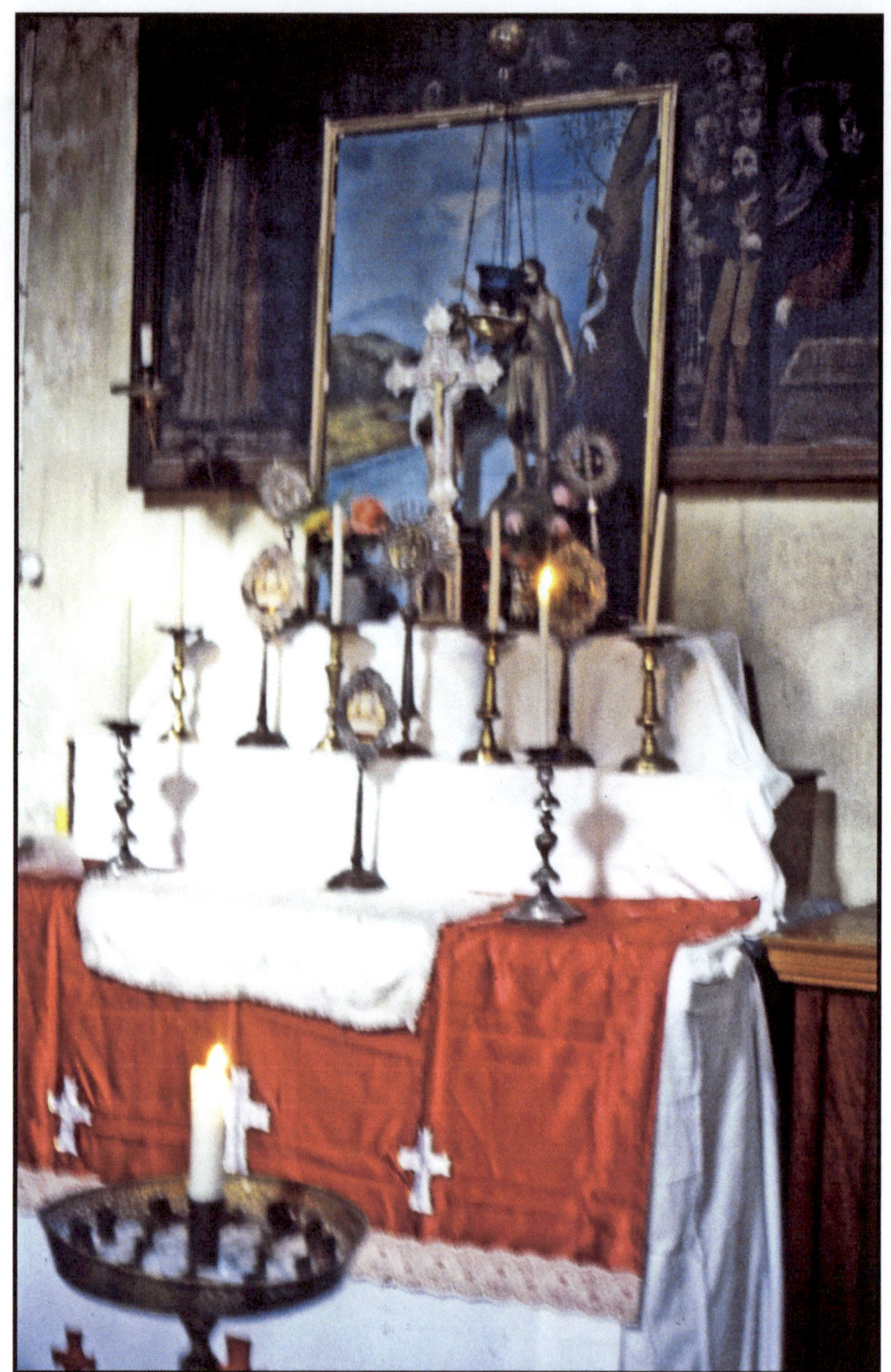

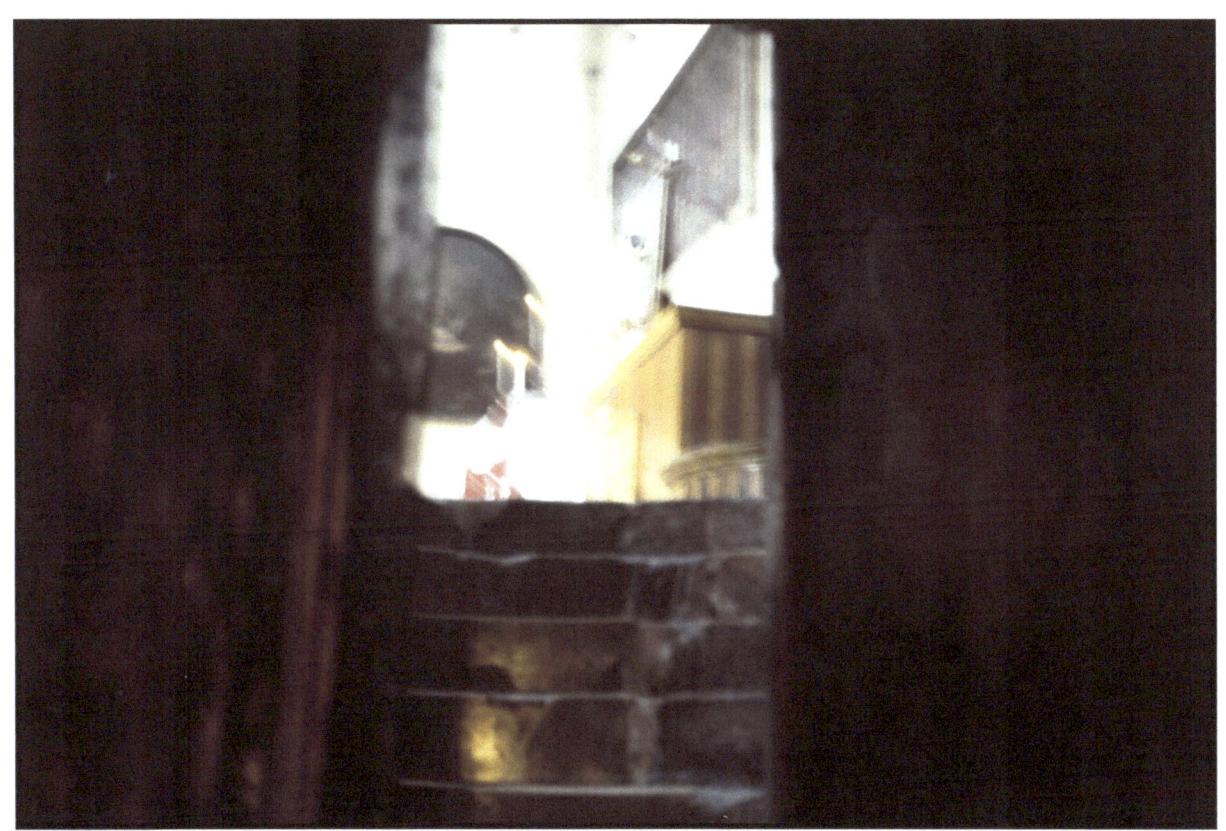

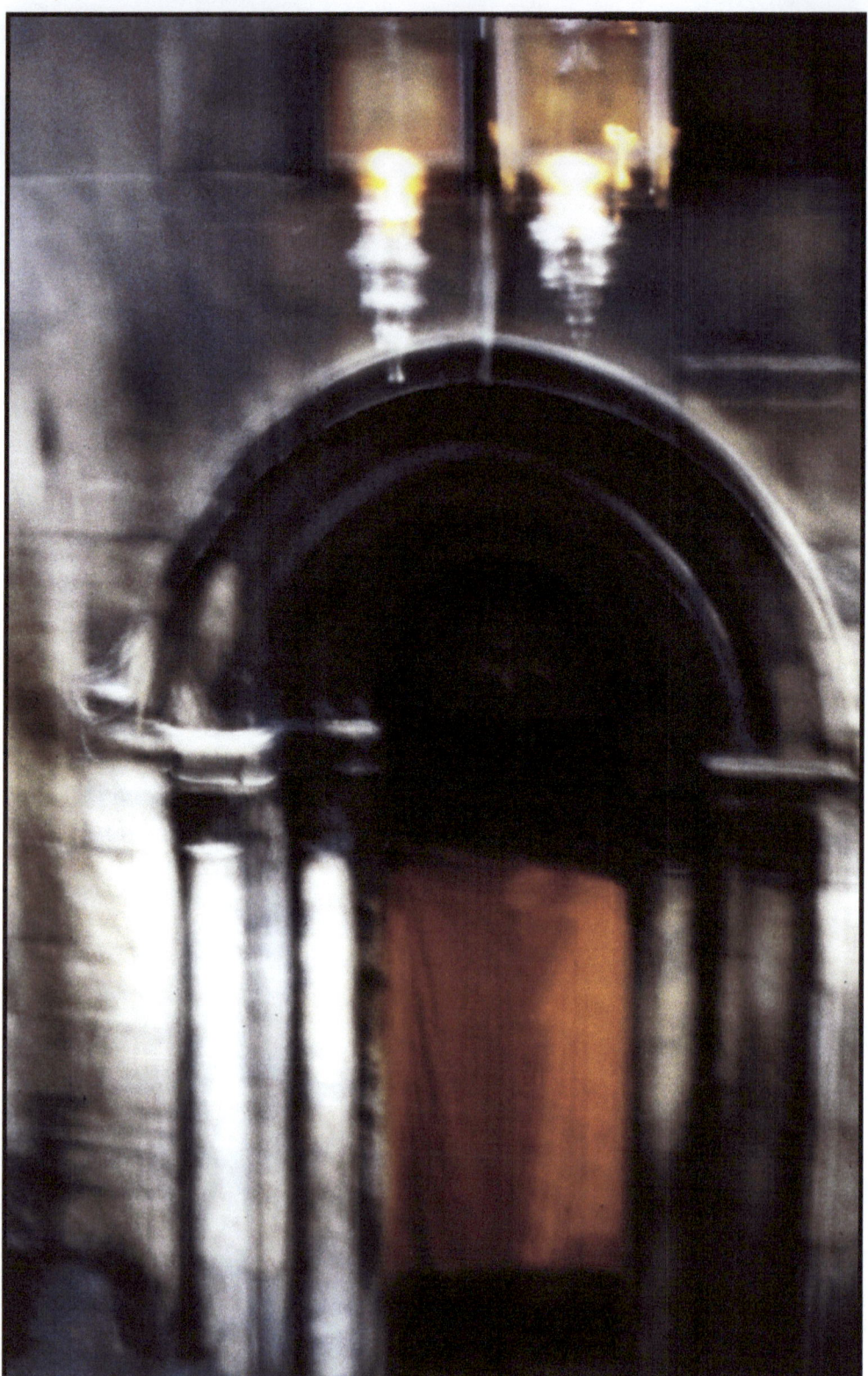

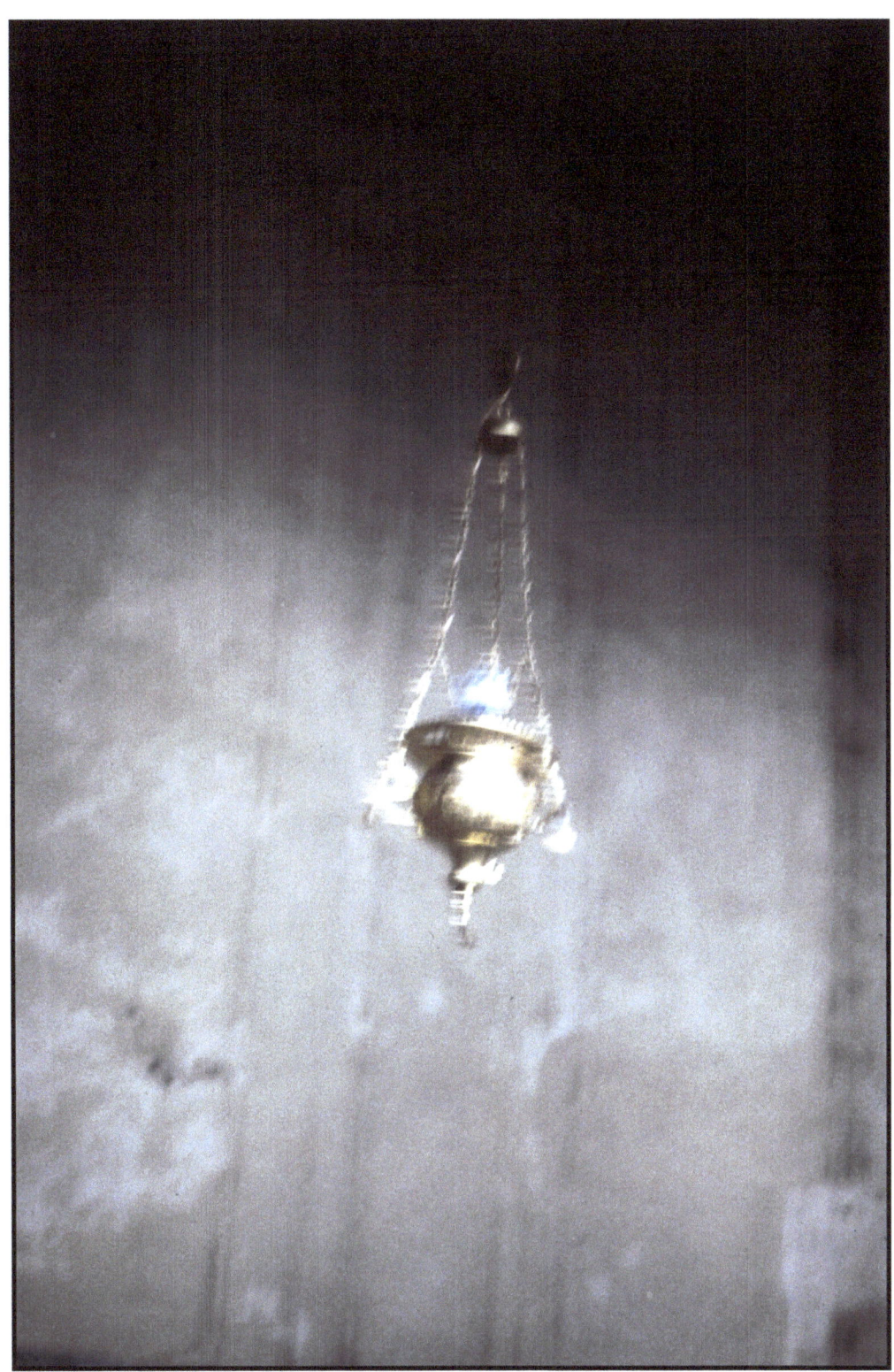

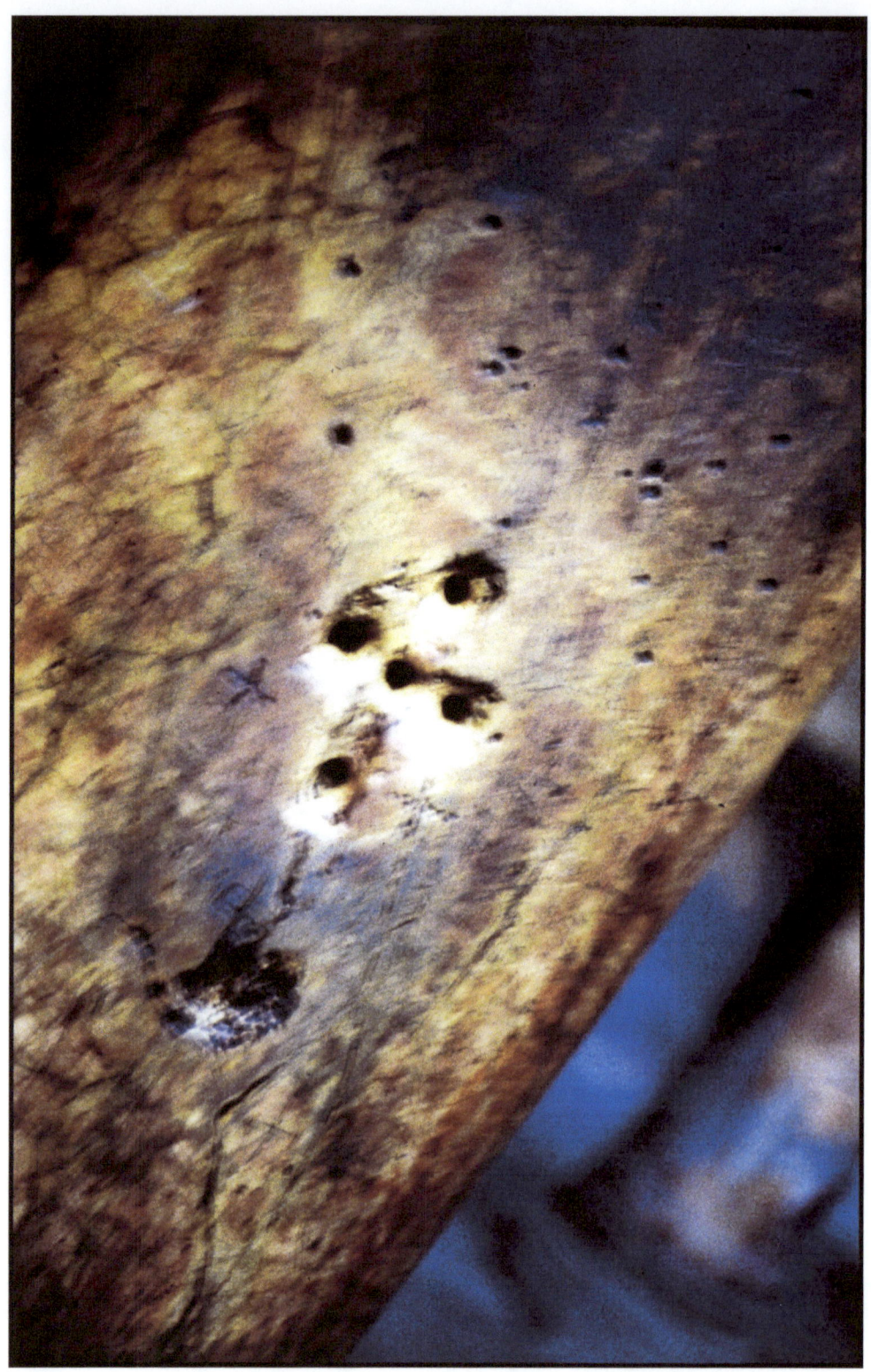

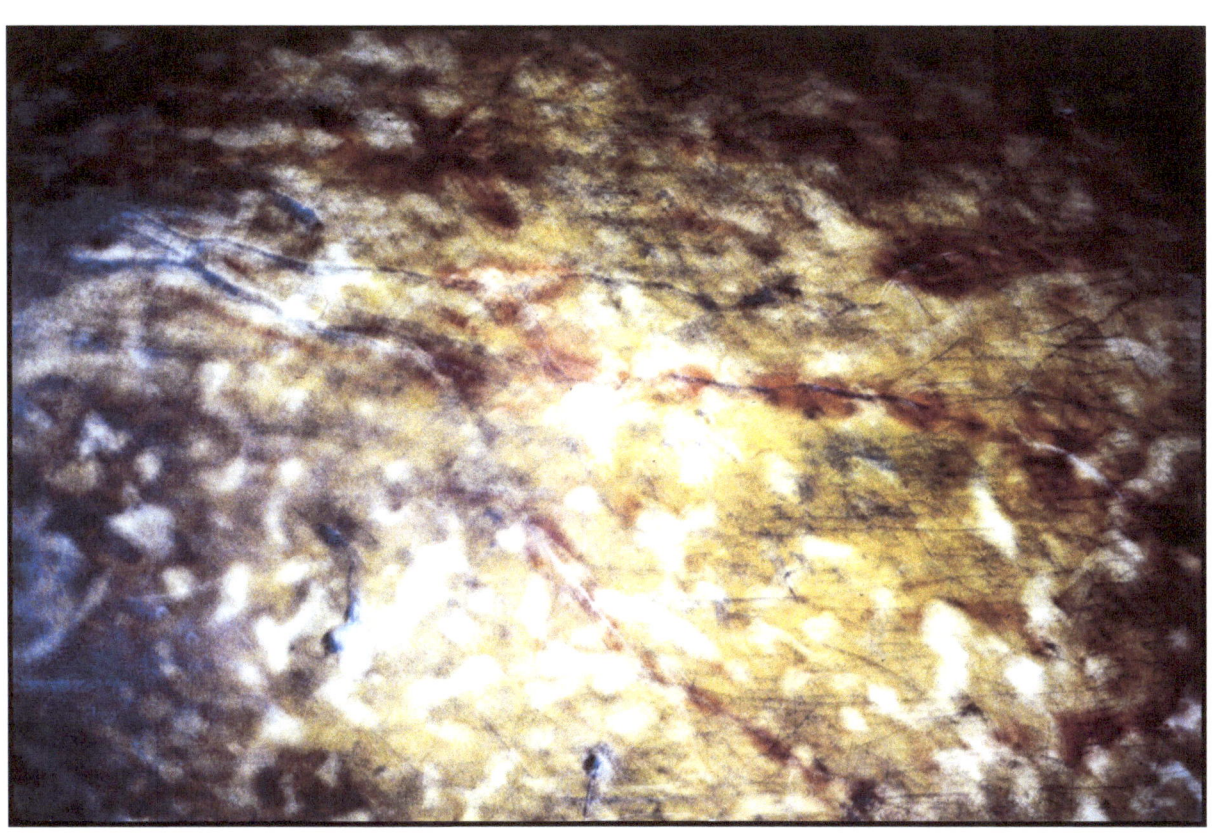

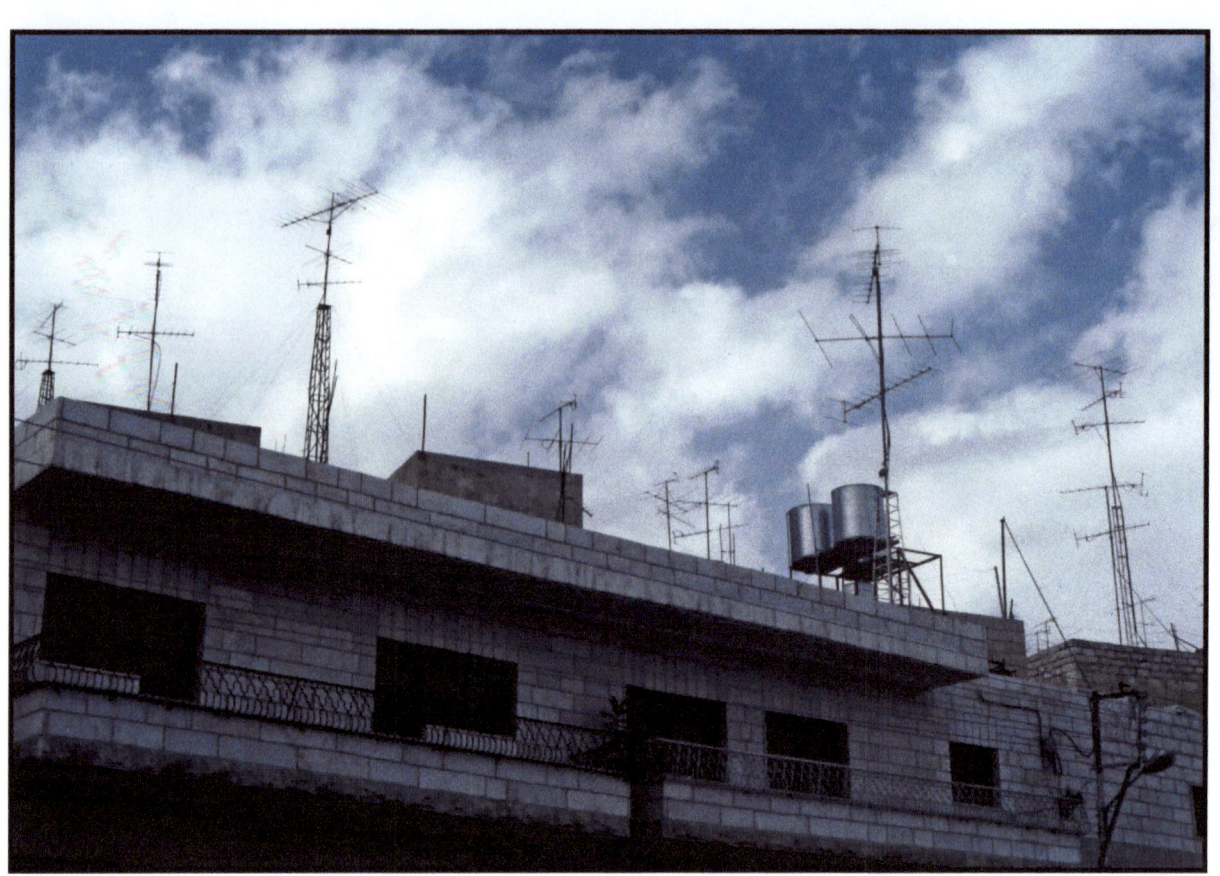

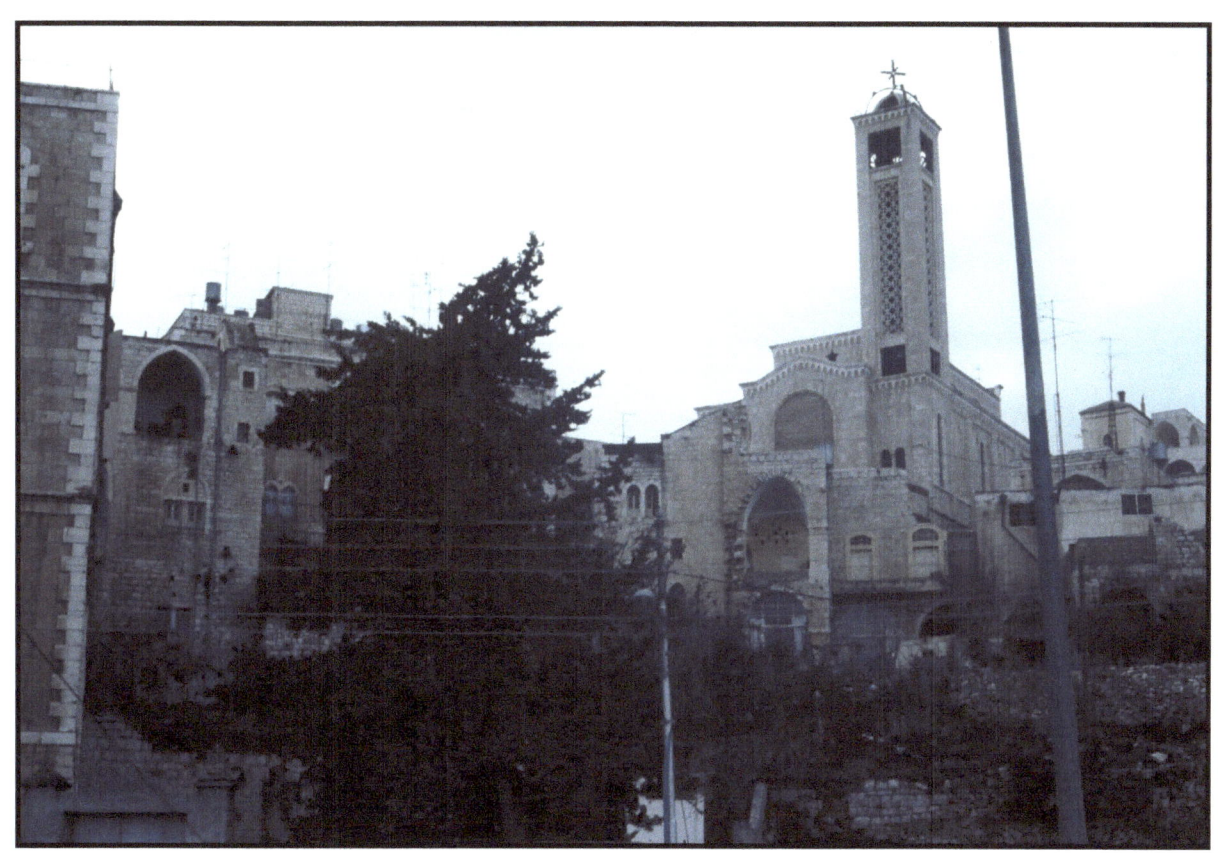

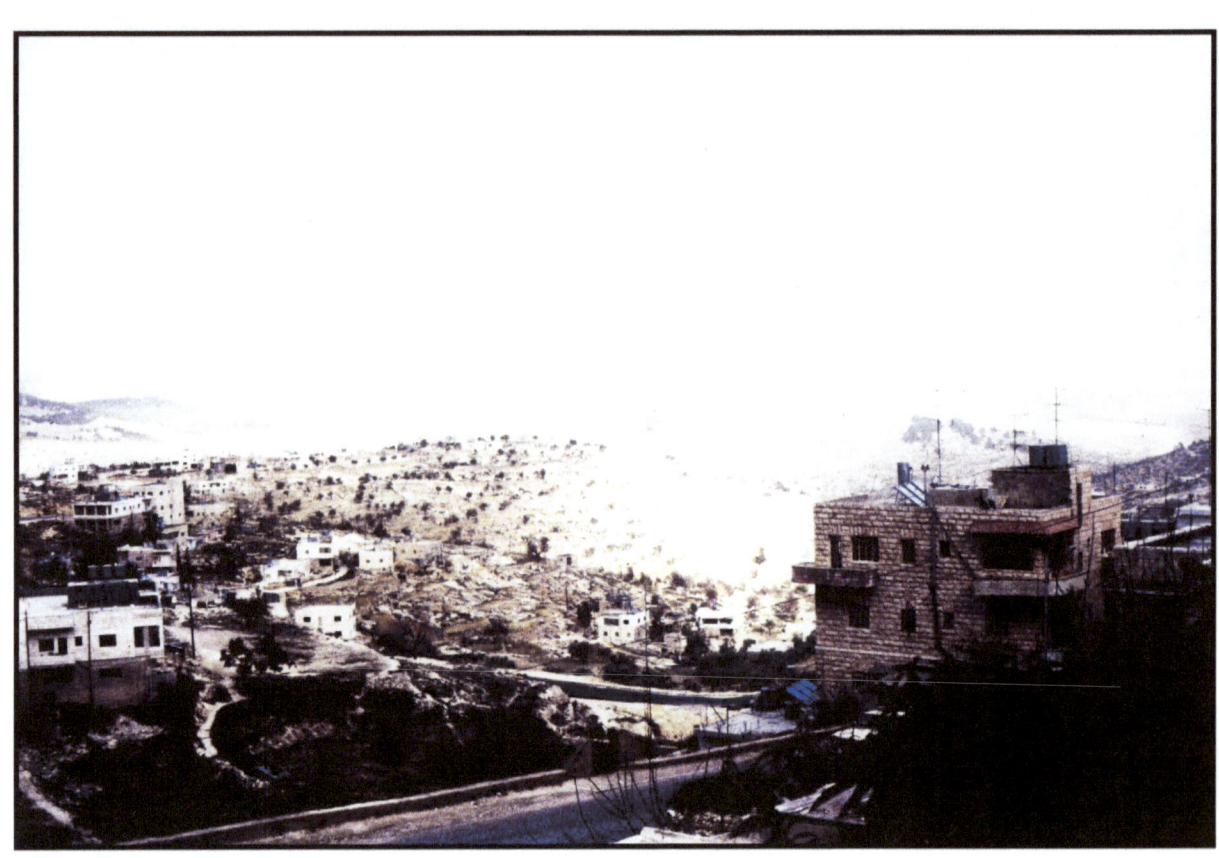

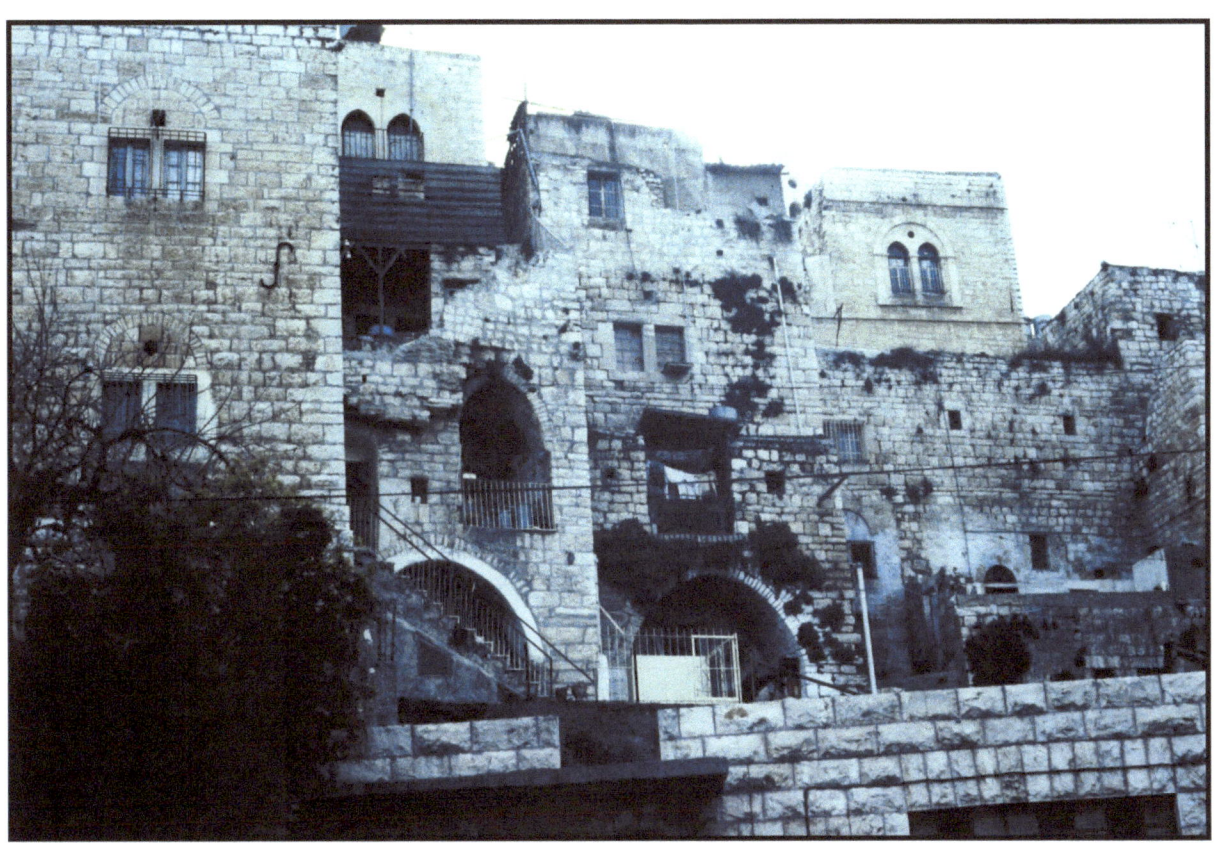

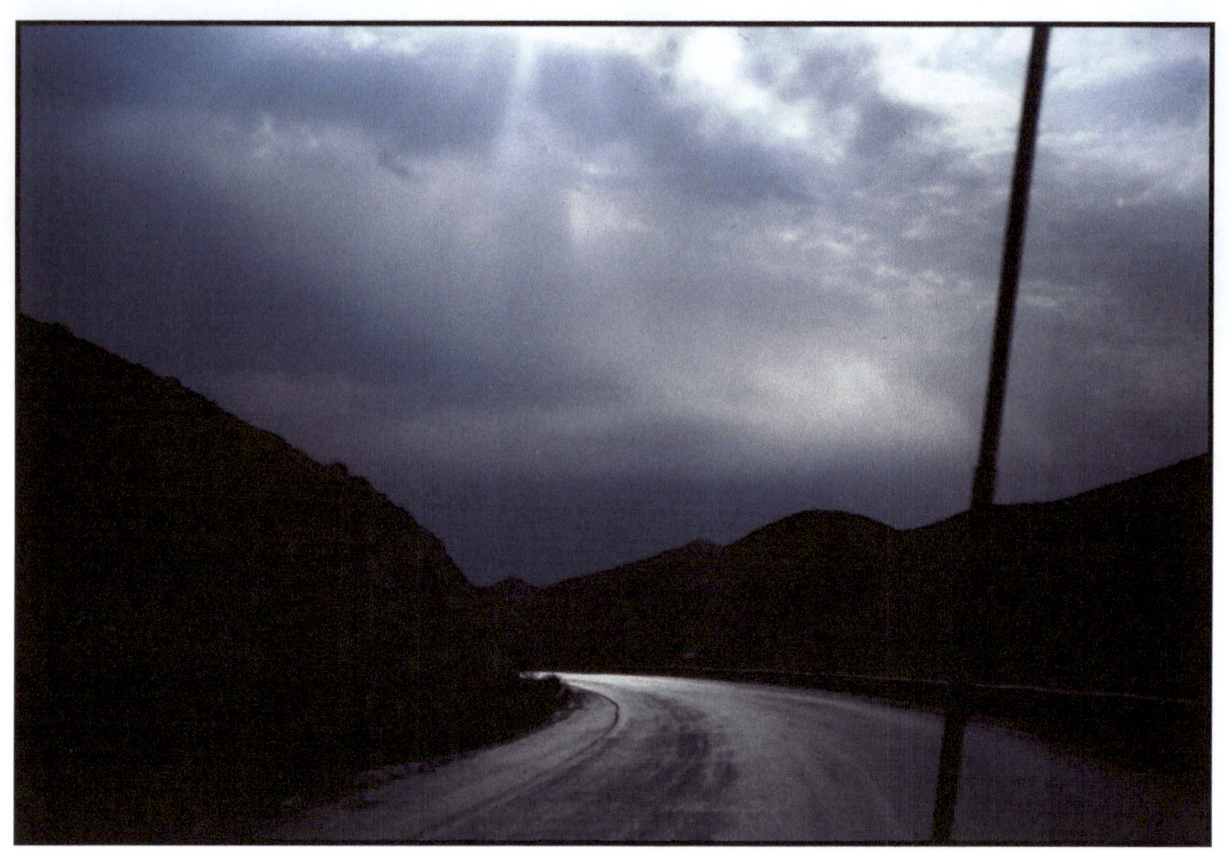

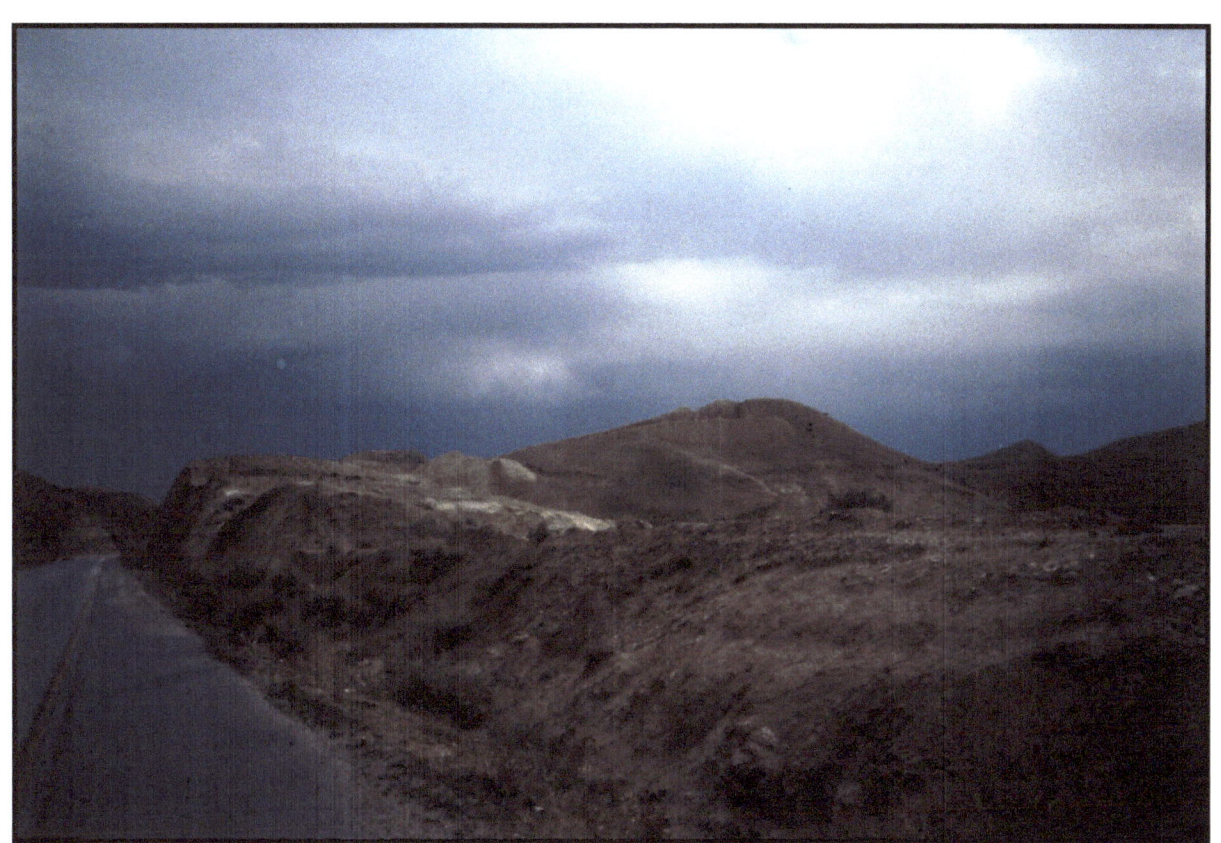

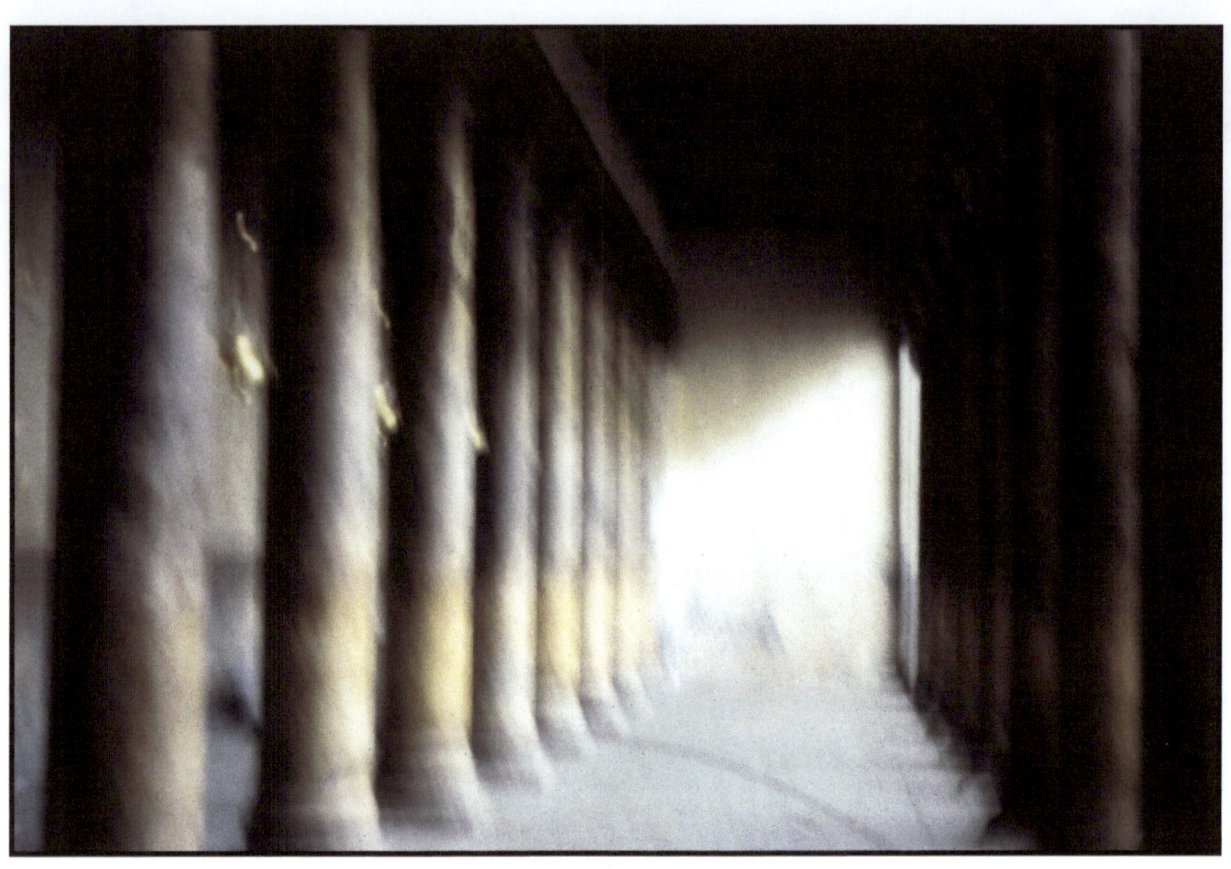

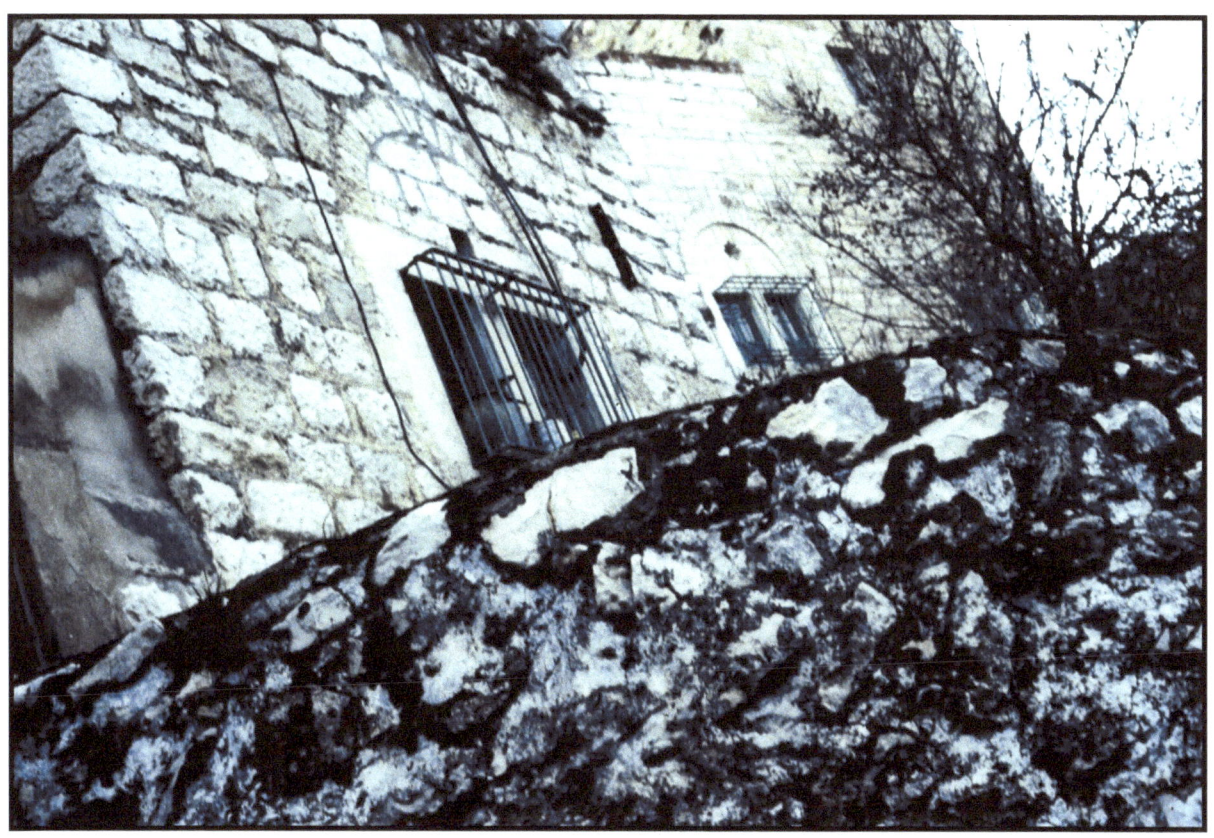

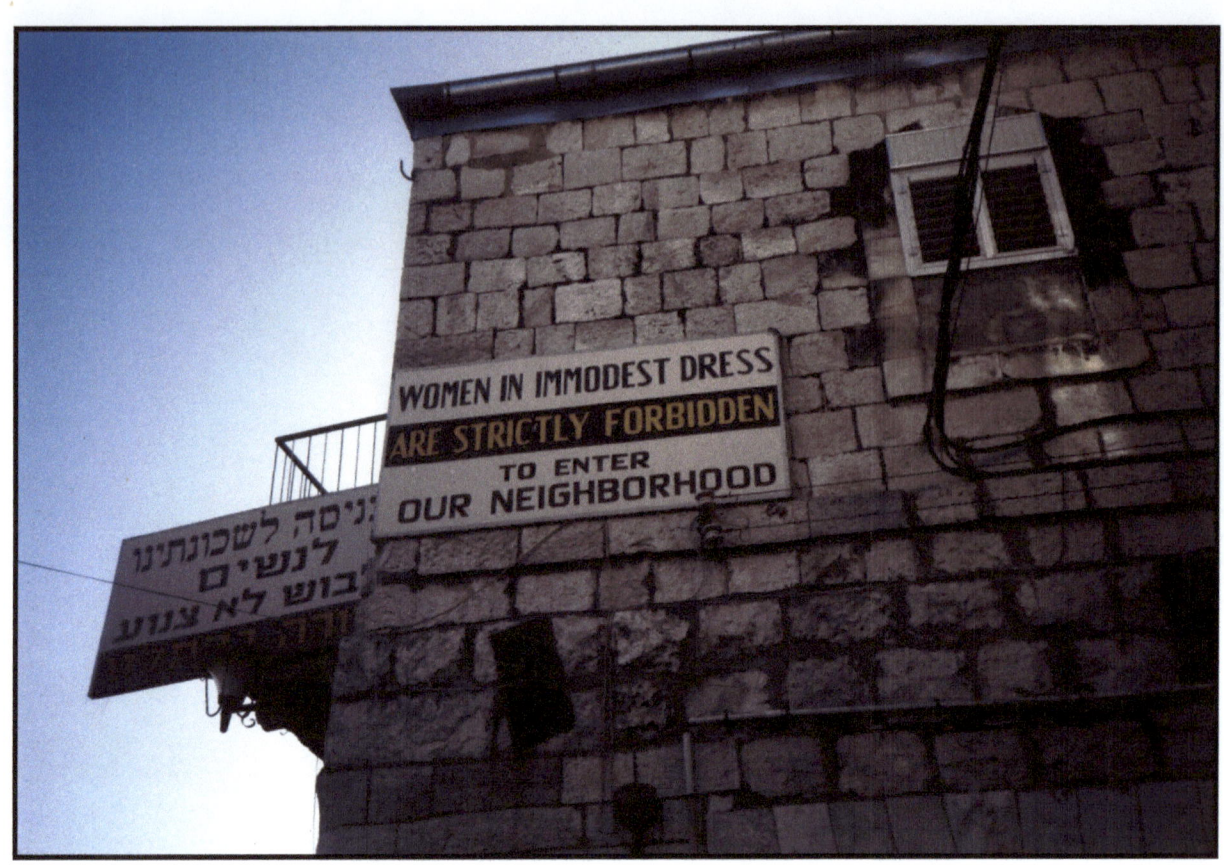

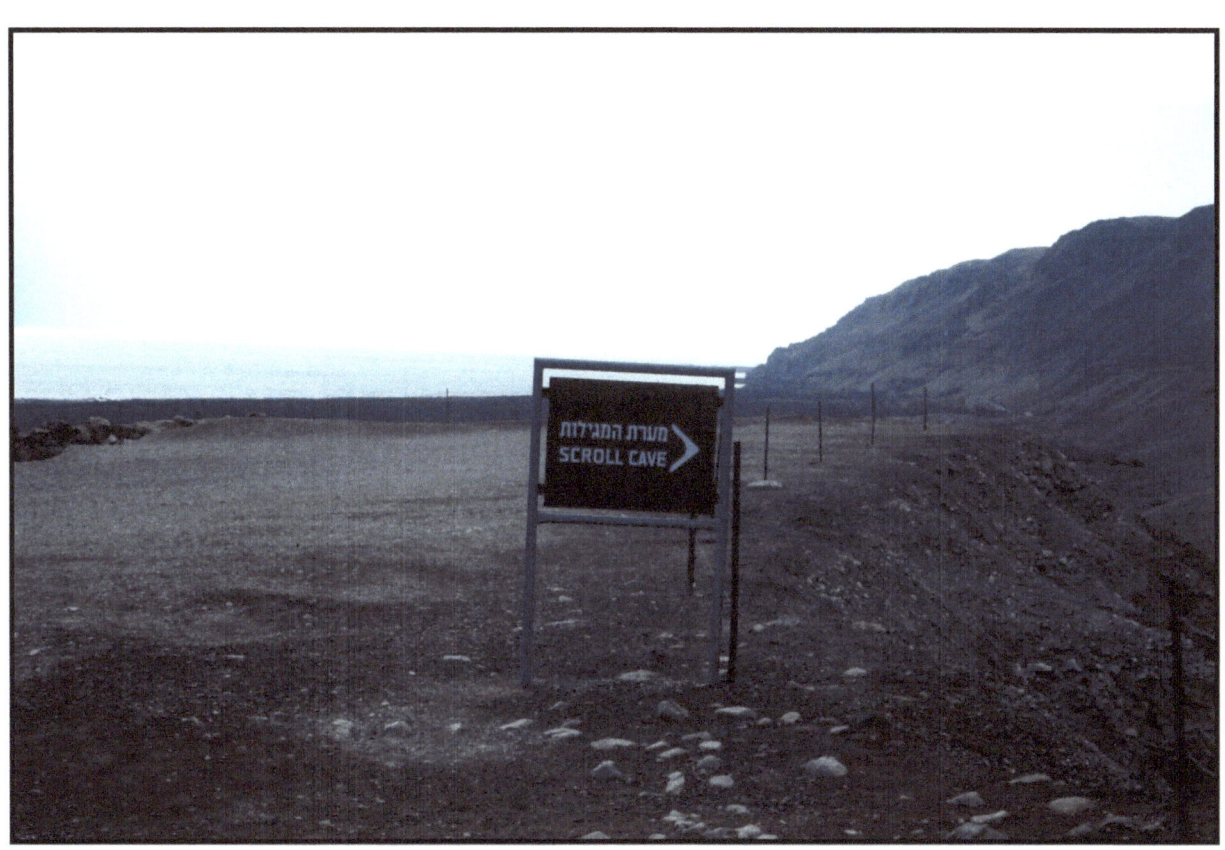

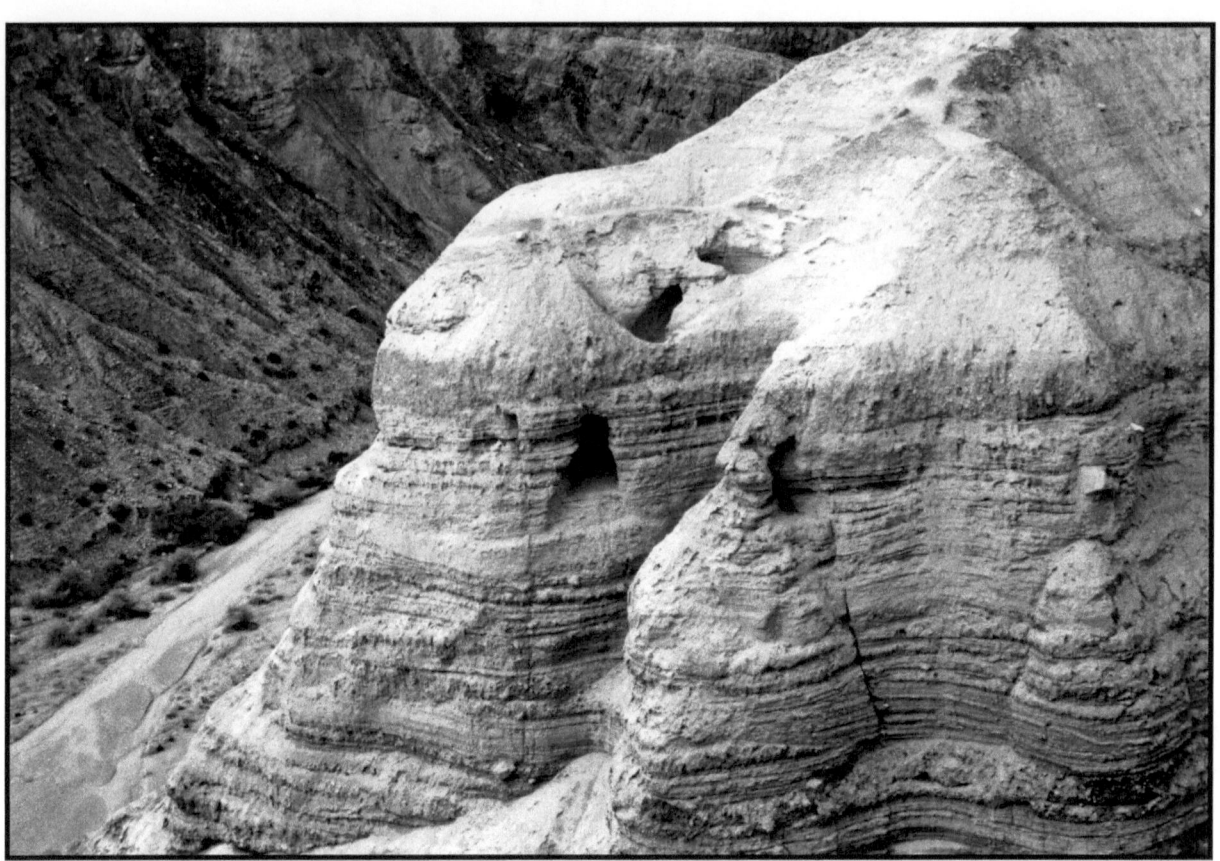

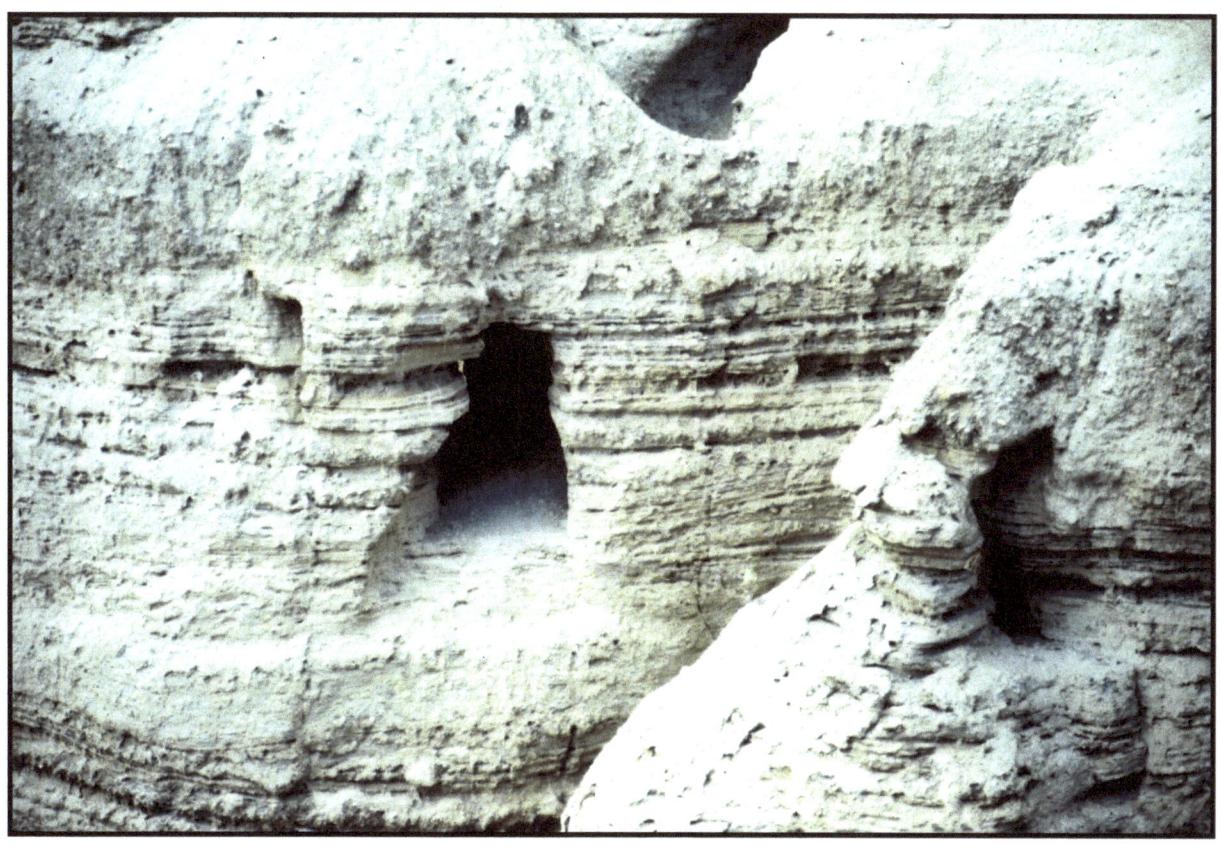

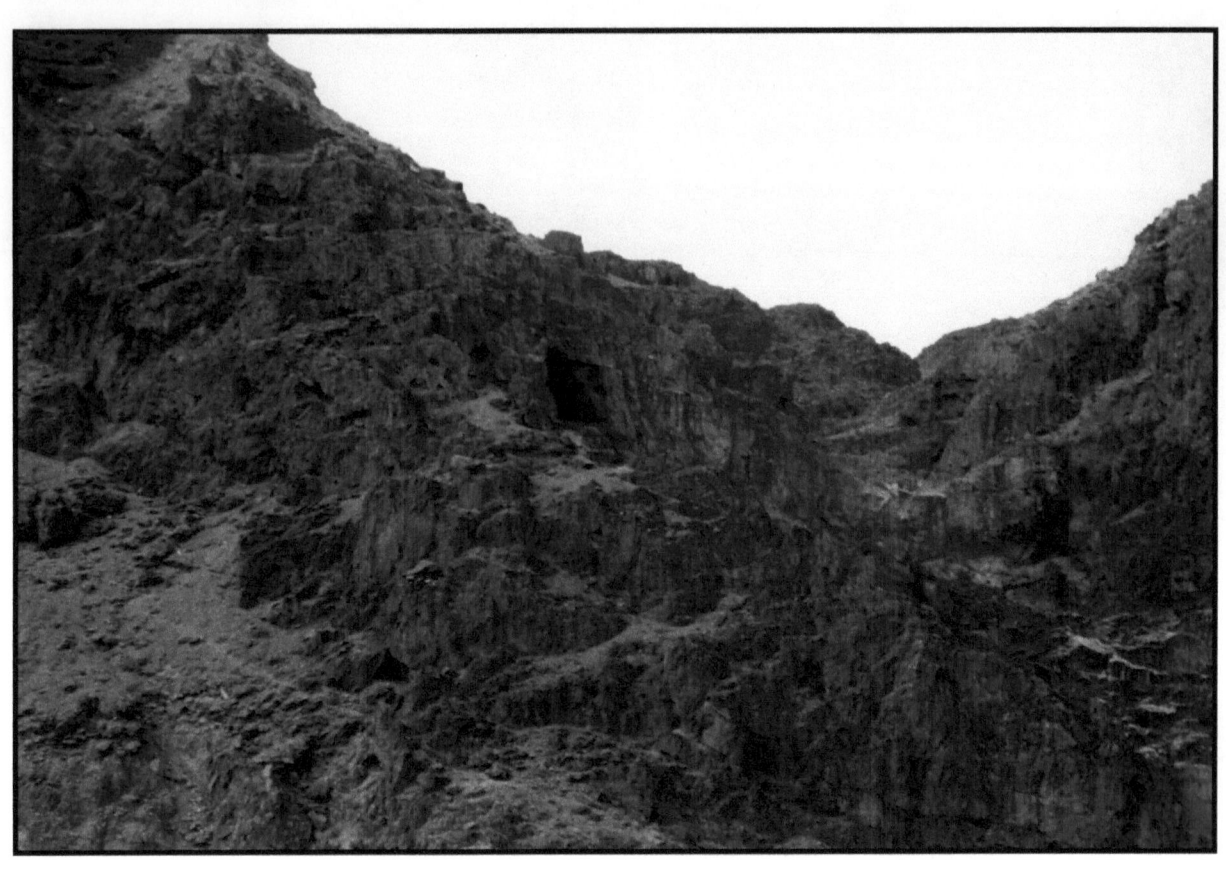

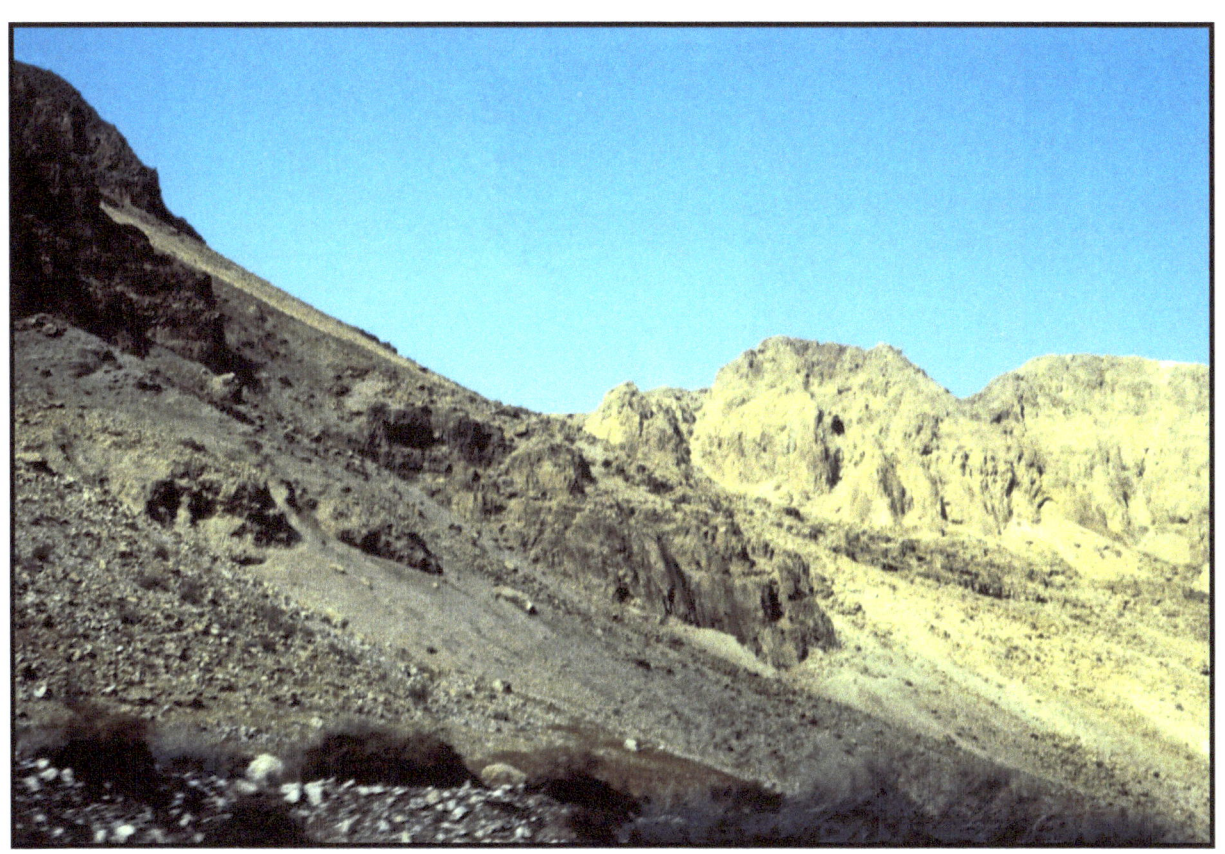

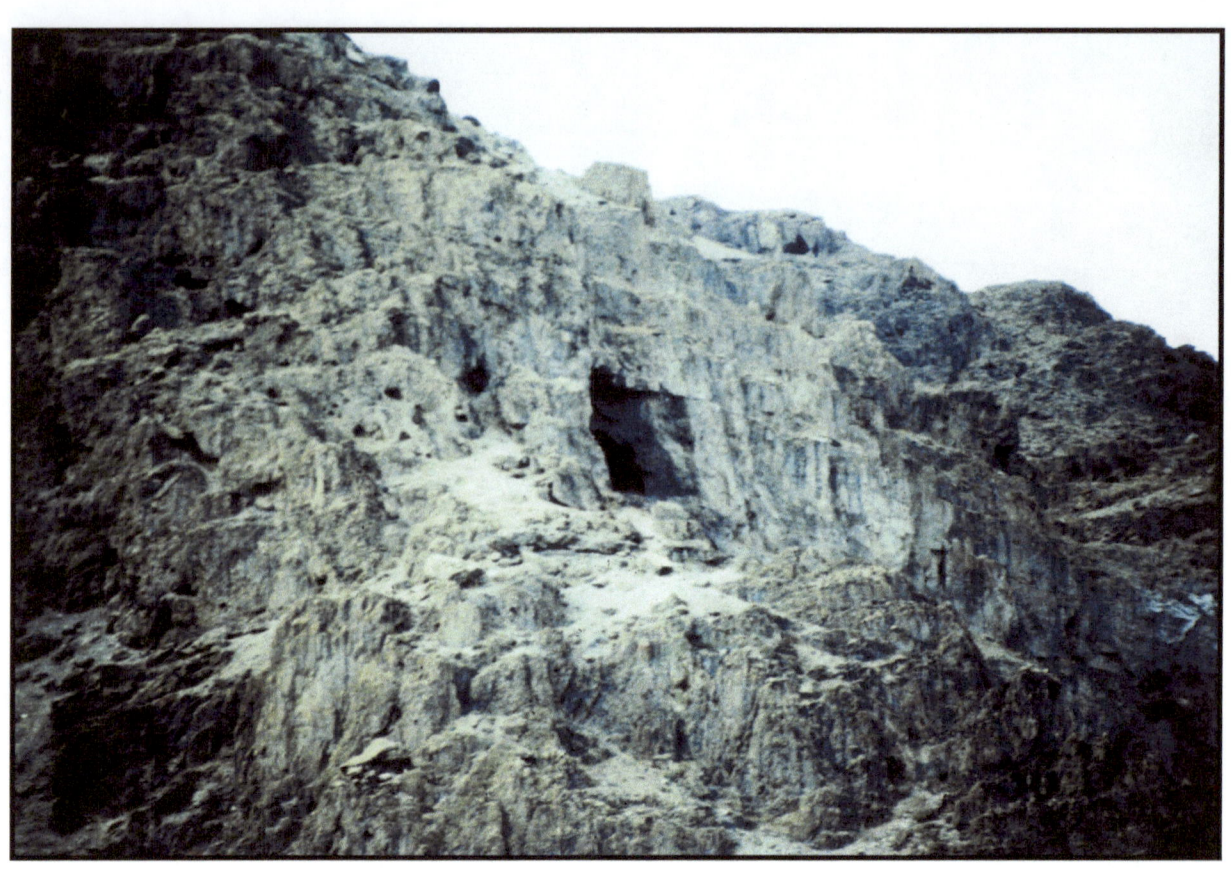

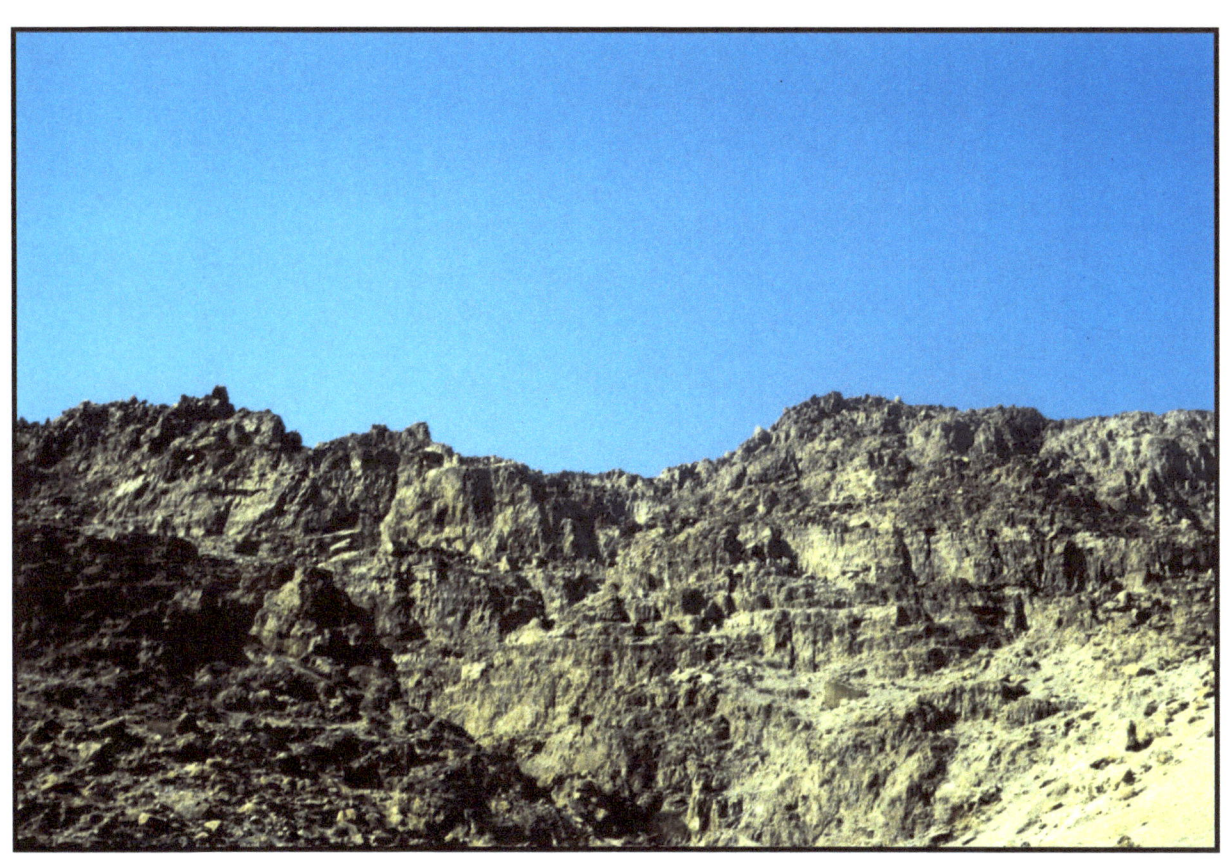

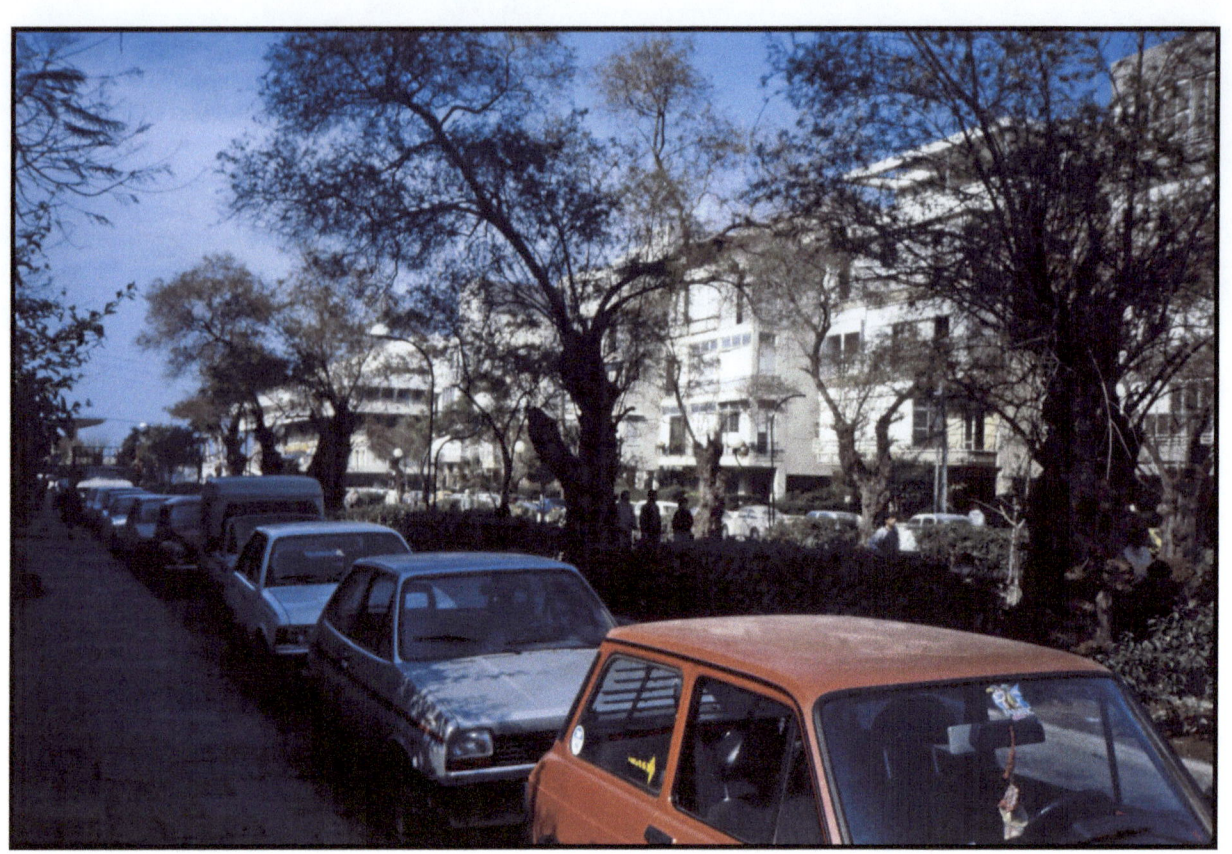

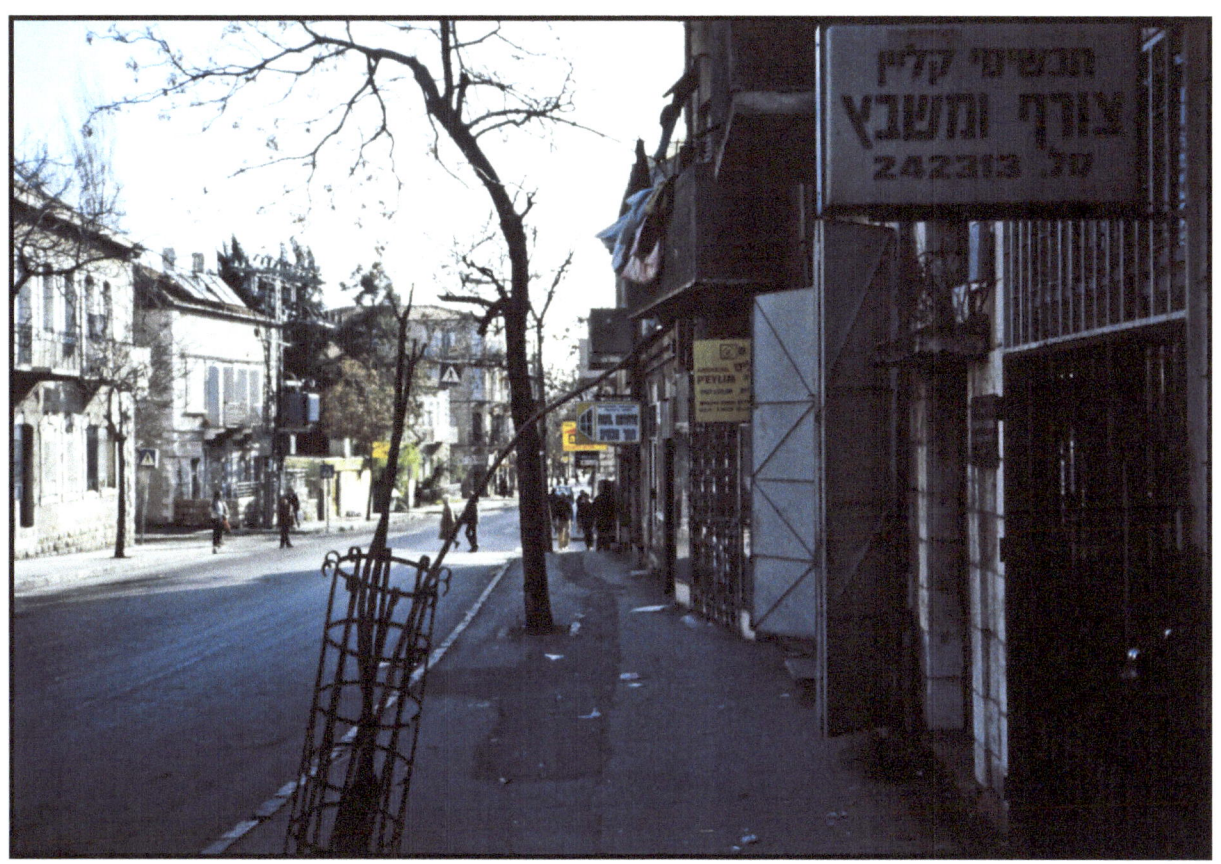

מצפים — תוך תפילה ולימוד התורה — לאחרית הימים.
רצה חגורל שאחריתם של מגיני מצדה ושל הישוב בקומראן, קשורות זו בזו קשר חדק; המרד חגדול נגד רומי.

QUMRAN

SITUATED ON THE NORTH WESTERN SHORE OF THE DEAD SEA, SOME FIFTY KILOMETERS NORTH OF MASADA, ARE THE RUINS KNOWN TO THE ARABS AS KHIRBET QUMRAN. IN THE CAVES NEAR THE RUINS, THERE CAME TO LIGHT IN 1947 THE MOST DRAMATIC DISCOVERY IN THE HISTORY OF THE JEWISH PEOPLE — THE DEAD SEA SCROLLS. EXCAVATIONS SHOWED THAT THE BUILDINGS AT KHIRBET QUMRAN HOUSED THE SPIRITUAL AND ADMINISTRATIVE CENTRE OF A MYSTICAL JEWISH SECT — APPARENTLY THE ESSENS. THE SCROLLS FORMED A PART OF THEIR LITERARY HERITAGE AND MANY OF THEM WERE COMPOSED BY THE MEMBERS OF THE SECT. SCHOLARS ARE DIVIDED IN OPINION AS TO THE IDENTITY AND DATE OF THIS SECT. THE EXCAVATIONS AT MASADA PROVIDE A PARTIAL ANSWER TO THESE QUESTIONS. AMONG THE MANY SCROLL FRAGMENTS FOUND THERE, A SECTARIAN SCROLL FRAGMENT PERTAINING TO THE QUMRAN COMMUNITY CAME TO LIGHT. IT APPEARS THEREFORE THAT IN THE FINAL PHASES OF THE REVOLT, MEMBERS OF THE QUMRAN SECT JOINED HANDS WITH THE ZEALOTS, THE DEFENDERS OF MASADA, IN THEIR DESPERATE STRUGGLE AGAINST ROMAN MIGHT. THE DISCOVERY OF THE SCROLL AT MASADA PROVIDES DEFINITE PROOF THAT THE DEAD SEA SCROLLS PREDATE THE DESTRUCTION OF THE SECOND TEMPLE.

THE SCROLLS SECT LIVED A FULLY COMMUNAL LIFE. THIS FACT IS REFLECTED IN THE BUILDINGS UNCOVERED (SHOWN HERE IN SCALE MODEL). THE SECT'S MAIN PRINCIPLE OF FAITH WAS A STRICT ADHERENCE TO MOSAIC LAW AND BELIEF IN PREDESTINATION, ACCORDING TO WHICH ALL CREATURES WERE DIVIDED INTO THE SONS OF LIGHT AND THE SONS OF DARKNESS, DESTINED TO STRUGGLE AT THE END OF DAYS, IN HEAVEN AND ON EARTH, UNTIL THE SONS OF LIGHT SHOULD PREVAIL. THE MEMBERS OF THE SECT REJECTED THE TEMPLE PRIESTHOOD, ESTABLISHED THEIR OWN SOLAR CALENDAR AND SET FORTH STRINGENT LAWS OF PURITY AND IMPURITY. IN ORDER TO CARRY OUT ALL THEIR RELIGIOUS PRECEPTS, THEY SETTLED IN THE DESERT, FOUNDING A COMMUNITY BASED ON THEIR BELIEFS, IN PREPARATION FOR THE END OF DAYS.

FATE DECREED THAT THE DEFENDERS OF MASADA AND THE QUMRAN COMMUNITY SHOULD FIND A COMMON END. THEY WERE OBLITERATED IN THE GREAT REVOLT AGAINST THE ROMANS.

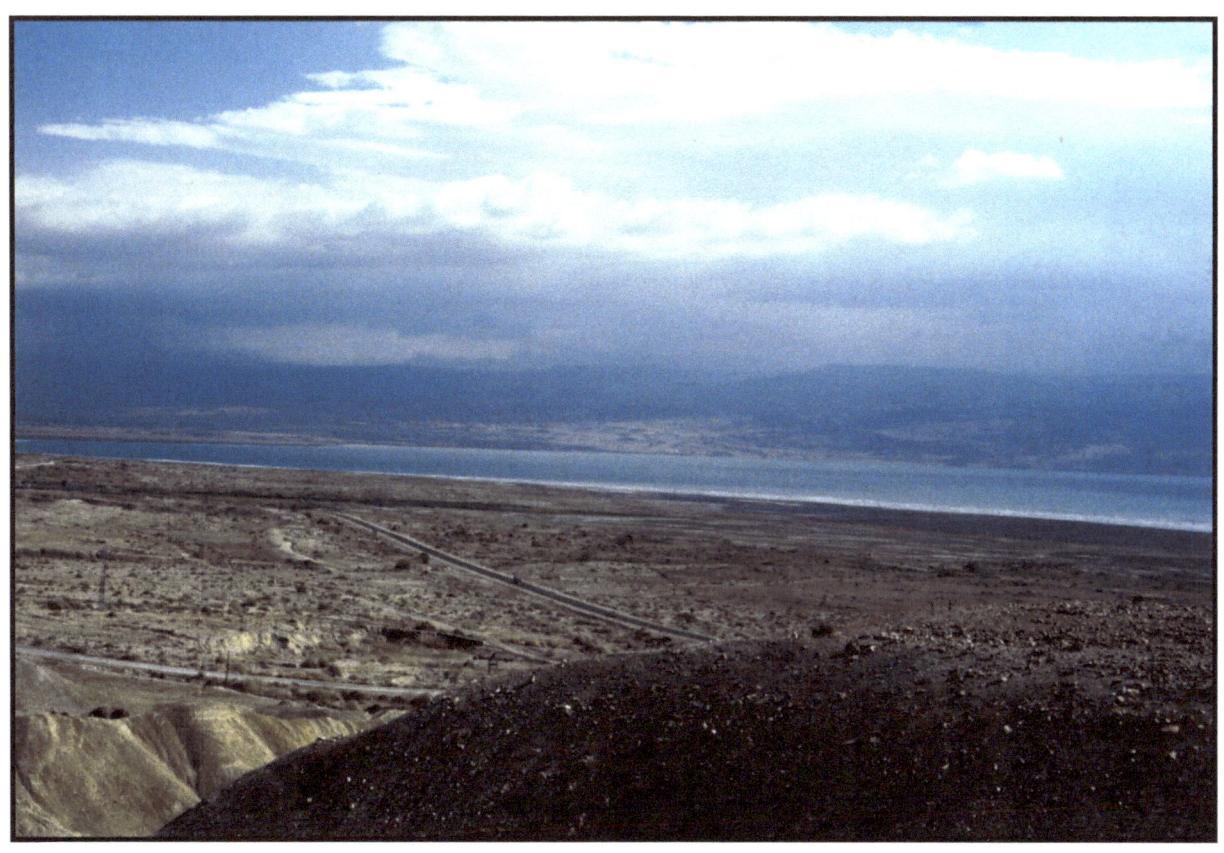

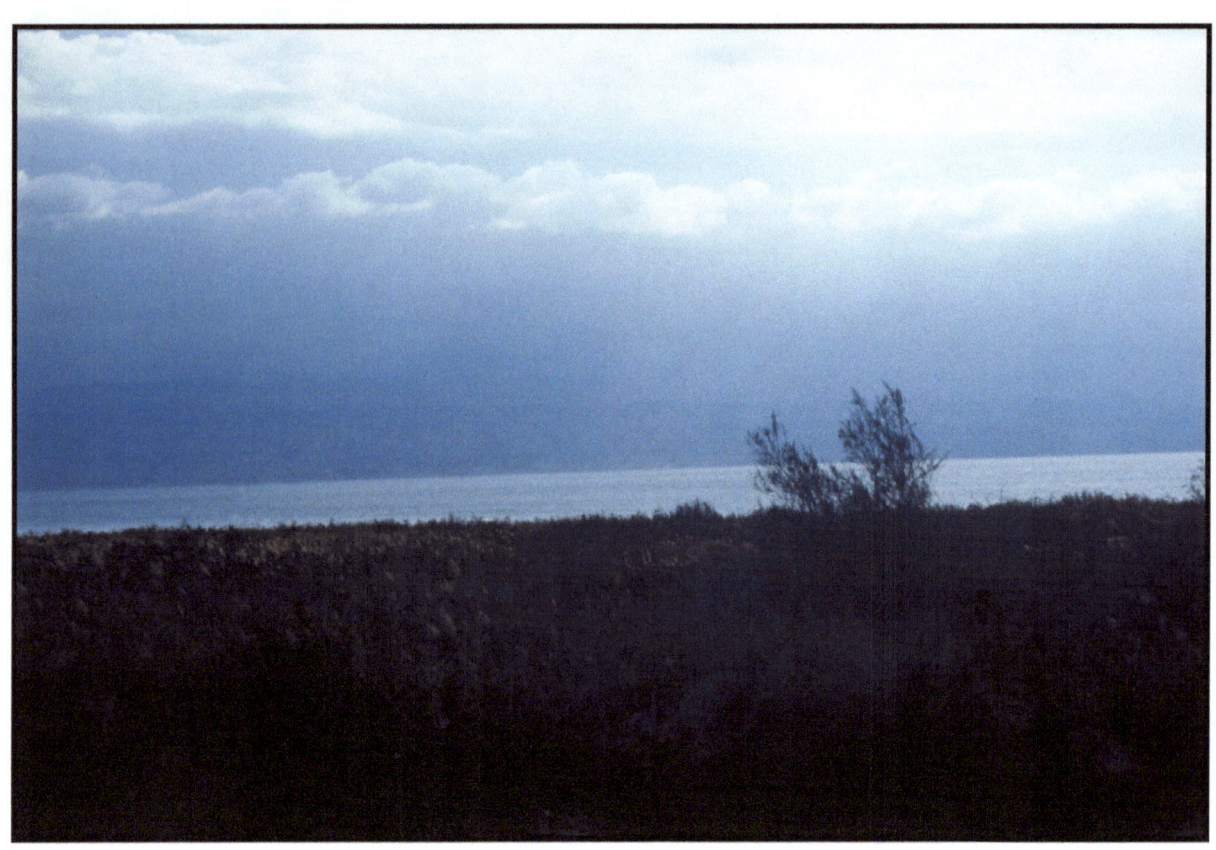

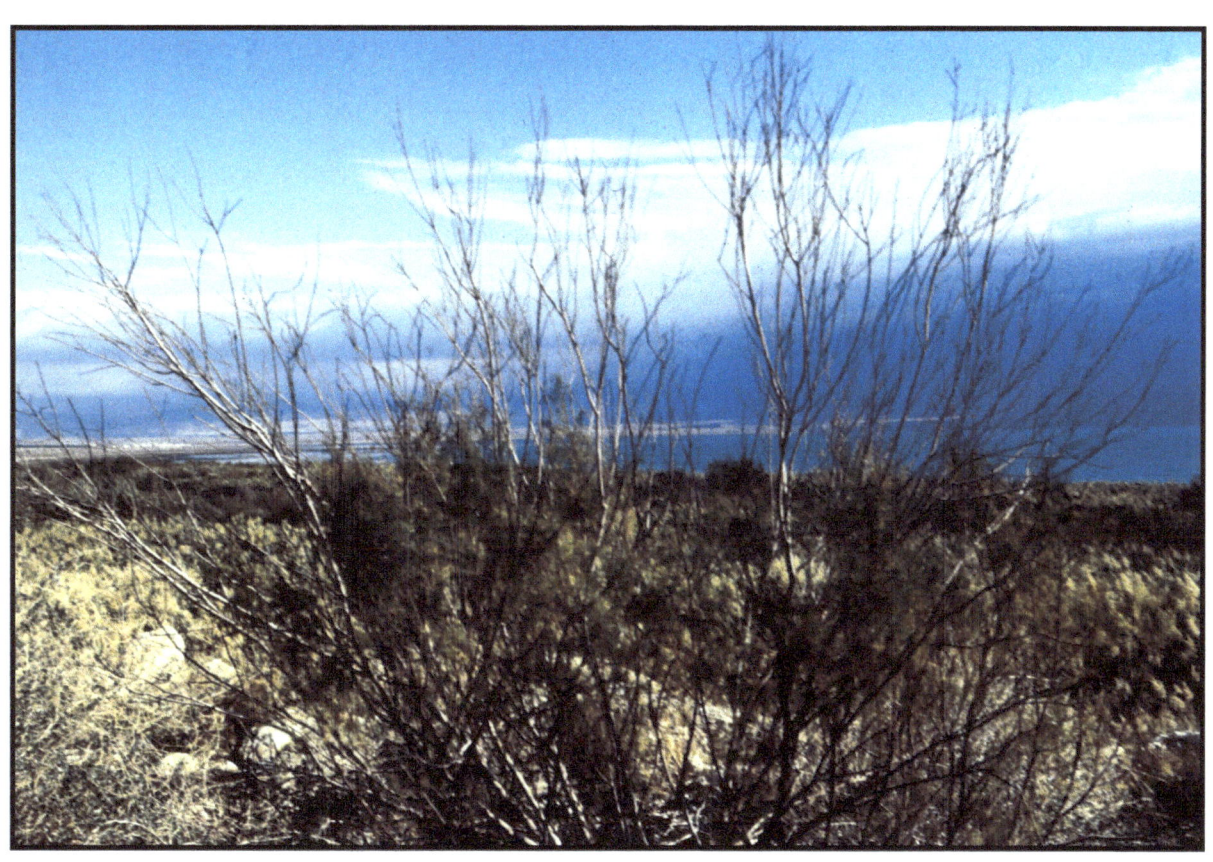

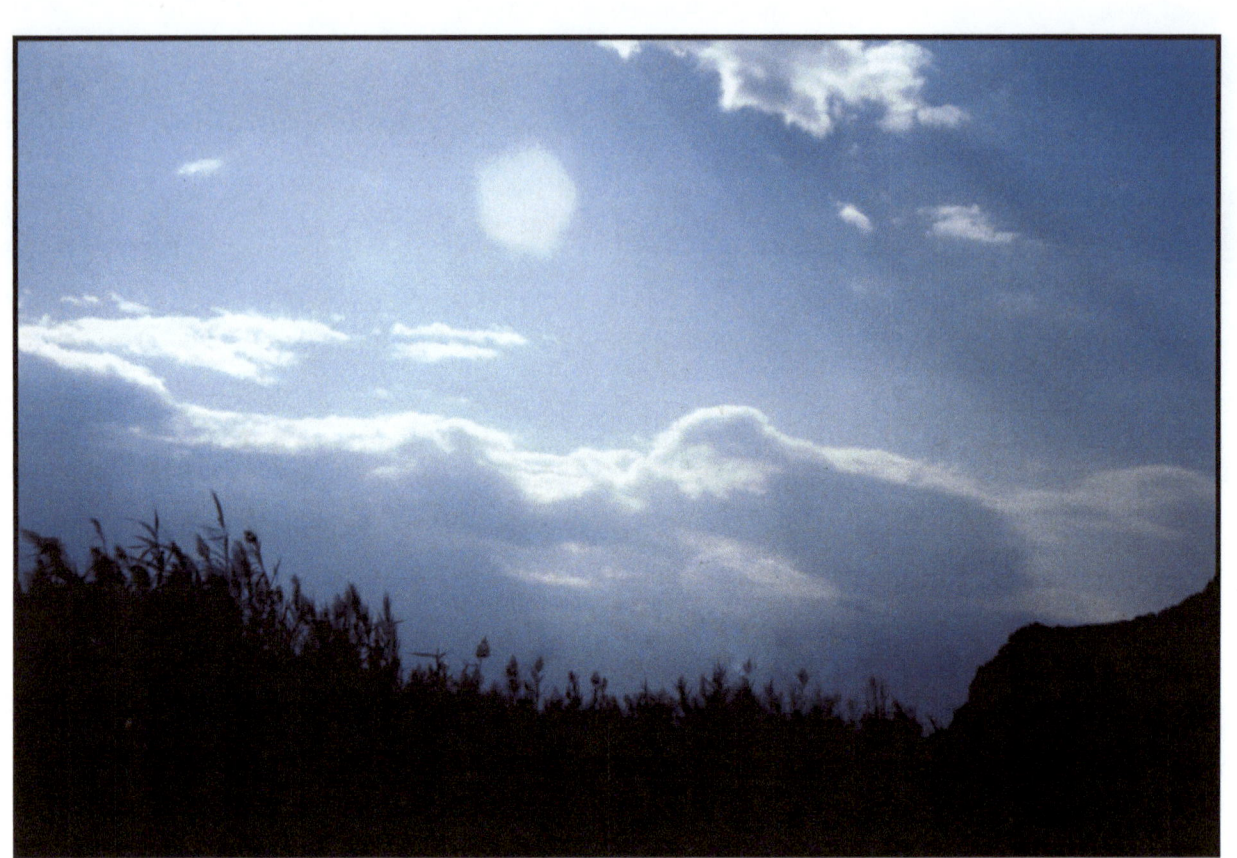

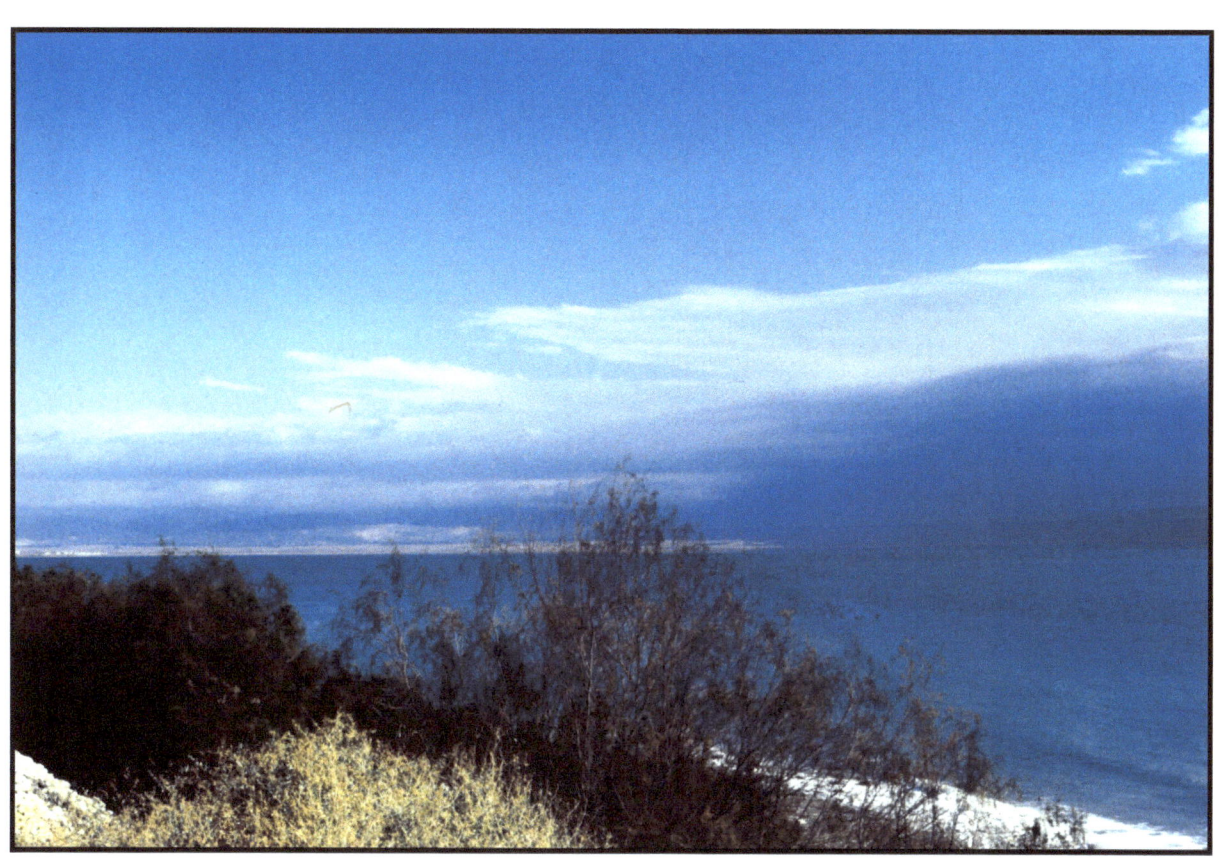

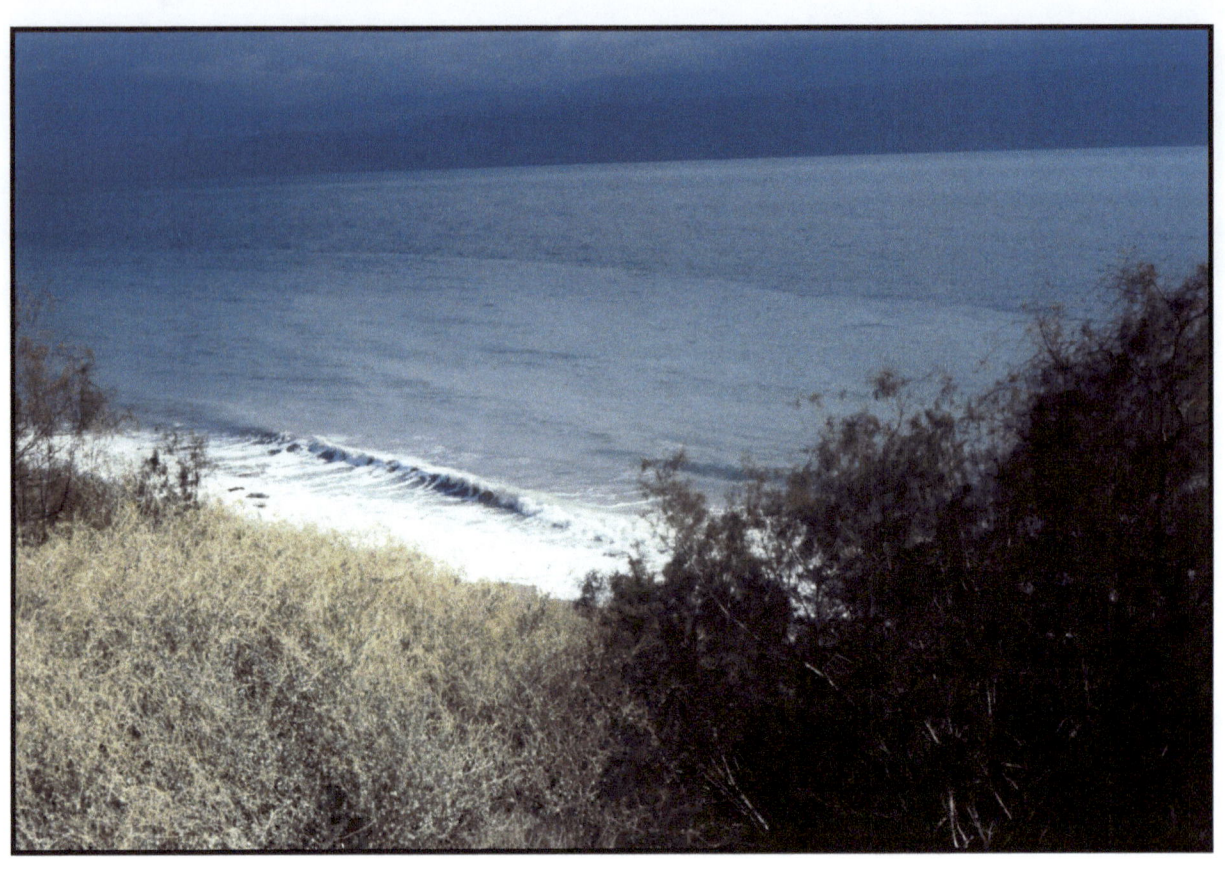

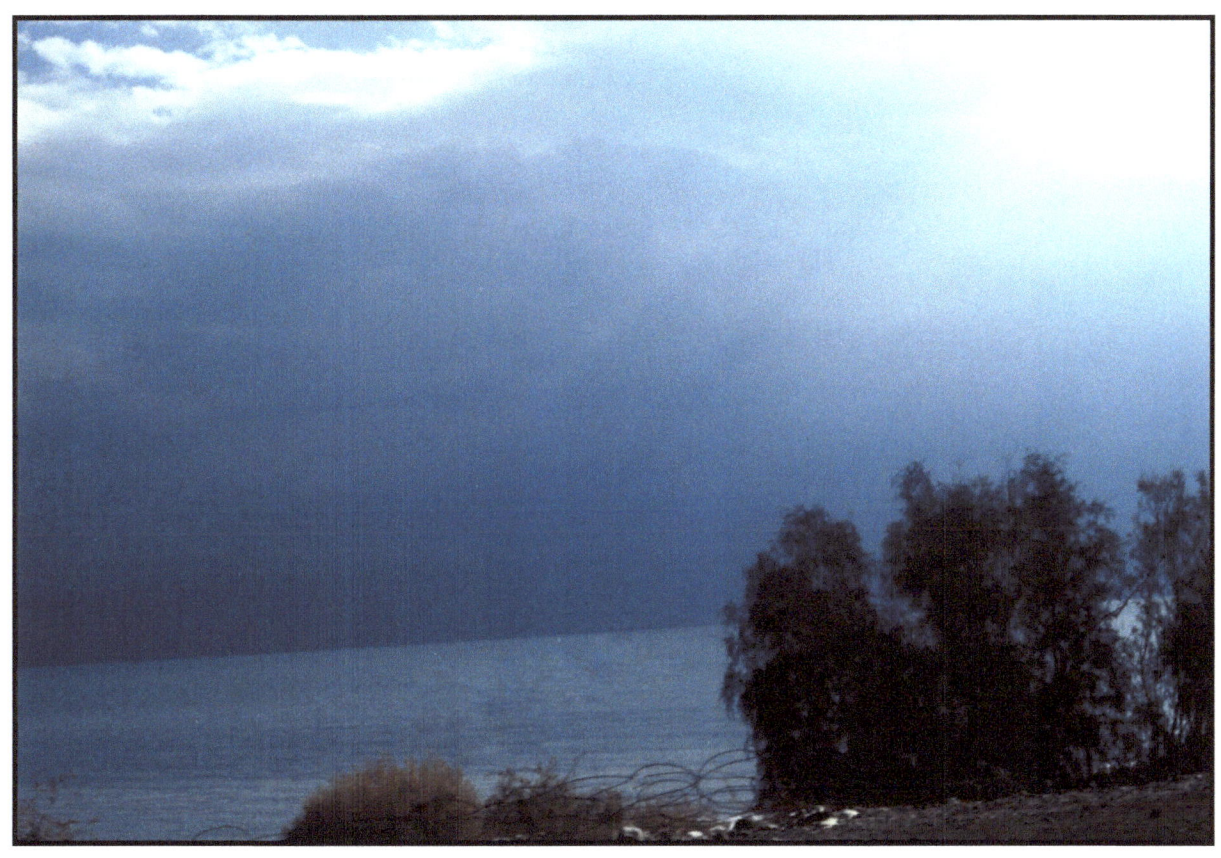

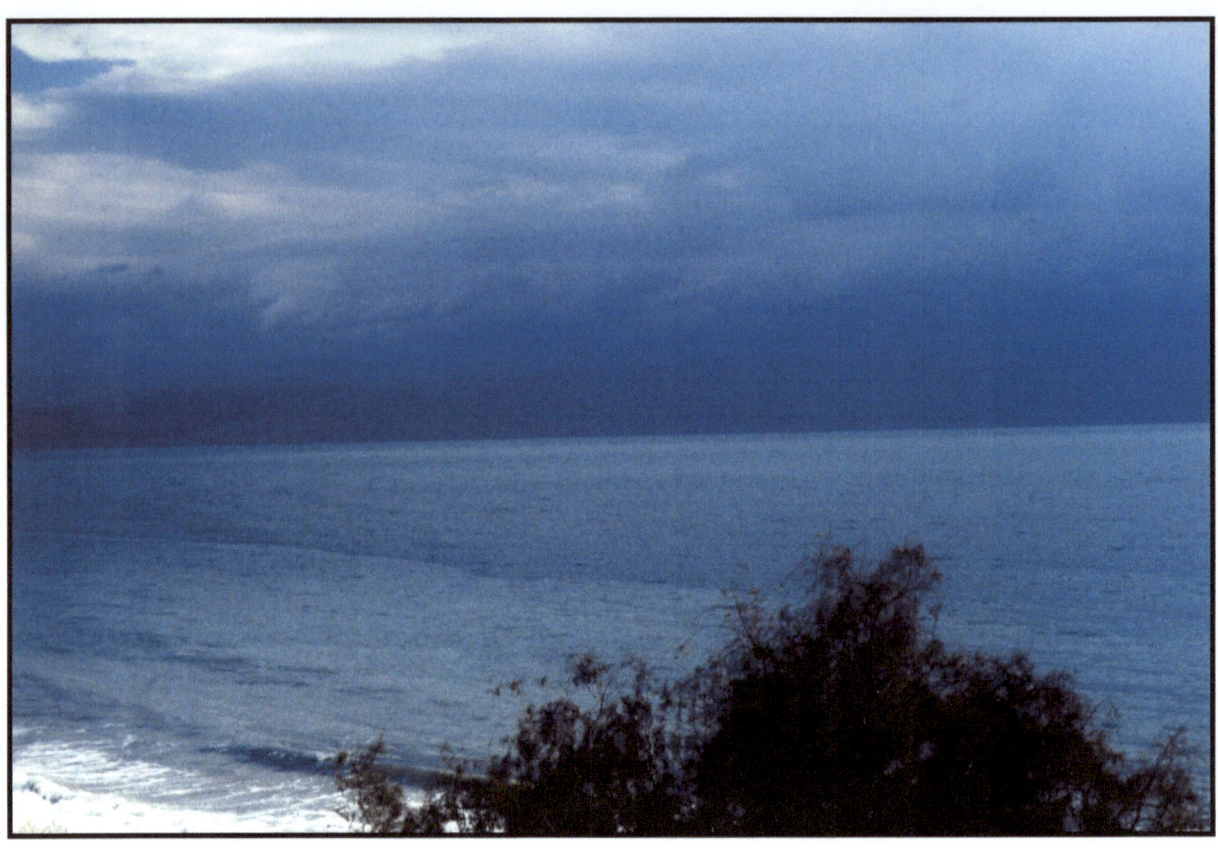

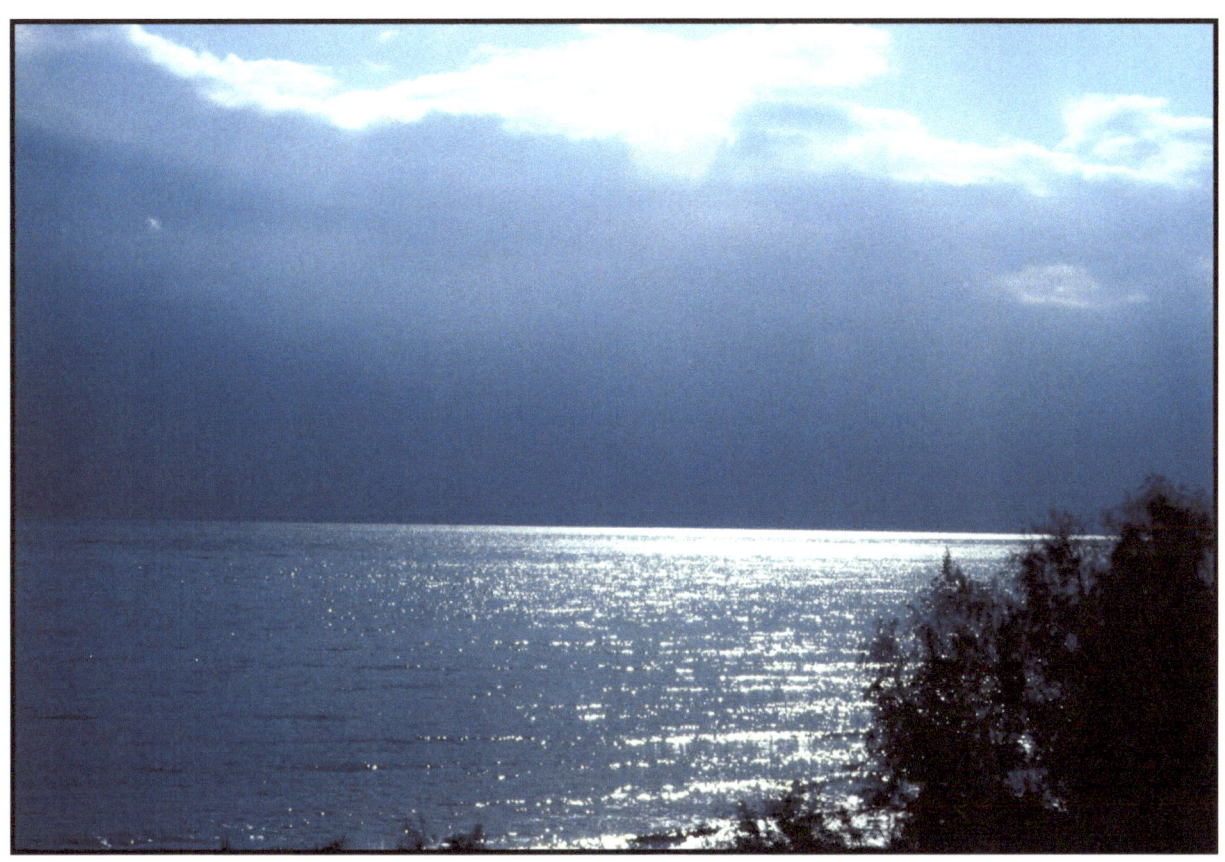

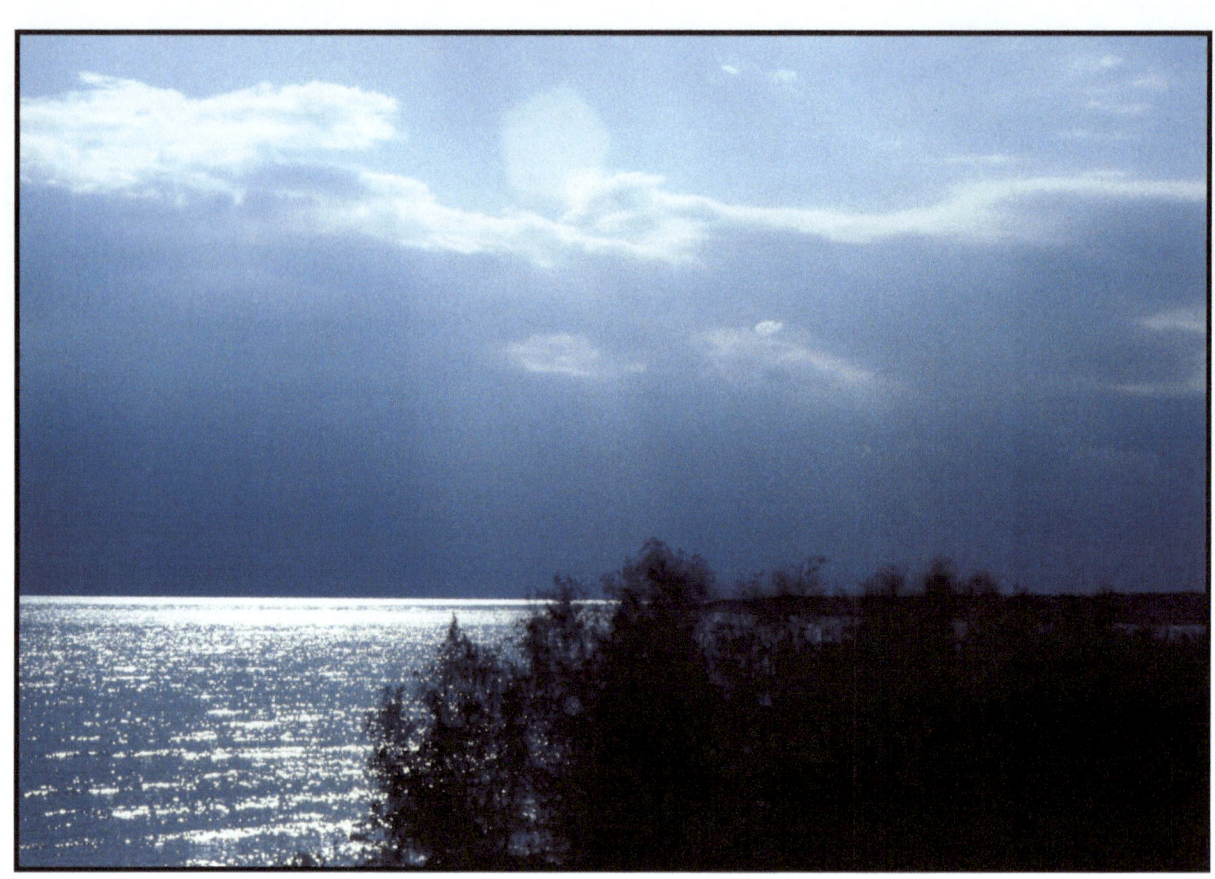

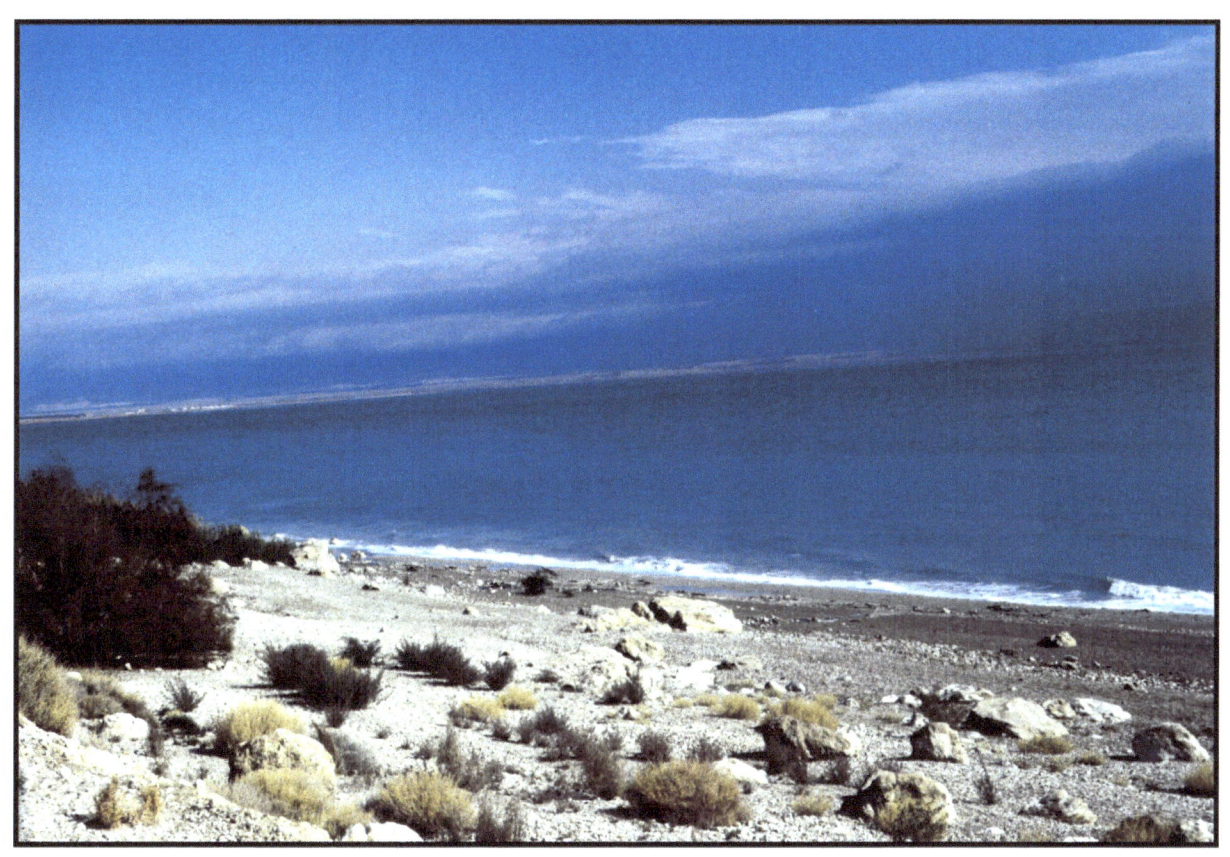

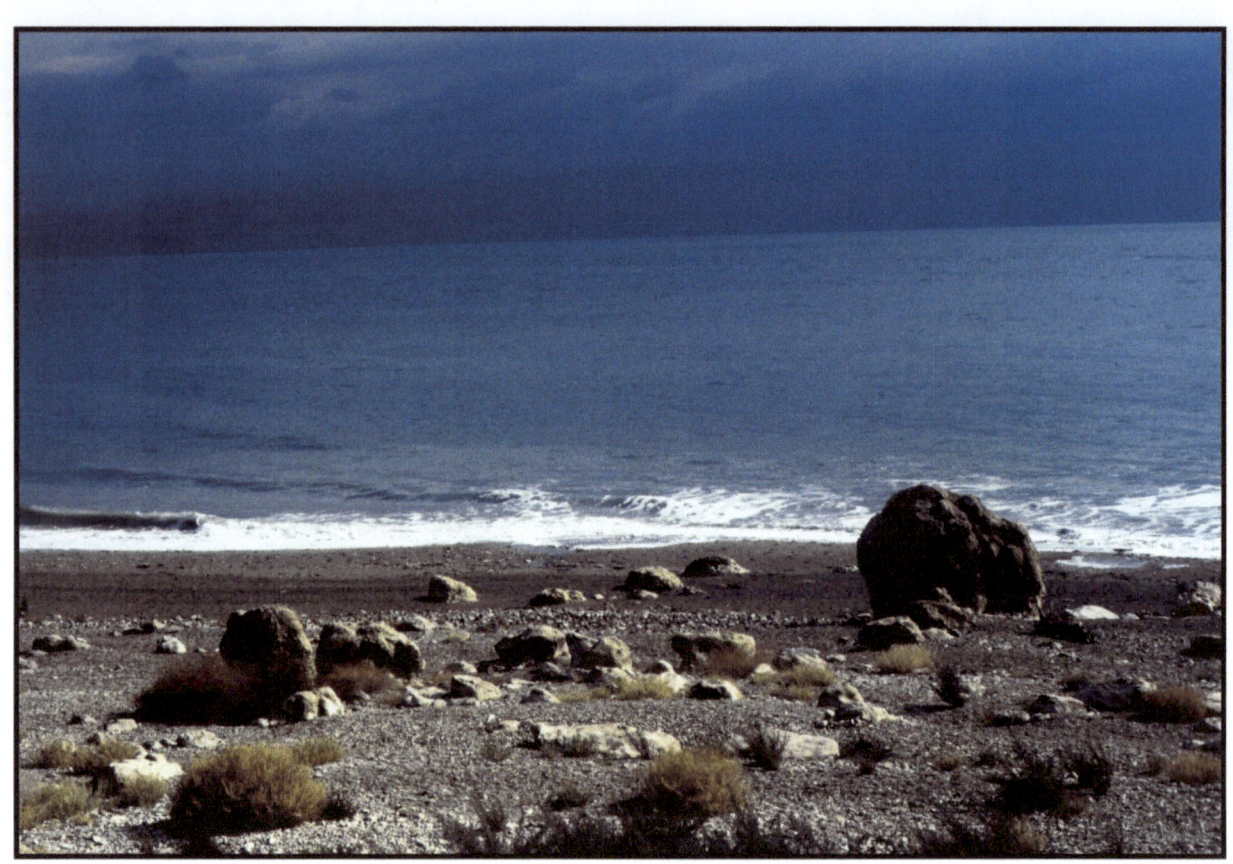

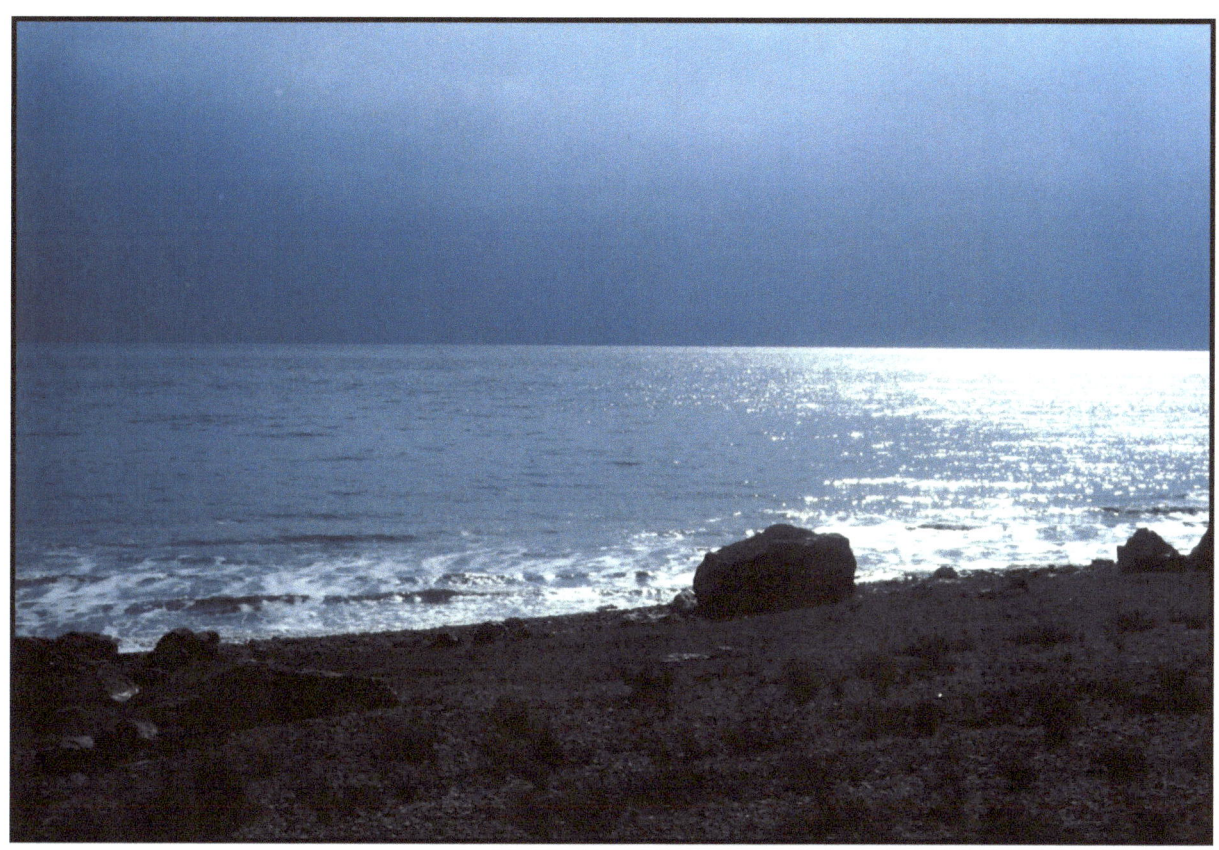

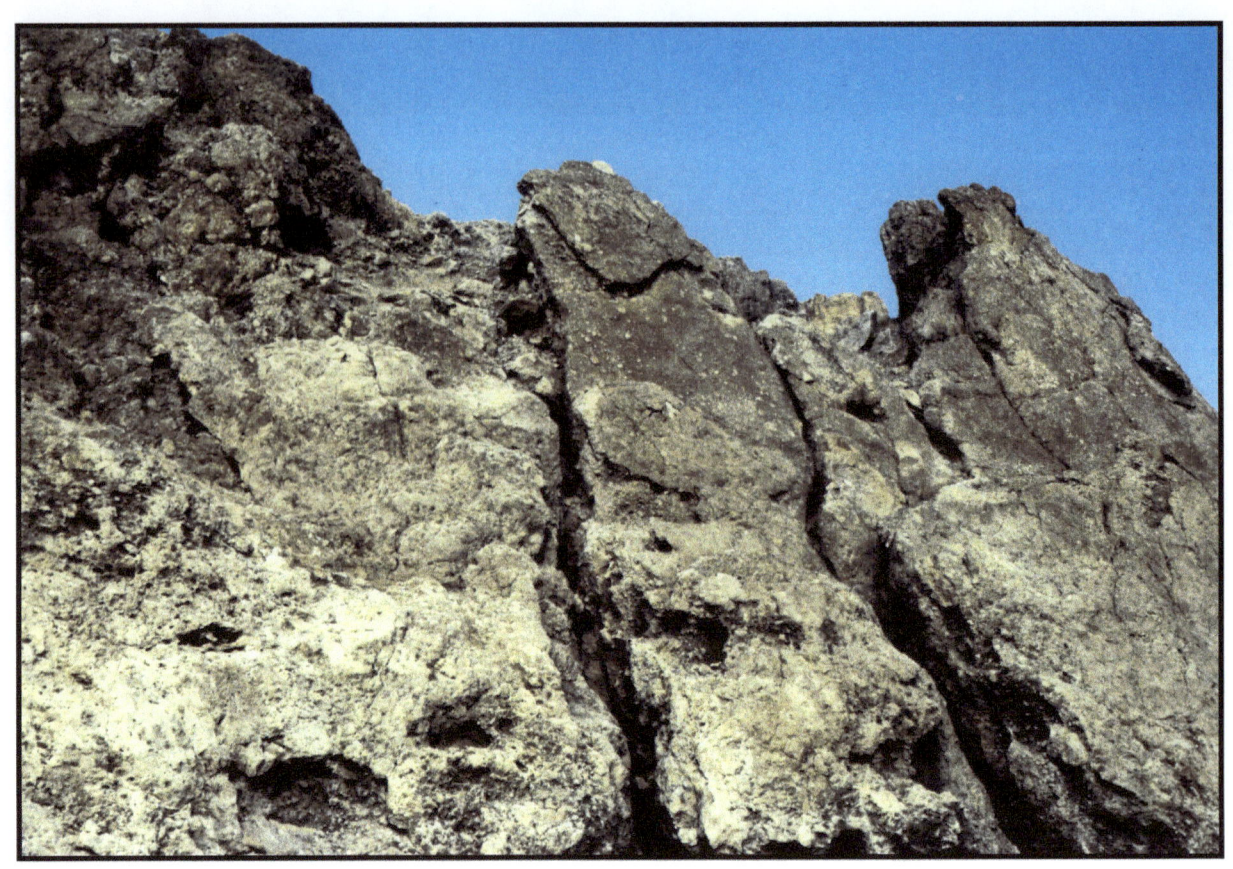

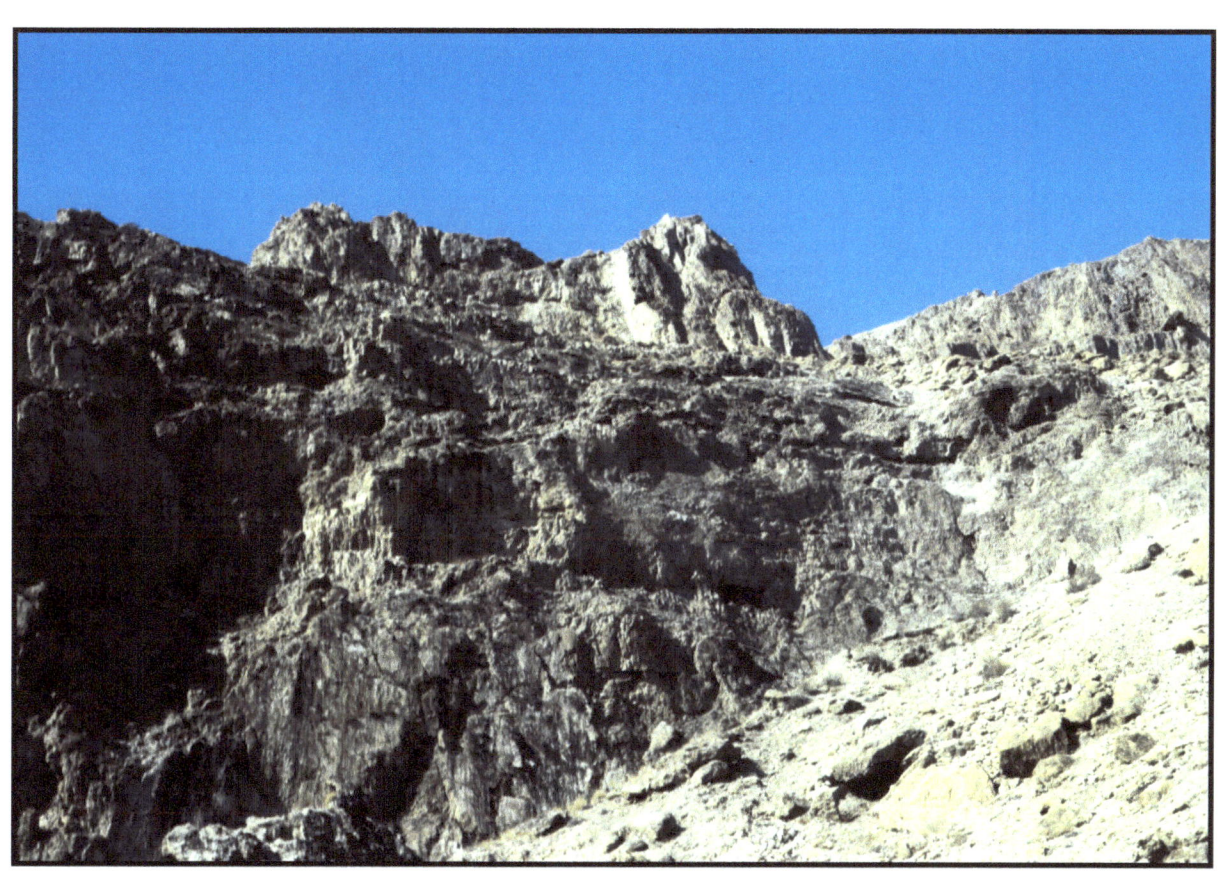

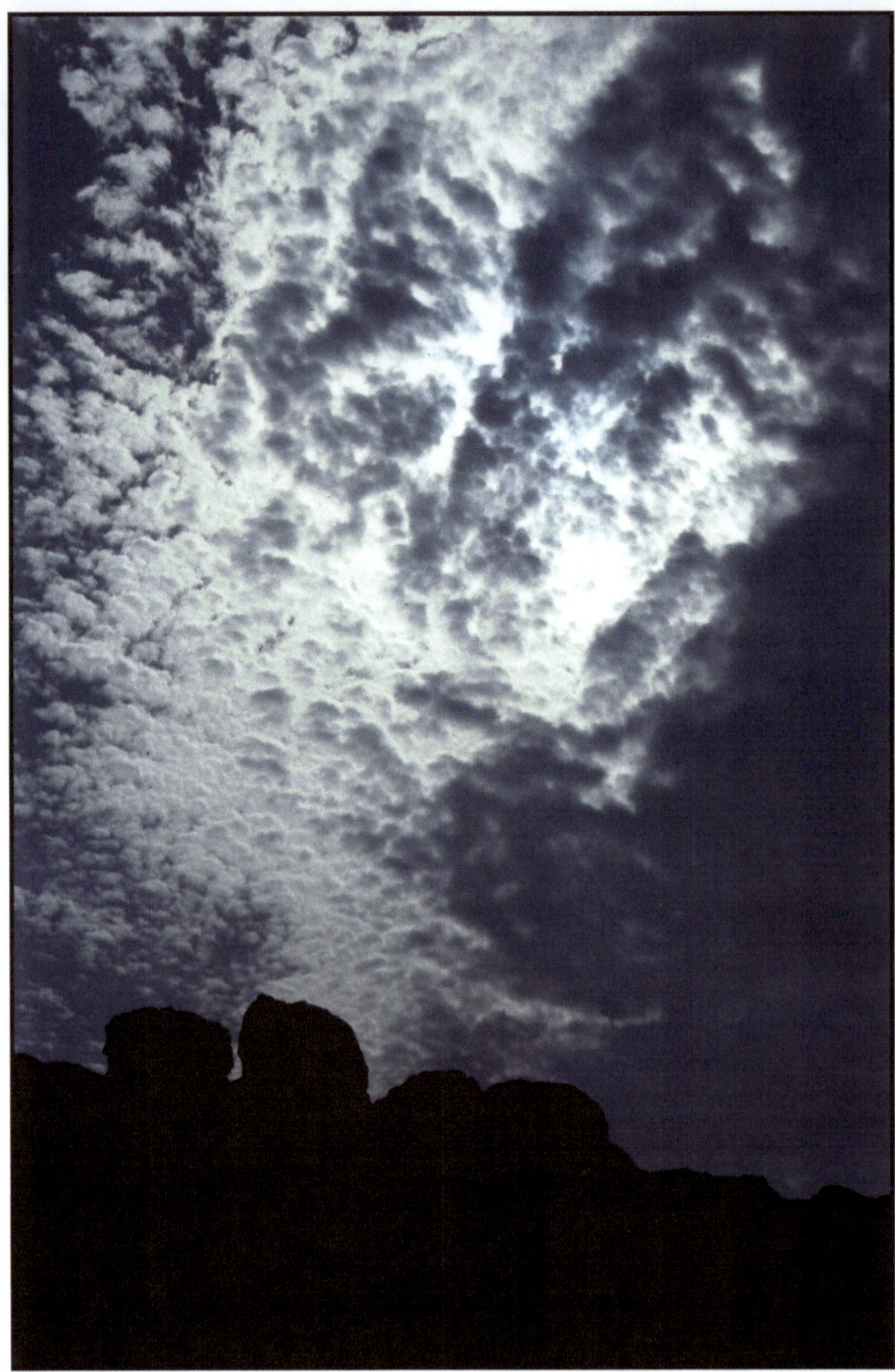

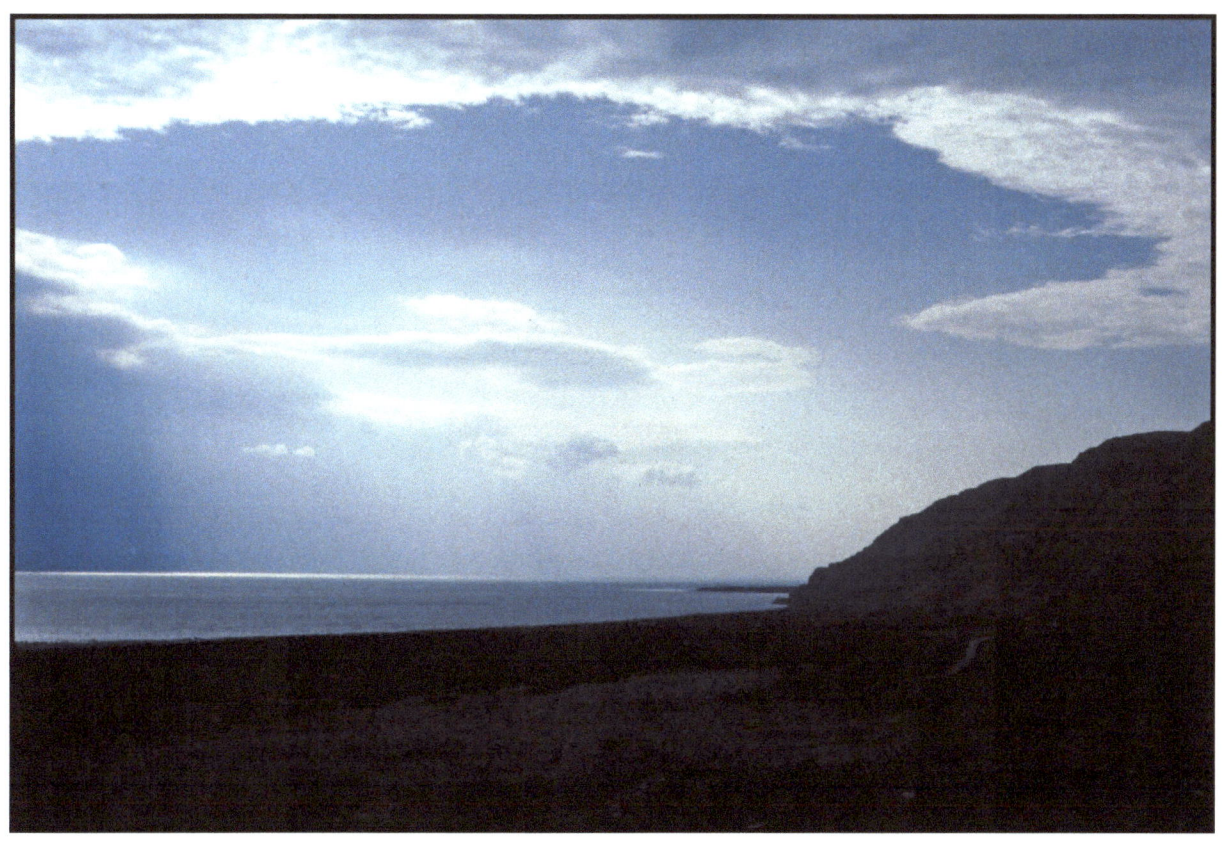

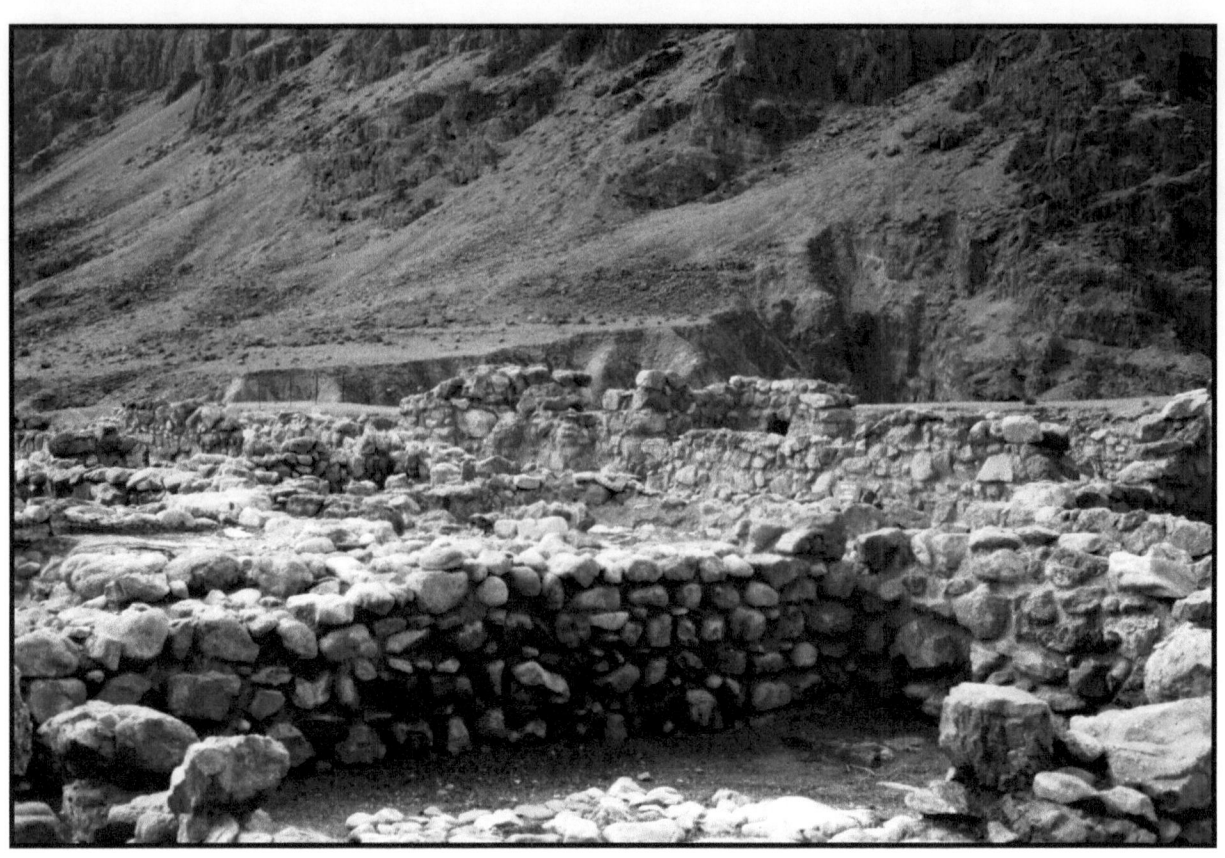

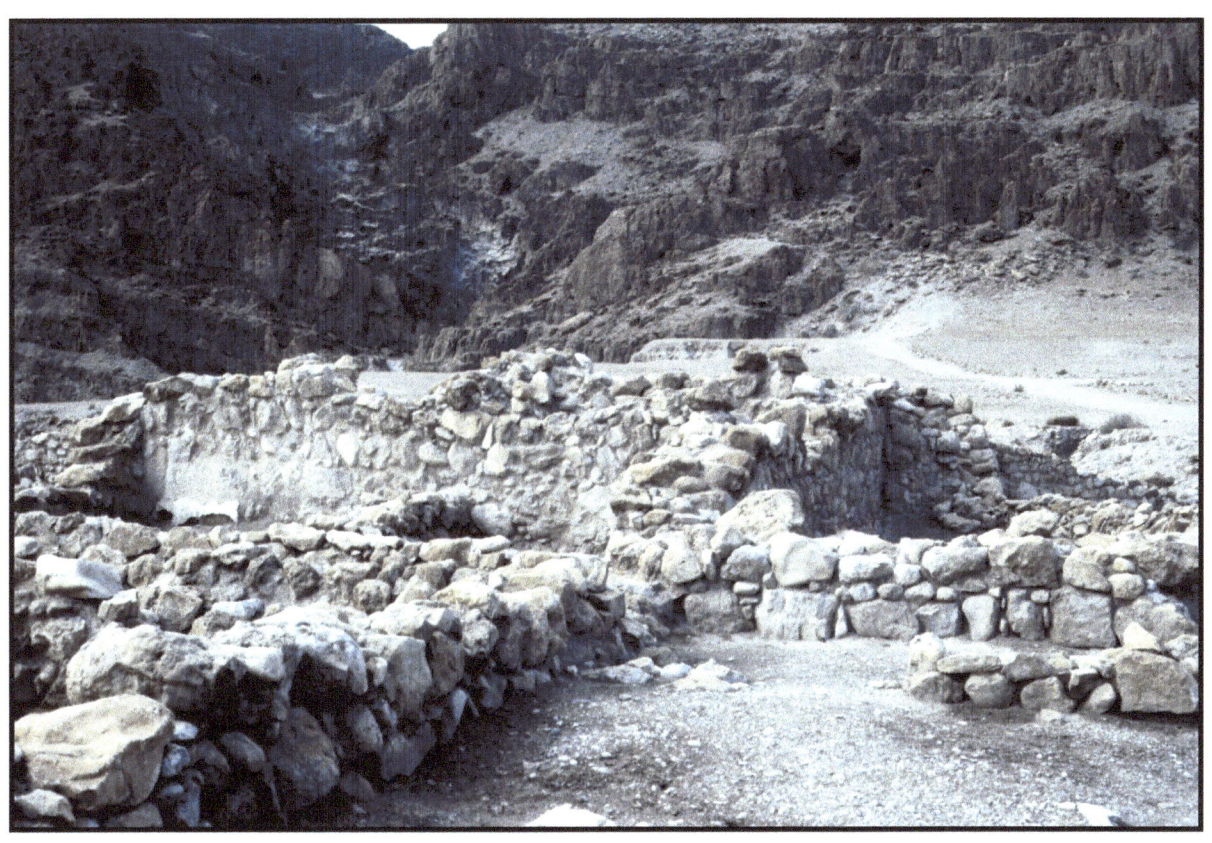

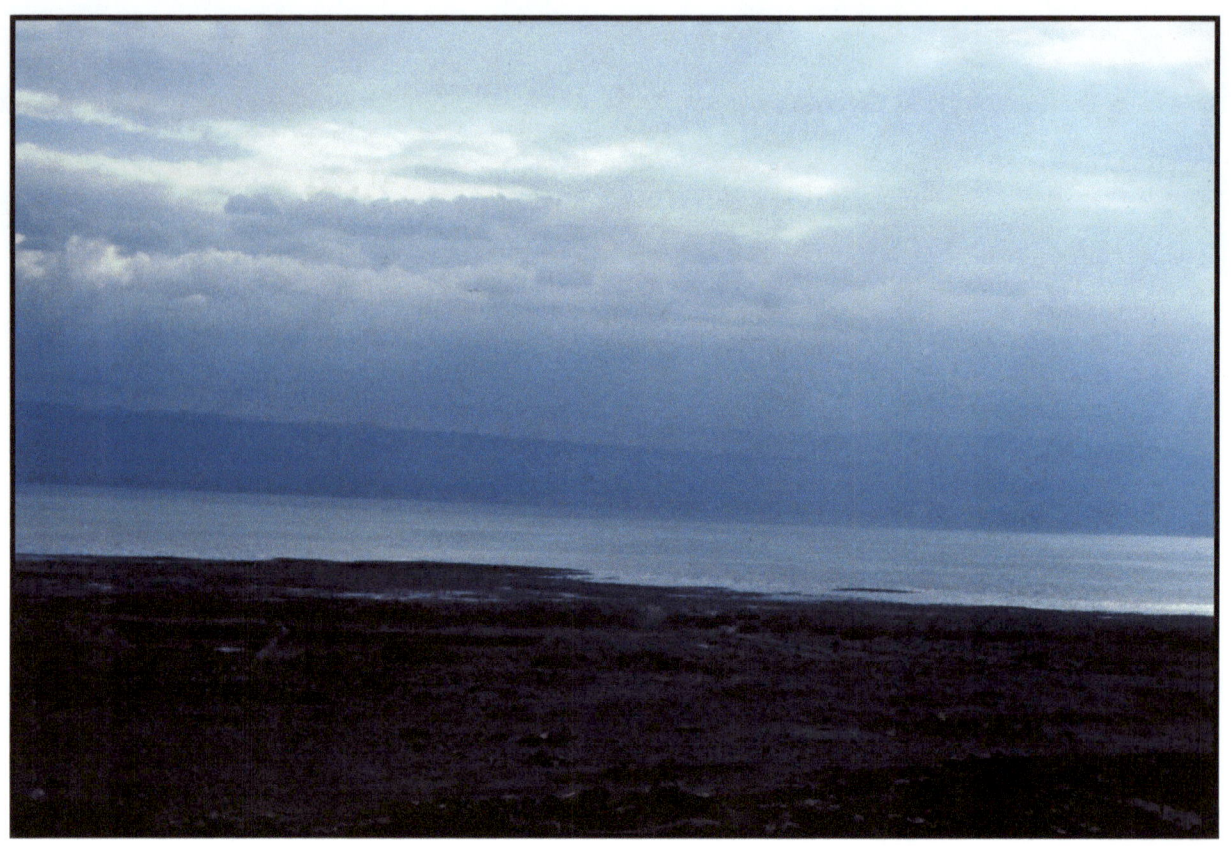

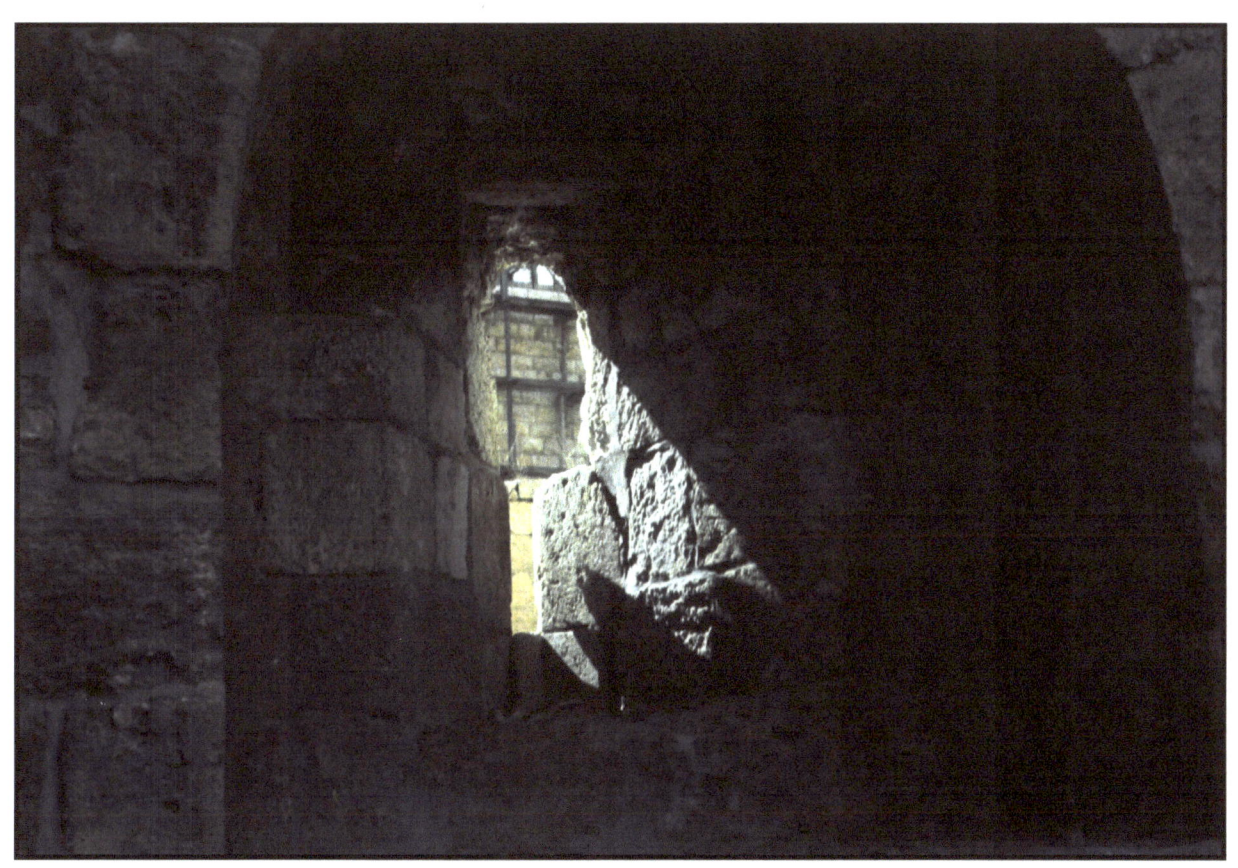

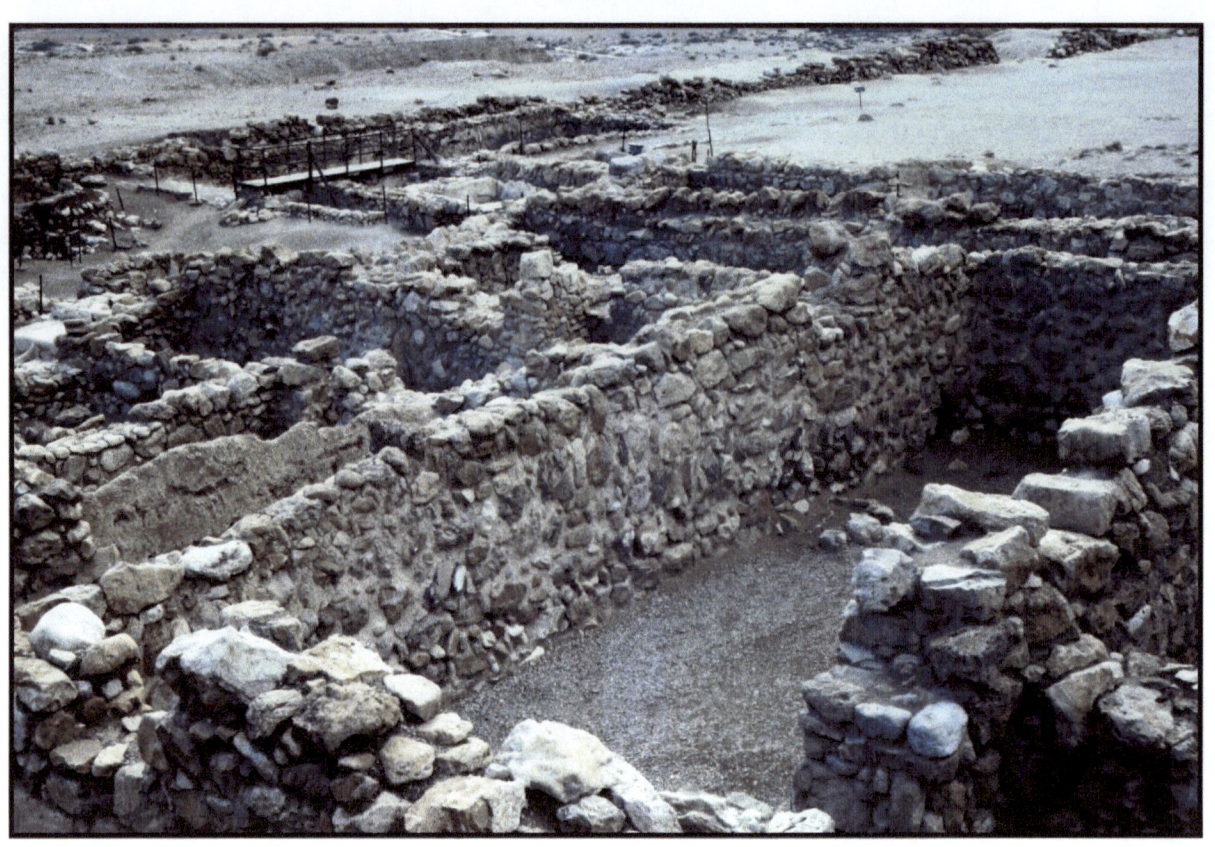

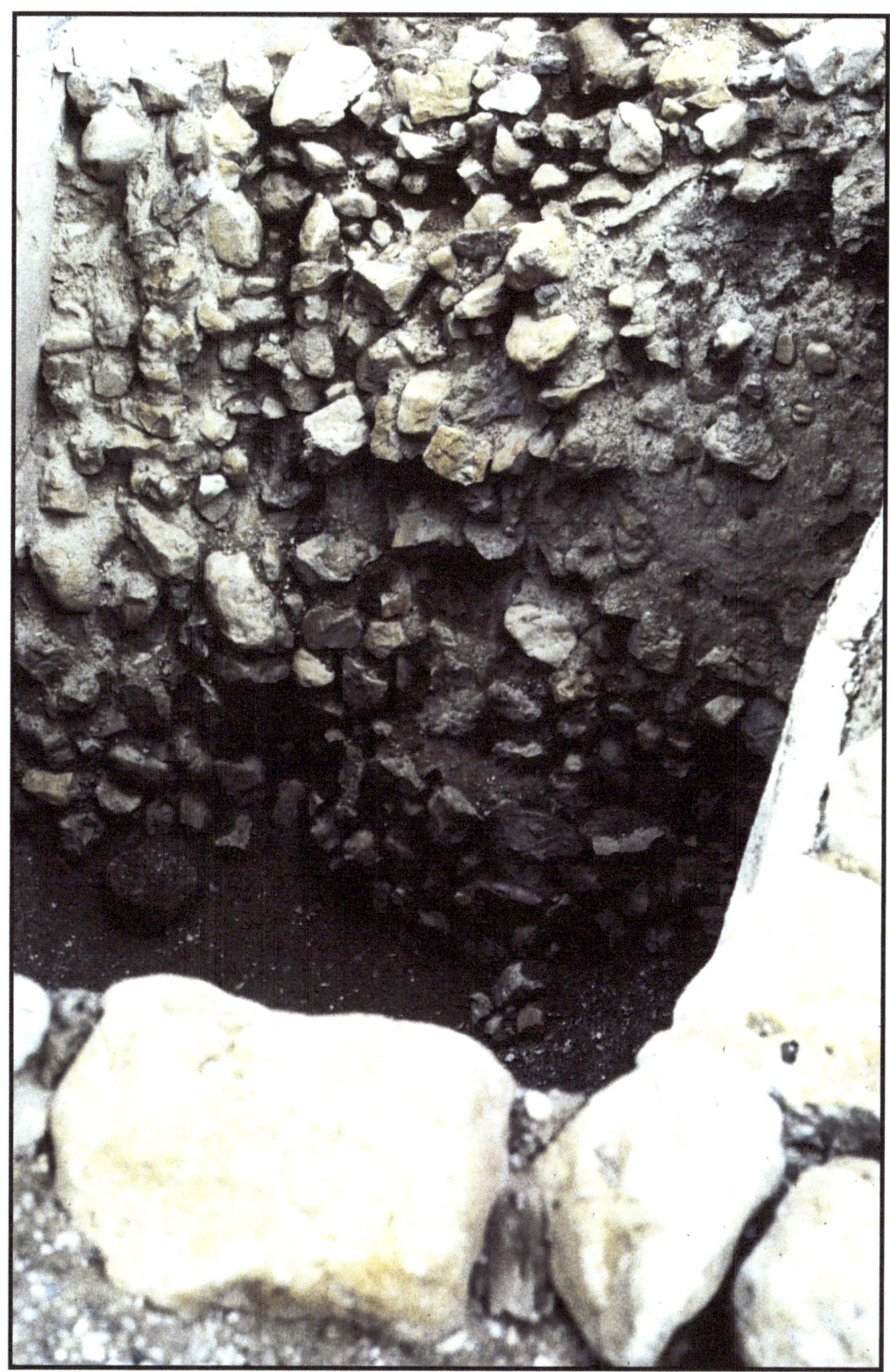

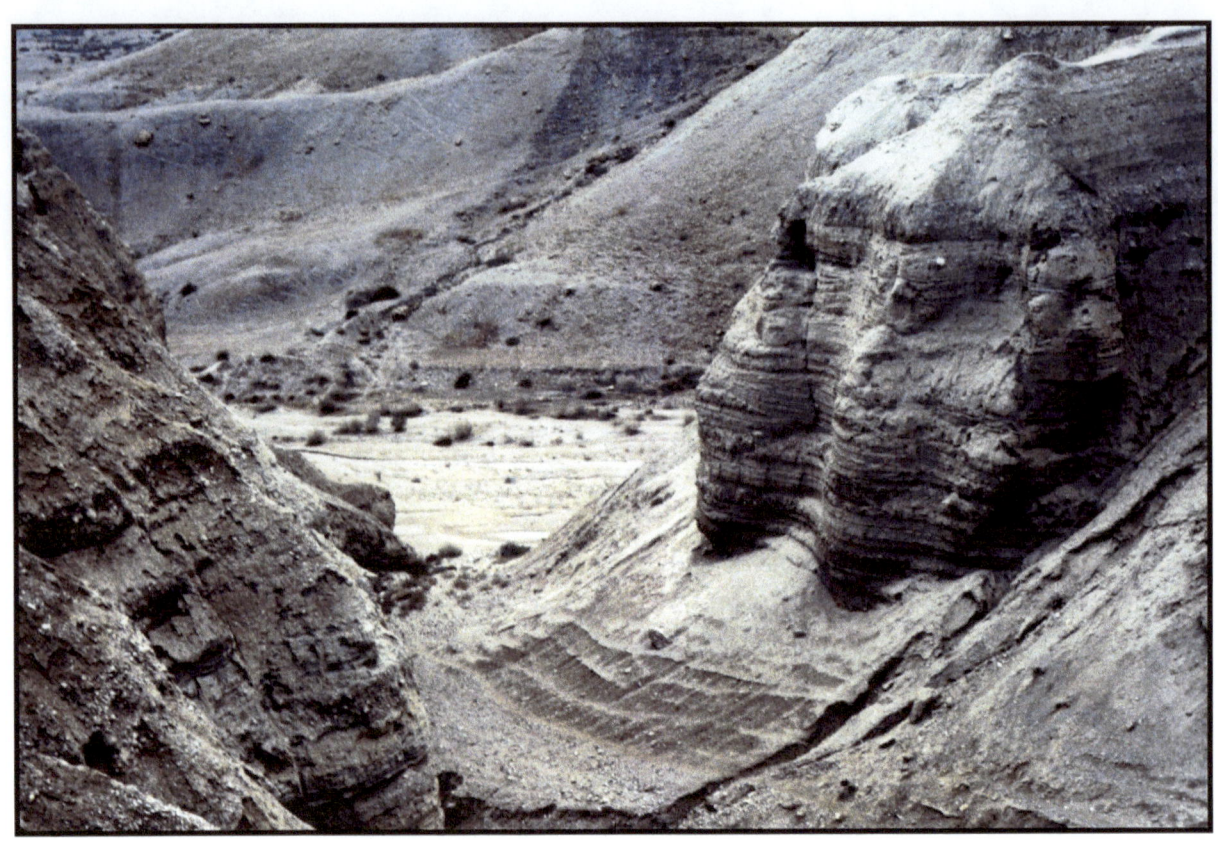

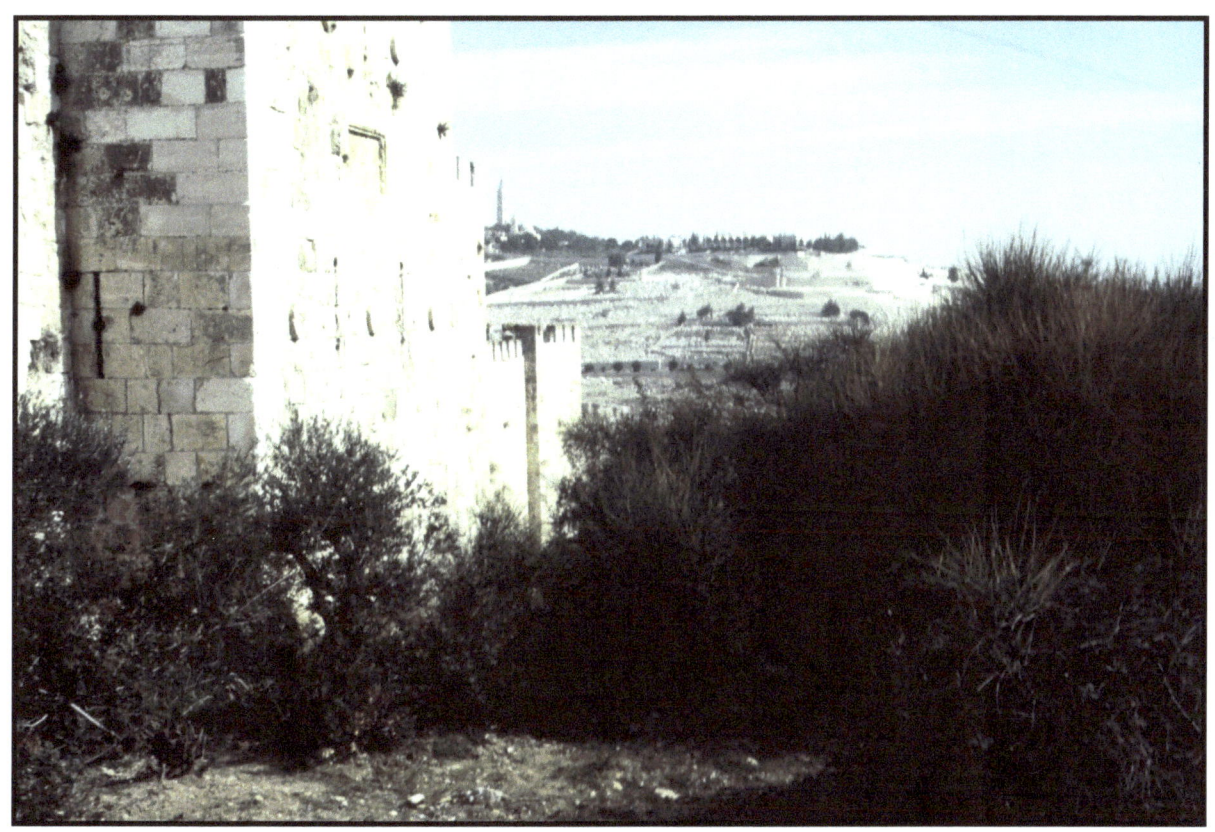

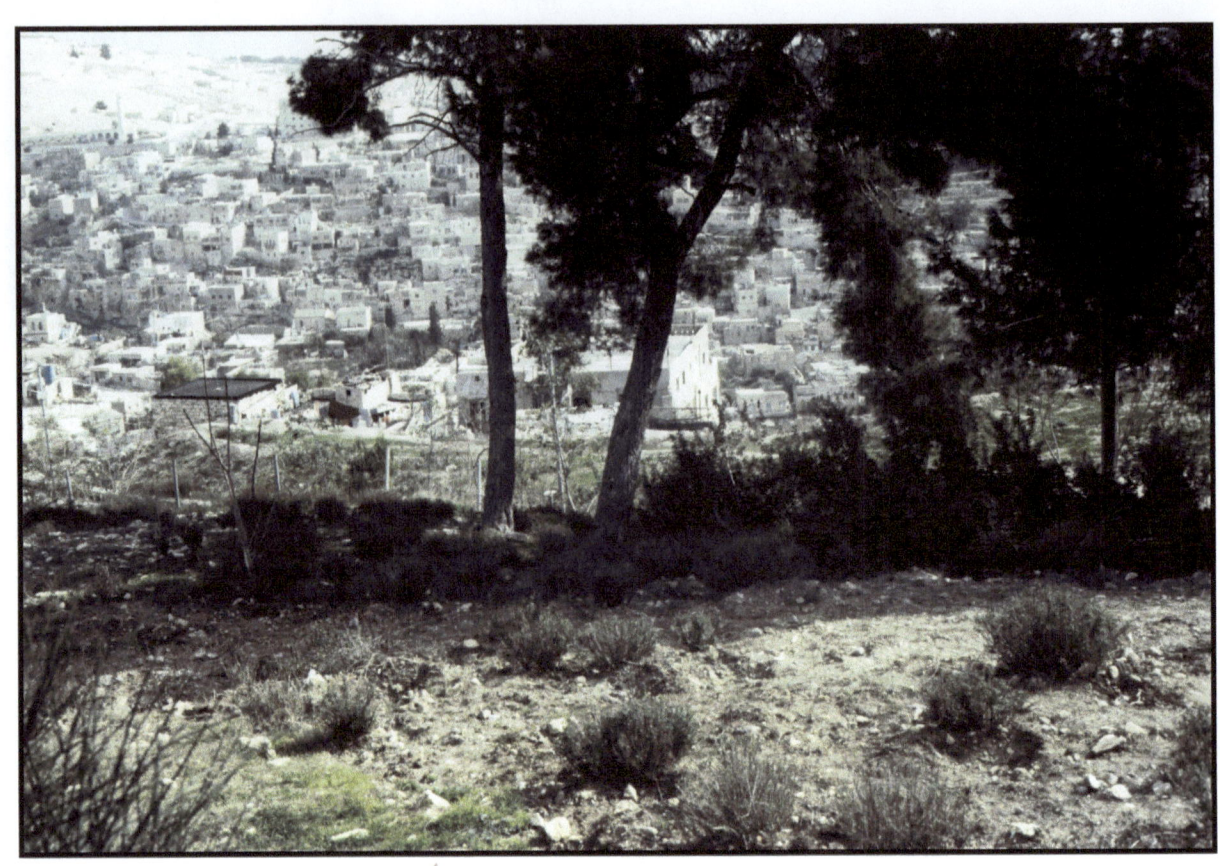

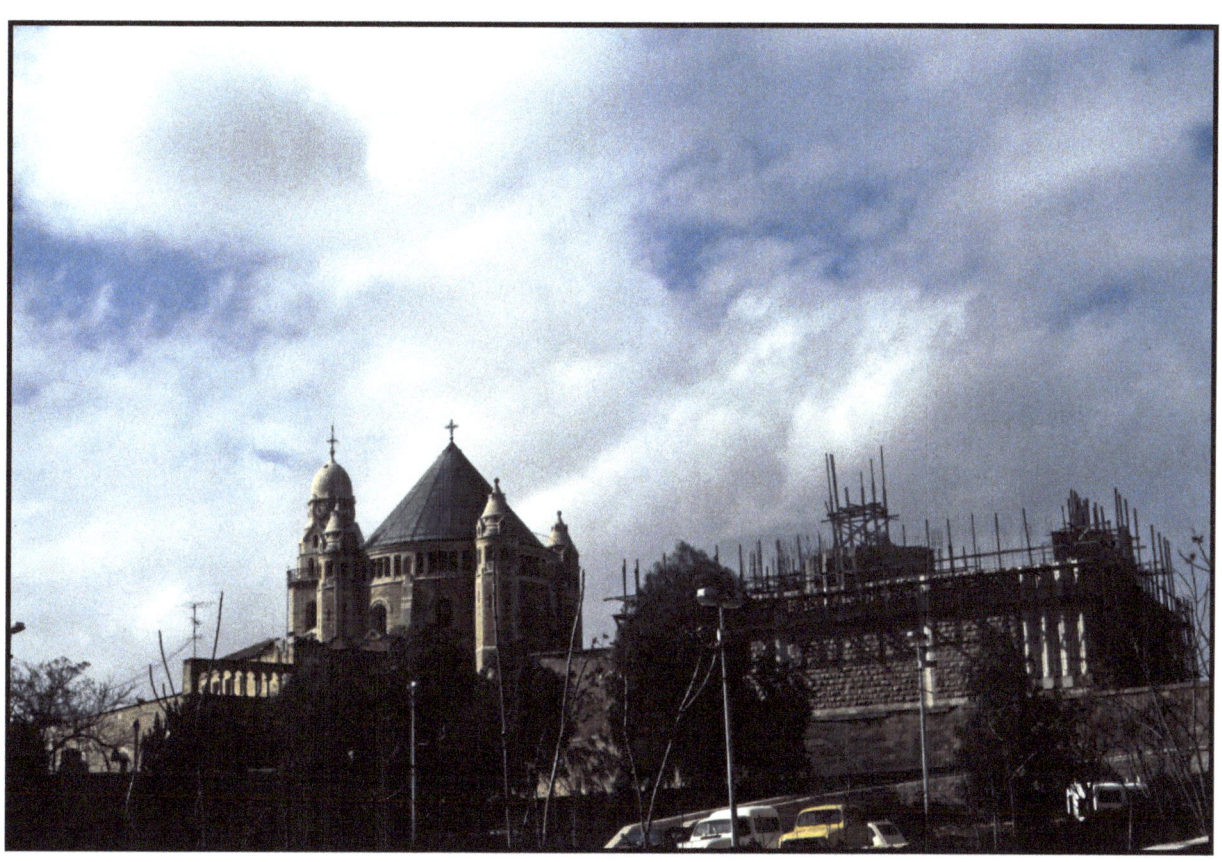

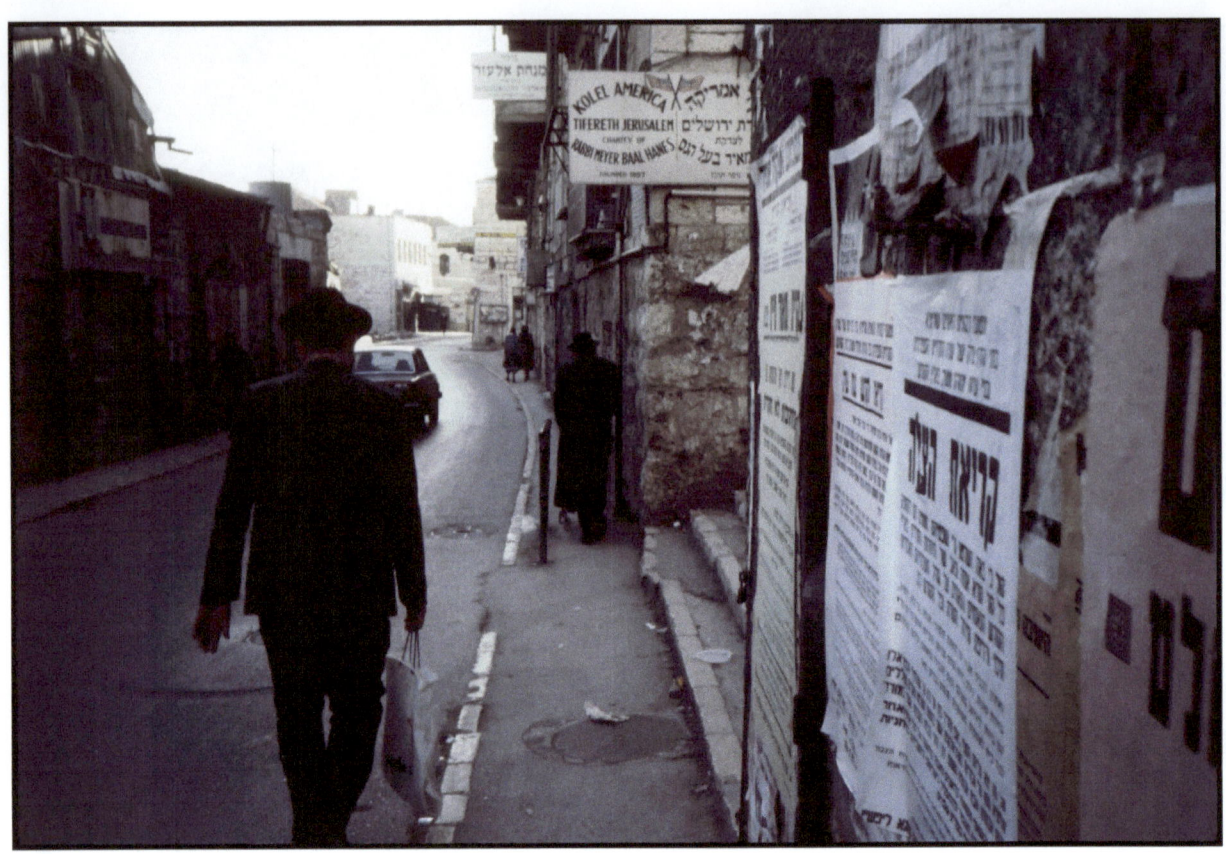

www.ingramcontent.com/pod-product-compliance
Lightning Source LLC
Chambersburg PA
CBHW051148220526
45473CB00003B/696